GOD CRAZY FREEDOM

Michelle Borquez Thornton
and the GCF Team

Carpenter's Son Publishing

Bella
PUBLISHING

PHOTOGRAPHY
David Edmonson

FRONT COVER
Back Row L-R
Marcie Schneider, Holly Renken,
Christal Tanks, Sharon Kay Ball

Front Row L-R
Michelle Borquez Thornton, Barb Pruitt

BACK COVER
Back Row L-R
Kim Vastine, Bonnie Keen, Jennifer Mallan,
Punky Tolson, Lisa Ostrowski, Alison Stevens,
Jo Ann Aleman, Paige Henderson,

Front Row L-R
Michelle Moore, Rebecca Gates, Julie Terwilliger,
Chanda Crutcher, Maree Socha (not an author)

Published by Bella Publishing in partnership with Larry Carpenter and Sons
Nashville, TN 37221

Bellawomennetwork.com
GodCrazy.org

Unless otherwise indicated, Scripture references are taken from The Holy Bible, New
International Version. NIV. Copyright 1973, 1978, 1984, by the International Bible Society.
Used by permission of Zondervan. All rights reserved.
Cover Art – Paul Lewis of Lewis Design and Marketing, Lewisdm.com

CONTENTS

Authors' Note 5

Introduction 7

Shame to Purity by Michelle Borquez Thornton 11

My Plan to God's Purpose by Paige Henderson 23

Rejection to Acceptance by Jennifer Mallan. 33

Emptiness to Intimacy by Punky Tolson. 45

Divorce to Wholeness by Sharon Ball-Dale 59

Singleness to Unity by Barbara J. Pruitt 71

Outcast to Beloved by Bonnie Keen 83

Control to Surrender by Natalie Gillespie. 95

Fear to Courage by Kim Vastine. 107

Abortion to Mercy by Marcie Schneider. 119

Abandonment to Forgiveness by Michelle Moore 129

Abuse to Favor by Jo Ann Aleman. 141

Condemned to Free by Chanda M. Crutcher. 153

Fallen to Restored by Julie Terwilliger. 165

Broken to Beautiful by Alison Stevens 175

Adultery to Repentance by Jeanne Kolenda. 187

Confusion to Peace by Lisa Ostrowski 199

Addiction to Freedom by Holly Joy Renken 211

Striving to Grace by Rebecca Gates 221

Death to Life by Christal M. N. Jenkins 231

Anonymous to Chosen by Julia Walker Crews 241

Closing. 251

God Crazy Freedom Authors

Front Row L-R
Marcie Schneider, Paige Henderson, Holly Renken,
Julie Terwilliger, Michelle Borquez Thornton, Barb Pruitt,
Michelle Moore, Chrystal Jenkins, Sharon Kay Ball

Back Row L-R
Chanda Crutcher, Kim Vastine, Punky Tolson, Rebecca Gates,
Lisa Ostrowski, Alison Stevens, Jo Ann Aleman

AUTHORS' NOTE

We are so excited to share with you, sweet sisters, our stories of healing from our hurts, habits, and hang-ups. In order to let the personality of each author shine through, you will probably notice right away that our writing styles, our "voices" on the page, are different. We have purposely left them that way in order to present you with our most authentic selves. We all have a story to tell, our victory to share, five devotions, a God Crazy Freedom Challenge, and a God Crazy Freedom prayer. Some of us included scriptures or inspirational quotes in each of our devotions; some of us came up with catchy titles. A few of us shared original poetry or repeated phrases for emphasis. Some of our challenges are short and to the point. Some require multiple steps over many days or months. We quote verses from different versions of the Bible. Each of our stories is unique, yet God reveals many common themes in our lives. Every word has been prayed over by each writer, the editors, and the God Crazy Freedom team. Each of you, dear readers, has been prayed for too. All of this is our humble gift, a love letter (and labor of love), to you. We pray that as you turn the pages, this book will become a roadmap, a study tool, a guidebook you can return to again and again – whenever the enemy tries to trap you in your past or keep you from constantly moving through your present and into the God Crazy Freedom of your future.

INTRODUCTION

*H*ow do we run free if we are bound up by the chains of our past, our pain, our unforgiveness, our jealousy, fear, anger and resentment? How do we run free when there are chains of guilt, despair, regret, and shame, wrapped around our ankles? Jesus wants us to run free into His arms, yet how can we ever totally grasp the boundless love, victorious freedom, and miraculous abundance He longs for us to have when we are emotionally crippled? When we are so hung up by our hang-ups that we can hardly move?

For many years fear had a terrific grip on my life. It was so strong that I could not even speak a prayer request in Sunday school without trembling. Today, I can tell you that no longer does fear have me in its grip. No longer does the shame of my past keep me from walking out my future. No longer does the guilt of my mistakes keep me from seeing the enormous value I have because of what Christ did for me. No longer do I sit and wonder why God loves me, adores me, and cares for me. No longer do I allow the accuser, the voice of lies, to bind me back to my past. I am free!

I am now running headlong, with childlike abandon, into the arms of Jesus. I know He is always there, always waiting for me to come to Him with all that I am, flaws and all.

How do I know? What made the change in me?

I know because Christ experienced the same rejection, the same feelings of isolation and loneliness, and the same despair. In his weakest moments His greatest enemy, Satan, came and taunted Him, trying to destroy Him in an effort to derail the greatest mission ever. Jesus came to give us freedom. He came to give us life. Forever. It is done. It is finished. The blood of Jesus

Christ has overcome every lie the enemy tried to bind us with. It breaks the handcuffs of low self-esteem, the ugliness of addiction, the straitjacket of heartbreak. So why do so many of us remain in bondage?

Because deep heart bruises, damaged emotions, and dark places in our lives where we have made choices apart from God can only be healed if we reach out to break the chains and run toward our healing. Memories of the wounds in our past can haunt us forever if we are not able to forgive, surrender the outcome to God, seek His will in the situation and allow Him to avenge the past.

Holding on to anger that eventually turns to resentment and bitterness allows a fortress to be built around your heart. Eventually, you cannot get out, and no one can enter. Surrendering the outcome of our lives to God, forgiving one another and our enemies, keeps us alive and free. Why would anyone choose to live in prison and let his enemy run free? Forgiveness sets us free. Forgiveness will set you free.

Focusing on perceived injustices, whether they are real or not, keeps us rooted in deadly emotions. We return again and again to our anger, and that enslaves us to our past. When we learn to surrender everything that hasn't been fair, all our injustices, to the God who loves us more than we can imagine, we are set free. When we forgive those who have trespassed against us, we are set free. Jeremiah 33:3 promises that God then gives us a hope and a future.

Let go of what you cannot control. God is a much better avenger. He will bring justice to all when we see Him face to face. It's a new day, friends! Whatever is behind you, leave it back there. It's time to walk in the freedom, the God Crazy Freedom, the Lord desires for us. Don't get stuck in the past and let it keep you from your today and your future.

That's easy to say, right? But how do we do it? How do we break free from these things that have kept us enslaved for so many years? How do we rid ourselves of the familiar, the coziness of our guilt, the comfort of our pain and pity? How do we shed the self-righteousness of our anger and unforgiveness? How do we move on from what was done to us or said about us, and the wrongs that have never been made right?

The stories you are about to read are the voices of those whose heart bruises are evident but whose victories brought healing! We walk in freedom because we are in the best company. The same kinds of injustices, abuse, abandonment and downright evil that we have experienced are the same evils and attacks that Jesus experienced when He came as a man to earth.

And in His darkest moment, while He was hanging on the cross of Calvary, He looked up to the Father, and what did He say? Did He ask God to strike everyone down who had hurt Him? Did He renounce all of mankind? NO! What did He say?

Father Forgive Them ...

And Jesus said, Father, forgive them for they know not what they do.

Paid In Full.

Father, into Thy hands I commend My spirit.

I am the Alpha and Omega, the beginning and the end, saith the Lord.

My dear sisters, do not be afraid to take a hard look at the hard places, because they are the dark soil that can bring up new life. The most painful places, when healed, create growth, accomplishment, success, and new life.

It won't be easy at times, because all freedom comes at a price. Jesus paid with His life for our freedom. The price you must pay is the acceptance of Him and a desire to fight to get close to Him and experience your freedom. Fight the negativity, shame, and all the lies of Satan the same way you would fight to get out of prison if you were incarcerated for no reason. If you were innocent and accused of a crime, would you sit back and do nothing or would you fight the charges against you and do everything you could to get out of jail? Jesus already paid the price for your sin, for all sin, but we have to accept Him and His truth into our lives and allow His truth to reign and rule in our hearts.

If you dare to accept Christ, dare to love, dare to forgive, and have the courage to let go, then you will see the freedom my friends and I have seen. You will no longer have chains around your heart, and you will finally be able to walk in all God has for you.

Do you find this difficult to comprehend? We understand. That's why the **God Crazy Freedom** team is opening up our lives in these pages and sharing our painful personal pasts, so that you can see the freedom we feel in our present and the excitement we have about our futures. We share our journey from heart bruises to healing victory so that you, too, might be free. Each story is topped by two words: the curse of the past vs. the freedom we found. For example, my story is titled: "Shame to Purity." Following each story is five days of devotions, personal challenges for you to take action and apply what you've read, plus a God Crazy Freedom prayer to draw you closer to the God who can't wait to watch you run to Him.

Our prayer as you read through this book is that you will begin your own journey to God Crazy Freedom. You are God's gorgeous girl, and He longs to show you how He sees, values and longs to heal you from your hurts, your bad habits, and all your hang-ups. We pray you begin the steps of moving beyond victim into the victorious. We also pray that as you walk out this process, God would comfort you, give you strength to withstand the darts of the enemy, and catch you in His wide open arms as you go from halting baby steps to a full-on sprint. It may feel like a marathon, but, Girlfriends, you can do it. We'll be cheering you on all the way as you find the God Crazy Freedom to walk our every ounce of your purpose and potential.

From our hearts to yours,

Michelle Borquez Thornton, president, God Crazy Freedom Experience; Creator of The Freedom Series; and Author *Forever God Crazy* and *Overcoming the Seven Deadly Emotions*

And the God Crazy Team.

SHAME TO PURITY

by Michelle Borquez Thornton

My love for fashion didn't come until I was in high school. As a little girl and preteen I was a total, all-out tomboy. While other girls were worrying about their makeup and hair, I was thinking about playing soccer with the boys. I look back on some of those childhood photos and hardly recognize that little girl. Today, I am as feminine as can be. As the lead *fashionista* of a fashion company, I'm hardly a tomboy now. Although, I am occasionally still called a guys' girl because I do love a good soccer game or rock climb. I even love me some football (smile).

Yes, it was in high school when my love for fashion hit me; and it was in high school that I began wearing the heavy, unwanted cloak of shame. I can see now that small heart bruises began when I was a young girl, a little tomboy filled with innocence and wonder and fun. I had a typical home life for the average middle-class kid. My mom didn't work, Dad brought home the paycheck, and life was mainly about survival. Dad and I never talked about deep things, nor did mom and I really at the time. They were caught up in in their world, trying to stay on top of five kids, a home in the suburbs, and just everyday life. Also, my dad was angry at life at that time, and as the oldest child I think he took some of that out on me. Those were the first heart hurts.

I think most of us are born with insecurities, and some of us grow up more insecure than others (or maybe some of us are better at pretending than others). I was very insecure as a young girl. I always focused on what I didn't have. I wasn't the best-looking girl. I didn't have a rich family, and I most certainly didn't have any fashion sense. I felt like I was always swimming upstream trying to "be" somebody. So every chance I had to swim with the right crowd and fit in, I was there. I felt like an outsider, but I was there.

The combination of my insecurities and the fact that my parents hadn't really prepared me for boys would lead to a string of heart bruises so deep they would take years to heal. These events colored my high school years and beyond and really warped my thinking well into my young adulthood.

The first deep bruise came in junior high school. A bunch of people had been invited to a party by some of the coolest boys in my school, and I was on the "in" list. I could not have been more excited. I asked my parents if I could go, but in my mind there could not be a "no." This was my chance to shine. They were reserved, but they agreed to let me go.

What I didn't know was that these junior high boys' parents had gone out of town for the weekend and left them alone. When I arrived at the party, there were only two girls there. Many had been invited, but only two of us had been able to come. That was the first night I was introduced to drugs and alcohol. I felt out of my league and definitely uncomfortable, but my insecurities made me stay. I wanted so badly to fit in.

Nothing happened to me physically that night, but the aftermath was as painful as a physical attack. The next day at school, the boys from the party told everyone that they had slept with me and the other girl. I was absolutely crushed. I had never experienced betrayal on that level. Emotionally, I was not able to process such a deep heart bruise. The rumor was a complete lie, but I felt as dirty as if it was truth.

I had barely kissed a boy, and now my reputation was destroyed at the tender age of fourteen. Moving into high school I felt those rumors follow me. I stayed away from boys for the most part and tried to move on, but the blanket of shame I now wore would not be removed for decades to come.

That first betrayal led to other deep heart bruises, such as rape and abortion. Eventually, my little heart became so bitter and angry. My innocence had been stolen by lies in junior high and continued to be stolen little by little over the course of the years to come. It's amazing how much damage can be done in just a few years. I was made to feel unworthy, and over time I embraced the unworthiness betrothed to me. I walked with my head held high, but my heart was bowed low beneath my feet. I never felt good enough or worthy enough and would spend the next years of my life working desperately to prove I was those things. I used my performance and outward image to cover nicely over my cloak of shame. I learned to wear these outer shells well.

I came to know Jesus Christ as my Lord and Savior at the age of twenty. This little broken girl found hope and meaning once again in life. I embraced my Christianity wholeheartedly and wanted nothing to do with my broken past. I thought I'd bury it and put on a whole new wardrobe. I learned the Christian lingo, walked the Christian walk, and I thought I wore it nicely. I learned to do all the right things to be acceptable and admired. I moved into leadership and excelled in life. I even fell in love and got married, had four children, and lived in the beautiful home with the white picket fence. I led worship, led Bible study, homeschooled my kids, and worked to make right and pay penance for all I had done in my past. But shame is an interesting thing; it's easy to hide when you learn to make yourself look good on the outside. It can go undetected for years … and in my life it did. The deep heart bruises I carried were far from healed.

I love the scene in *Les Miserables* when Jean Valjean, the ex-convict who served years in prison for stealing bread, is caught stealing once again from "Monseigneur Bienvenu" (Bishop Myriel). Bishop Myriel forgives him and covers for him. He tells Valjean that in exchange for his freedom, Valjean must go live his life and give back to society. A reformed, forgiven Valjean does exactly that, quietly but in a way that impacts people through all he does and eventually brings notice to him.

Officer Javert, a man of the law who takes pride in his flawless record, catches on to Valjean. He had lorded over Valjean when Valjean was imprisoned and even beaten. The two men are brought together again, and Javert makes it his life's mission to find fault in Valjean and put him back in prison. Javert believes that people don't change. However, once Javert comes face to face with Valjean's compassionate and loving nature, he is forced to realize that his notions of law, justice and human nature are not true. He finds himself at a loss and commits suicide so Valjean can go free.

I sobbed after watching this film. It reminded me of my own burden of sin I carried for so long, and the freedom Jesus granted me when he set me free at the age of twenty. Justice and the law were things I had embraced as a new believer, focusing on performance and serving my penance instead of truly understanding God's grace for me. I had no idea of God's depth of love for me, His unconditional mercy He had so freely given based on His death and resurrection. I had no idea until my perfectly constructed cloak was pulled off of my life through an unwanted divorce, revealing the deep shame I felt underneath. My perfect marriage of thirteen years, my carefully constructed image of the good Christian I could be, was over and I was left to pick up the pieces.

I couldn't understand how God could allow this to happen to me. I had done all the right things. If there were a set of boxes to check on how to live the Christian life, I would have been able to check every one. It just didn't make sense. It didn't add up. This caused a crisis in my faith that would last a year. I stopped going to church and really had no desire to hang around anyone who called themselves a "believer." I was angry with God, yet I knew the world had nothing to offer me.

It was in this place of unworthiness that I finally saw Jesus. Before my divorce, I knew a form of Christianity and truly loved the Lord, but I didn't know His incredible love for me. Now, in the midst of my trial, in the midst of the darkest season I had ever encountered, Jesus came and met me. He pursued me in my unfaithfulness, and this truly baffled me. Without realizing it, I had based God's love for me on how well I performed, how good I could be. The better my world looked, the more desirable I felt I was to God. I was His shining star and He could use me to show the world how great He could make someone look. *Wrong.*

MY VICTORY

Shame was the very last deadly emotion enslaving me that had to go. I had been enslaved by fear, anger, stress, and pride before; and God had freed me from all of those pretty early on in my life. But for some reason, the cloak of shame I had worn for many years, like a warm familiar blanket in the midst of a cold winter, was hard for me to rid myself of. I had even rationalized that as long as it was there, it would somehow keep me humble. Lies, lies, lies. Every deadly emotion is rooted in a lie.

In my book *Overcoming the Seven Deadly Emotions*, I wrote this about shame;

> *"At the very root of shame is a sense of self-loathing. A feeling of unforgiveness for the sins of one's past or the sins of someone else we endured. Shame gives the burden-carriers the feeling that something is wrong with them; something is not right with who they are. Shame can come from messages we have told ourselves or even messages others have told us throughout our lives. There is such a thing as "healthy shame": an awareness of conscience telling us that when we sin we should feel ashamed of what we did. But once we repent, the shame should leave us because we have been cleansed by the blood of Christ. The burden has been lifted.*

Our desire to be martyrs or the lies we continue to believe keep us in bondage when we've really been freed. This is the greatest loss of all. What a waste of the great life we have been given if it is spent in remorse and regret rather than freedom and grace."

I was unable to truly walk out my purpose until God freed me from the shame, and He used someone else to help me get there. Just like in Luke 5:19 when the friends of the paralyzed man lowered him down through a roof so that he might be healed, I needed someone to help me in my paralytic state.

> *When they could not find a way to do this because of the crowd, they went up on the roof and lowered him on his mat through the tiles into the middle of the crowd, right in front of Jesus. When Jesus saw their faith, he said, "Friend, your sins are forgiven.*
> (LUKE 5:19-20)

Jesus goes on to address the Pharisees who are appalled that He would be so bold to grant someone their sins forgiven and Jesus responds: *"Which is easier: to say, 'Your sins are forgiven,' or to say, 'Get up and walk'?"* (Luke 5:23)

As I pressed through for my healing, God began to reveal His love to me in an even deeper way. One afternoon in prayer, the Lord gave me a simple illustration. He showed me a brilliant diamond with no flaws. It was so radiant I could barely look on it. Suddenly, as I fixed my gaze, admiring the diamond in all its brilliance, what seemed like a flood of blood came pouring over it. It was washing over the diamond like a river of water washes over a rock bed. Even though it was being covered with the rushing blood, the brilliance of the diamond was so great; it shone through like a magnificent light. I could see it shining through, radiant for all to see.

This is such a simple illustration, but seeing this in prayer helped me to see so clearly how God looks at us. None of us is worthy for God's gaze to be on us. We are all sinners and have fallen short of the glory of God. God sent His son Jesus to wash us clean with His blood, the blood that was sacrificed for us on the cross at Calvary. This blood is what God sees us through. When we accept Christ into our heart as Savior, He looks on us through the river of blood that washes over us and cleanses us of our sin.

This picture set me free forever. No longer did the blanket of shame cover me and keep me paralyzed from my purpose and destiny. No longer could the enemy, the accuser of the brethren, use my past against me. I am free indeed, and while there are moments when shame tries to attach itself to me once again, I immediately recognize the lie and think back to how much Jesus loves me. He made the ultimate sacrifice for my life, so that I might be forgiven and His mercy and grace extended to me over and over again when my heart repents.

DEVOTION: DAY ONE

What shame are you holding onto? Are there secrets you have never told anyone, keeping the blanket of shame tightly knit around you? Today is the day of your freedom. There is no reason to walk in shame any longer. Why?

I am God's child. (John 1:12)

I have been redeemed and forgiven of all my sins. (Colossians 1:14)

I am free from condemnation. (Romans 8:1-2)

I am free from any condemning charges against me. (Romans 8:31-34)

I cannot be separated from the love of God. (Romans 8:35-39)

I have been established, anointed, and sealed by God. (2 Corinthians 1:21-2)

I can find grace and mercy in time of need. (Hebrews 4:16)

These are just a few of the reasons you no longer have to wear the blanket of shame. When you accept Christ, you are a new creation. You are no longer connected to the shame of your past, the guilt of your past, the sins of your past. You are forgiven, redeemed, and now you will begin walking through the restoration of your heart. He desires to heal your memories. Will you allow Him to heal you?

Today, begin the process of admitting. The first step to getting beyond the pain of shame and the guilt of your past is admitting and accepting it. Admit to the Lord today all you have done and ask for His forgiveness.

Write down on a piece of paper:

I forgive the girl of my past for _____.

Sometimes, even though we think God has forgiven us, it takes forgiving ourselves.

DEVOTION: DAY TWO

Well, we have repented, which literally means a *change of mind*. We've asked God to forgive us, yet the shame still feels so real and so present. It took me many years to let go of the shame. I hope it takes less time for you. It really is a perspective change. It's realizing you are not good enough; you are not ever going to be good enough. Our righteousness is as filthy rags:

> All of us have become like one who is unclean, and all our
> righteous acts are like filthy rags; we all shrivel up like a leaf, and
> like the wind our sins sweep us away. (ISAIAH 64:6)

You are right. You are not good enough. But you are worthy. How can you be both at once? Because His strength is made perfect in your weakness. You can't do it yourself. I can't do it myself. If we could, God would not have sent His son. Close your eyes. Think of the most beautiful picture of nature, or a diamond, or something you deem of great value. Are you seeing it? Now imagine the blood of Jesus pouring over it like a river. When God looks on you, He views you through the same river, the river of life. Jesus shed His blood so that we might be free. Why, then, do you remain in bondage? It's time to be free from the past guilt and shame and move ahead to begin to fulfill the purpose God has for your life.

DEVOTION: DAY THREE

Are you looking good on the outside but inside hurting badly? Let's move beyond those heart bruises and reach for the freedom found in a life with Christ. What does this look like? What lies are you still hanging on to? What lies are still engrossed in your every day thinking? The first step to getting rid of the lies we believe is to expose them. Begin by confessing them to the Lord, and then find someone safe, someone you trust and who has possibly walked the same road as you. Broken people are advocates for the broken. They are most likely going to be safe, simply because they understand the steps you are taking. They have walked the same journey.

Here are some amazing first steps in God's Word to overcoming shame:

Exposing the lies – *I have no greater joy than to hear my children walk in truth.* (John 3:4)

Repenting of your past sins – *Let us therefore draw near with confidence to the throne of grace that we may receive mercy and find grace to help in our time of need.* (Hebrews 4:16)

Realizing who you are in Christ – *The King delights over his daughter with singing.* (Zephaniah 3:27)

My prayer for you is that God gives you strength for the journey because the steps to becoming whole and healthy once again are not without pain. It's never easy to look at your past and move beyond it, yet the freedom experienced once you do is so worth it. We must remember we have an enemy who goes around like a roaring lion seeking whom he may devour:

Behold Satan has desired to sift you as wheat, but I have prayed for you, that your faith fail not, and when you are converted, strengthen the brethren (daughters). (LUKE 22:31-32)

May your faith not fail as you walk on this journey to overcome shame in your life. Remember, He is with you and He will never leave you nor forsake you.

DEVOTION: DAY FOUR

In an interview I did with author Stormie Omartian, a victim of abuse, she told me that it took her more than a decade after she came to know the Lord to feel free from the pain. "It was fourteen years from the time I received the Lord until the time I felt no pain," Stormie said. "If I had to point to one time in my life when I really got free, it was when I was able to forgive my dad for allowing my mom to do those things to me. That was major – it was a hidden forgiveness I didn't realize I had but it translated into a lack of trust in my husband and a lack of trust in God." Stormie's inability to forgive was keeping her from freedom.

What are you holding back? Is there someone you need to forgive today? Is there something you need to let go of? As long as you are holding on to the past, it will continue to hold on to you and keep you from being free from the shame and guilt. Fully overcoming in the area of shame means looking at any areas of our life that may be keeping us from the freedom we are fighting for.

Take a moment and pray about who you may be holding in contempt. A teacher, a parent, a friend who betrayed your trust… just take a moment and ask God to reveal it to you. Use the Word to guide you. The Word of God has power, but if we are not able to fully have the faith to believe in its power, then it remains powerless in our lives. Allow God's Word to empower you for the journey. He came that we might have life and have life abundantly. Are you ready for the abundant life?

Meditate on these scriptures: Ephesians 1: 4-12, John 3:1, Colossians 3:3, Psalm 32:1, and John 3:16.

DEVOTION: DAY FIVE

When Christ comes into your life, you are made new, and the old things pass away (2 Corinthians 5:17). We have put on the mind of Christ, to think His thoughts, to know His heart concerning us. This comes by praying, praising Him, and meditating on His Word. It is important to say His promises out loud until they become established in our hearts and minds.

The Word of God means nothing of value to us until we realize its value in our lives. It can be difficult to believe at first because of all our old thought patterns and the lies we have based our life on. These thoughts speak loudly in our minds, but if you persevere and expect God to honor His Word, the Word you have planted in your heart will begin to take root and grow. Be patient. The roots are underground, but at the right time they will begin to sprout and produce life in you. For as long as you live, no matter what trial you go through, you will need to turn to the Word of God first and continue to seek Him with all your heart, mind and soul.

Allow His words to wash over you daily and take time to worship Him. It is in the midst of many personal worship times that I was able to find healing.

Lord, thank you for "purging me with hyssop, and making me clean and washing me that I shall be whiter than snow" (Psalm 51:7). Continue to pour out your love, filling our hearts, that we may be secure in Your loving embrace. In Jesus' name, amen.

GOD CRAZY FREEDOM SHAME CHALLENGE

My dear sister in Christ:

You no longer have to walk with a limp or feel disqualified in any way. You are forgiven, your sins are forgotten, and now you are free to walk out the purity and purpose God has for your life. This is not a sinless life, but a life of walking in the spirit and overcoming sin. Sin no longer enslaves us, derails us, deceives us so easily because truth now reigns and shame no longer has a grip.

My challenge to you is for you to really begin to focus every day on what is ahead of you and not what is behind you. To daily meditate on God's Word and, memory by memory, ask God to continue to heal and restore.

Don't be afraid to talk with someone about the things you have been holding in secret. It is so important for you to express these to someone you deem safe who can love you in the process. I suggest someone who is a counselor or ministry leader and is mature in her walk with God.

Every day, take another step towards your freedom. It isn't an overnight process; it's a lifetime of healing and pressing through the difficult moments to the victory. You *will* be victorious. Greater is He that is in you, than he that is in this world. He overcame the world for us, and when we truly receive this truth we are then able to move beyond the lies.

For many years I struggled with the greatest lie of all. The lie that I wasn't worthy enough. This one lie kept me in bondage and prevented me from being fully effective to walk out my purpose. Whatever your lies are, take them captive one by one and speak them out so they are exposed. Then study the Word of God and seek the truth about each of the lies you believe and speak it daily.

Ask yourself, *Are these lies rational or irrational? Are they a counterfeit to what God has for me?* When we expose lies, they lose their power over us. My challenge to you, my friend, is to speak out the lies and expose the secrets, so you can walk in freedom and fulfill the purpose and potential God has for you.

God Crazy Freedom Prayer over Shame

Lord,

You know every dark secret I hold, every moment of shame, every accusation made against me. You know the moments of failure and times when sin has had a grip on me so strong I have been unable to break free. Lord, you see my dark thoughts, my feeble ways, and most of all my inability to come to you in my moments of shame for fear you will reject me, not love me, not deem me worthy. Lord, forgive me for my lack of faith, my lack of will, my lack of determination to fight and press through the pain so I can find the victory. I need you desperately to carry me through, to strengthen me in my weakness, to renew my mind and heart so I can walk in the purity you so desire for me. Lord, I long to see myself through your eyes, like the beautiful daughter you describe in Psalm 45:13-15: "You, my child, are a daughter of the King and all glorious within. I clothe you in clothing embroidered with gold and lead you to me in purity with gladness and rejoicing as you enter the palace of the King."

Lord, help me to see my value, my worth. Look into my heart and heal my heart bruises, my pain, my despair, so I can begin to live out the beautiful plan you have for my life.

In Jesus' name, Amen and Amen.

My Plan to God's Purpose

by Paige Henderson

It was a cold-sweat kind of dream. The big ship was upended and sinking fast in the dark, and I was paddling for a spot on a lifeboat just a half-dozen strokes away. *I will not die today*, was all I was thinking as I mustered what was left of my strength to survive. The lifeboat I was heading for was sort of egg-shaped, not the long, multiple-life-preserving kind that are really on those big cruise ships. The lifeboat I was struggling for only had one seat; it was just a wooden version of an inner tube, really. I was pulling hard against the waves to get to the boat when I sensed the splashing of another lifeboat seeker off my starboard. It was another woman.

No! I repeated my mantra, *I will not die today. She might, I won't.* In one continuous stroke, my arm paddled one last time and reached the rim of that little ark just as another hand thudded against the side. I looked up and saw the face of the one who wanted my seat.

She was … *me!*

I knew instantly what the stakes were: two of me, one seat. *Who I Was* and *Who I Could Be* were nose-to-water-dripping nose, struggling against the waves and wind. I was staring into the calm and confident eyes of the woman I longed to be, but I just couldn't let go of who I had created. Who would I be if I wasn't … me? *Let me live*, she spoke to my heart.

I snapped awake.

The next few years of my life would be a showdown between my identity and my purpose, between who I thought I was and who God called me to be.

I know the plans I have for … me!

I was born to two fabulous people who knew Jesus, loved Jesus and raised me without a single moment when I didn't know about Jesus. These two fabulous people created a perfectly protected environment with lovely traditions and fond family vacation memories. They appropriately disciplined me, encouraged me, and never missed a concert, a sporting event or a contest of any kind. They were kind and fair. I had two sisters and my own room, some pets along the way, a good American bootstraps work ethic, and room to play and create. I was denied nothing that the budget could afford, I was not abused, never felt abandoned, and felt not just loved, but also liked by these fabulous people.

Except for a few minor stupidities that resulted in some cheek-coloring embarrassments, my childhood was perfect. So why am I writing a story of overcoming? What great obstacle did I have to be victorious over?

Me.

Now, that's a stronghold that rarely comes up in the deep conversations of overcoming deep stuff. It's the stronghold of having nothing to overcome. This stronghold has to do with where you're born, who your parents are, where you went to church, all the good stuff you know, and how you've never had to walk in places where others have had to walk.

We talk a lot about those who have "issues" and the great victories that are won in laying aside the curses and vows and fears and addictions and all manner of yucky stuff that comes from those "issues." I've had the privilege of having a front row seat to see God work miraculous deliverances and instantaneous healings.

Now, in no way do I want to diminish those mighty struggles to overcome what you've done and what's been done to you. But no one addresses those of us whose greatest struggle is believing that the absence of "issues" means that everything is okay and that you've done well in creating an impervious identity.

Keep it to yourself, it's my life.

It's the ugliest thing Jesus dealt with and the ugliest thing I've ever had breathing down my neck. "I am the master of my fate; I am the captain of my soul" is not in the Bible, you know. That's from William E. Henley's poem "Invictus." Since it was the way I was living, I really wanted it to be biblical, or at least a very good idea.

On the other hand, I thought, "I am crucified with Christ," which is truth, was a terrible idea. Why would I need to be crucified? Who would want to do such a wasteful thing? I am cute, smart, confident, creative – a real asset to the Kingdom. I made the right decisions, was seen at the right places, attended the right church and had the right friends. I had the right job, volunteered for the right committees and maintained the right level of influence. I married the right man and we lived in the right house with the right exterior base coat and the right living room arrangement according to the right decorator magazine. I set the right table and taught the right Bible studies.

Jesus was sure fortunate when He found me! I would be the first Christ-follower who would not ever need to be crucified to ... *anything*.

Wow! I can't even believe I said that. I can't believe that was in my heart.

This was a battle: my identity was at war with my purpose. In the one corner, wearing the multi-colored boxing shorts was a bouquet of pretty identities: singer, actress, speaker, writer, teacher, sponsor, etc. The sum total of what I did. My life as a human *doing*. In the other corner, wearing plain jogging shorts, a single flower of Obedience. The blossom of becoming a human *being*.

A "yes" to the Great Adventure of Obedience, leaving behind the kingdom I'd built, could ruin everything. But I think that was actually the point God was trying to make. I really feared what God would do to me if I were completely yielded to Him. I had this great life that I honestly thought I'd played some big part in creating, and I really didn't want Him to mess it up.

Faster, faster, I think I'm gonna crash.

So I began the negotiation: performance for obedience. As long as I could sing and dance really loudly, maybe I could distract Him from what He was planning to do to me once I completely yielded to Him. Be good enough, cute enough, smart enough and invaluable enough, and I would never have to give up control. I wasn't exactly sure what God's purpose for me was, but I was fairly sure that I would lose my identity if I really yielded to it.

Where had I gotten *that* stuff? The truth was ugly and exposing it was like yanking a band-aid: I didn't trust God, I was gaudy in my pride and my Nice Life was actually just "stanky" rebellion.

I had lined up my pedigree, my identity, against His purpose for me and silently declared that I knew best what the sum of my life would be. I thought the life of blessing that had been given to me was about me. It never dawned on me that it was about nothing more than His glory, His purpose, and "the kind intention of His will." Bad things happen to good people and bad people. Good choices don't immunize you against bad experiences; bad choices don't guarantee you a messy life. You don't earn blessings, you aren't owed them for a great performance or for services rendered or because you are So-and-So's daughter. I had completely missed the greatness of God in my life because it was really the greatness of Me. I had stolen His glory, yapping about how great my choices were and how glorious my decisions – and I believed my yapping. Yuck!

Then I tripped over some verses that Paul wrote that described what I couldn't seem to put into words. In Philippians 3:1-8 he outlined his stellar pedigree – born to the right people at the right time, studied under the right teacher, joined the right sect, and made the right choices. According to the measure of the law, he was "blameless." But he'd throw it all away as excrement for just knowing Jesus. It didn't matter how great his life had been and how right his choices had been or what his identity had been, it was a smelly pile of nothing important compared to one moment of purpose in the presence of Jesus the Christ.

It doesn't mean a thing without You.

Jesus was a friend of sinners, not the ones who were raised and trained to be the consorts of the Messiah. Nope, they'd missed Him altogether. His face-to-face showdowns were with the self-sufficient, the self-proficient and the self-righteous. When you look at it like that, then the sin of "right living" (self-righteousness, actually) is worse than whatever "Oops, I missed the mark" you've done. Jesus went toe-to-toe with those who chose righteous identity over grace-filled purpose. Those who desperately clung to Him got His heart. Those who desperately cling to nothing because, well, they don't cling and are never desperate get … nothing.

MY VICTORY

So there I was, clinging to my pedigree in the dark. In a moment of absolute terror, I asked, "If I let go of ME, what will You give me for a life?"

"Everything," He said. "You haven't seen anything yet. Everything you think you know is just a replica of the real purpose that I have stored up for you."

She who saves her life loses it (Luke 9:24). I was paddling toward a lifeboat of death. I was trying to protect a life that He didn't want for me. I was preserving an identity and was about to miss purpose.

Oswald Chambers has two definitions in his *My Utmost for His Highest* devotional. One definition is for Individuality and the other is for Personality. Individuality is the "husk," he says, of the real life contained within. Individuality is "all elbows" and it pokes and jabs its way through life, making room for itself and its identity. But the Personality is the kernel of the real life inside that husk of protection. It is the Grand Adventure, the breathtaking beauty of "Yes." I wanted that. Personality is unique – not individual.

He made me in full 3-D color, so why would His purpose be flat and in black and white? Why would He take the swirl of my personality and replace me with a Stepford Christian? What He really wanted to do was loose me! He really just wanted to peel the husk off and let me breathe. My identity had me bound up like an old corset. I was completely limited by my own ability to think of all the things I could be. He wanted to cut those corset strings and let me, "Walk and not grow weary [breathless], run and not faint [pass out for lack of oxygen]." I only became free when I let go of Who I Was and embraced Who I Could Be, the woman that He had called me to be all along.

DEVOTION: DAY ONE

We are quick to encourage people to leave their pasts behind them and move forward. But what if what's behind you is good stuff? What if you have done nothing to be ashamed of? What if someone has not taken advantage of you or abused you? What if you have no skeletons in your closet?

Let me let you in on a little secret about Lot's wife and maybe why she looked back (Genesis 19:17-26). She'd left two married daughters back in Sodom, and maybe grandchildren. She'd left friends back there. Since there's no mention of her when Lot makes his initial choice of the pretty green land, leaving Abraham with the Other Land, it's not inconceivable that she may have been a local girl and this was her home, the place of her birth. Now it was going up in sulfurous, falling rock-lit flame. She looked back at what was her identity: hometown, friends, nice home, children, and grandchildren.

Her salty state wasn't just because she looked – it was because she looked in the direction of her treasure. And her treasure was back, not forward. When your treasure is back, but your purpose is forward, you will freeze like a salt lick and be useless in the Kingdom.

Read Matthew 6:19-21. What do you read that is especially applicable to you? Consider the context of our discussion here. Make the "two masters" of verse 24 your identity and your purpose. What's the Lord saying to you?

DEVOTION: DAY TWO

They go from glory to glory and every one of them appears before God in Zion. PSALM 84:7

Compare that verse to Proverbs 4:18 and 2 Corinthians 3:18. What do you see in all three of these verses?

Can you see the Christ-follower moving forward? What is she moving from and moving to? What is the Lord saying about you and your life in these three verses?

Not one of those verses intimate that "they go from disappointment to glory," "from bad stuff to good stuff," but rather from "glory" - good things, great memories, a job well done, a decision well made - to the next "glory."

We have to be transient people. We can't stay long in either pain or applause. The whole idea of the manna that God provided to the Hebrew nation during the wilderness wandering was to completely consume what had been given for that day so that the pots were empty to collect more manna the next day.

We are so ready to move on when the day has been a complete disaster. In fact, we can't get to sleep fast enough. But when the day's been stellar, what then? We want to take pictures, put them in a scrapbook, post them on Facebook, and top the memory off with a Tweet to a couple of hundred friends. Then we somehow want "credit" for the success. We quickly want to be excused from the wreck one minute, but awarded with a tiara and sash for the greatness of the next minute.

If God's throne is a throne of grace, then it is a place that equally receives successes and failures with the same value – God's glory.

DEVOTION: DAY THREE

"Follow me," was Jesus' simple invitation to His disciples.

They weren't on the run from their pasts. We actually know very little of their personal histories, and while that would be interesting to know, what we do know is that their lives were apparently not so bad. Some were fishermen, but we aren't told that their businesses were on the brink of collapse when Jesus showed up and rescued them from bankruptcy. Matthew was a tax-collector but there's not one mention of his suffering at the hands of the Romans. Judas and Simon were both zealots, and although they'd probably made some folks mad, as far as we know they weren't running for their lives.

So basically Jesus interrupted their great lives and called to them to drop their nets, calculators, and picket signs of success and follow Him to "greater things"(John 14:12). My translation of His invitation: "Drop who you are and come see what you can be."

There were no guarantees as to what this adventure would be. In fact, in the next three years, this ministry they'd signed up for looked pretty shaky, and all of their reputations were on the line. But Jesus called them by their purposes, not their identities – you will be healers, evangelists, church-planters, preachers, teachers, brilliant businessmen, etc. The identities of fishermen, tax-collectors, religious zealots were left way behind for the Adventure of "Yes."

DEVOTION: DAY FOUR

I think the discussion of identity takes on a different twist when we replace the word with "reputation." What kind of reputation do you have? What five words do you think (hope!) other people would use to describe you? Now, what if following Jesus requires that that reputation changes? It probably wouldn't be in a negative way, but just different. Are you willing to lay aside the name you've created for yourself in order to follow Jesus?

One day a man with a great reputation came to see Jesus because he was interested in being a disciple. He was a man with his finger on the pulse of life, and he wanted to be in with the In Crowd of Jesus. The scene is found in Mark 10:17-23. Read about this encounter with Jesus. What do you see in these verses that connect to the discussion of purpose and identity?

Did you see what Jesus felt in verse 21? Have you ever read this story with Jesus having a loving voice and not an accusing voice? Was Jesus trying to keep the man from being a disciple or was He trying to save this young man from himself and his reputation?

Now read the encounter that Jesus had with some other would-be disciples in Luke 9:57-62. Did they become disciples or not? What's the basis of your answer? What answer did each one give? Could it be that the response you imagine they gave is based on what you would have said in the same circumstance?

I don't see a response given by any of them. They were just as likely to have said "Okay" as "Never mind."

What do you say?

DEVOTION: DAY FIVE

Let's look at Paul's words again in Philippians 3:1-14.

Paul's identity was perfect. He was a rock star in his own culture. By the time he wrote this letter to the Philippians, he was not.

Following Jesus had cost him his identity and his reputation. Paul's identity was scary and his reputation was vicious. Christ-followers didn't want to be anywhere near him; ardent Jews flocked to him in droves.

The first time we meet Paul, his identity is "Saul" and he's the one presiding over the stoning of the first Christian martyr, Stephen. Presiding meant that he not only approved of what was happening, he held everybody's coats so they could stone him better. The Bible says that Paul was breathing threats against Christians because of his zealous love and devotion to Jehovah, His law and reputation. But he was wrong. His whole identity was based on wrong thinking.

His identity didn't have a leg to stand on the day Jesus knocked it down on the road to Damascus. Saul's very identity evolved that day, complete with a brand new name and a brand new purpose. God's purpose required a total revolution.

Are you sensing a total revolution in you? What does it involve? Write about what you're feeling. What is the old that's going to be revolutionized? What is the new thing?

GOD CRAZY FREEDOM CHALLENGE

Give yourself a tangible experience in letting go of your identity. Go to a local party store and collect some helium balloons. On those helium balloons write everything that has gone into creating your identity. On one balloon, write all the words that you would use to describe your reputation. On another balloon, write all your achievements and successes. (You may have to use two balloons for that one.) On another balloon, list your failures and regrets. Whatever you identify yourself with, put it on a balloon. Consider your family, your "right" choices, your career moves. Keep writing till you have nothing else to use to identify yourself.

Then let them go. As they float away, thank God for everything on them. Recognize that He is the source of everything you wrote on them, and He is the source of everything new that's coming for you.

GOD CRAZY FREEDOM PRAYER

Almighty God, I lay all I am at Your feet. You are the source of my life and who I am. I am fearfully, wonderfully and purposefully made and I give you all the glory for me. I thank you for the idea You had when You made me in secret. Even knowing my thoughts, my attitudes, my successes and my disasters, You made me and set me in motion to live with purpose. Your delight is a yielded life, and I want You to be delighted in Me. Here I am. Yours. I willingly relinquish who I think I am for who You created me to be, and I welcome a new Adventure of "Yes." In Jesus' name I pray, Amen.

My Choices:

I recognize that I am the Lord's and what He chooses for me and my life is not only acceptable, but perfect.

I hold loosely my successes and failures and will be ready to lay aside both in order to move from "glory to glory."

I will no longer elbow my individual way through life, but I will allow my personality to be purposefully used for God's glory.

REJECTION TO ACCEPTANCE

by Jennifer Mallan

I could feel my life unwinding.

Right there in the middle of my grandmother's living room, curled up on all fours on my Meme's plush, mint-green carpet. I felt rejected – unwanted, extremely misunderstood. My whole life, I struggled with the prevalent thought that nobody really loved me except my Meme. I believed that nothing could fill the deep emptiness in my heart. My spirit cried...

Notice me.

Love me.

See me.

I should have been on top of the world. I was twenty-one years old, about to get my business communications degree with honors. I had pageant titles and homecoming queen runner-up status under my belt. I had great grades and many accolades, and I had enjoyed working for famed Florida State University football coach Bobby Bowden throughout my four-year university career. I interned in the governor's office and worked for two of Florida's first ladies. I had wined and dined with famous people in fancy places. And I had already found the man I was in love with and would later marry.

Still, I kept striving, striving, striving. Driven by a performance-for-acceptance mentality, I always wanted to go above and beyond anything that was expected of me. I wanted, no, I needed to know I was worthy. But deep down I didn't believe it. Now I found myself in one of the darkest, most despondent, depressed places I had ever been. I felt the spiral downward. I felt numb. I didn't even know if I wanted to live anymore.

All my life, I had worked for validation, begged to feel connected and valued. Whether my mother and father couldn't say it or I couldn't hear it, I don't recall them ever telling me I was a good girl. My family had a hard time saying, "I love you." And the more desperately I cried out to be accepted, the lonelier I became.

You see, from as far back as I could remember, I felt different than everyone else in my home. I was adopted as an infant, and shortly after I came home my mother unexpectedly became pregnant with my brother. A sister came along after that, and evidently I didn't adapt too well. Having already lost my biological teen-aged parents, now I had an adoptive family who tried but didn't quite know what to do with me. I just wasn't anything like them. My brother and sister had pale skin, freckles and red hair. They were quiet and introverted. My skin was olive-toned, my hair dark and thick, and my emotions a roller coaster of highs and lows. I was a type-A personality, driven and determined.

My mother once told me I was an "angry" baby, and that she often couldn't figure out anything that would soothe me or stop my crying. There was no internet or Google to look up remedies or connect and partner with others in the same situation. Child development and attachment in adoption were subjects that were almost unheard-of back then. Now I know that sad babies and children from hurt and broken places often look angry. Then, I just felt alone and abandoned, no matter how many family members surrounded me.

As I sobbed myself to sleep at night, my little-girl heart cried ...

Notice me.

Love me.

See me.

But I didn't think anyone did.

My family moved many times during my childhood, which didn't help.

Every two years or so, my academically-minded father transferred to a different university for his degree, internship, or fellowship. I couldn't keep a best friend or stay plugged in to a local church, school or neighborhood. As soon as I began to feel settled, our family packed up and moved again. On top of everything else, my mother developed debilitating rheumatoid arthritis by the time I was seven. The disease left her crippled with pain, in bed early every evening and unable to engage with the security needs of a wounded girl who needed affirmation. My high levels of energy and exuberance were exhausting to her and my love languages of quality time and acts of service were the opposite of hers.

Our differences and the lack of attachment to any permanent place put a strain on our family relationships, and took a huge toll on my self-esteem. I loved people and was very outspoken, but I was constantly being told to sit down and be quiet. I was addicted to the approval of others, high on the façade of acceptance I felt when I received an award or got any form of recognition. On the outside, I was an achiever. On the inside, I felt like damaged goods, not good enough for my real parents to keep or my new parents to love. I looked like I could fit in anywhere, but I lived in constant fear of letting everybody down which would lead to more rejection and isolation. Above all, I longed to belong.

My soul's cry continued …

Notice me.

Love me.

See me.

Couldn't anybody hear me?

By the time I entered my teen years, I soaked up attention like a sponge. It didn't matter if it was positive or negative, healthy or unhealthy; I took what I could get. Any attention was better than no attention. I won the lead roles in every high school drama production. I loved putting on another person's personality; it was such a relief to live vicariously through my characters. I could take a break from being me for a while, escape from all the raging thoughts and emotions within my heart. I also began dating boys who – let's just put it this way – didn't always treat me very nicely. I hopped on a six-year crazy cycle of codependency and abuse. I didn't know I was worthy, so I didn't expect the guys in my life to treat me with respect. I continued to garner praise for my performance at school, all the while enduring torturous physical and emotional abuse in my personal life.

And my spirit cried ...

Notice me.

Love me.

See me.

When I was seventeen, my quest for connection led me on a search for my biological family. Meme had kept my biological mother's family address, and after all those years they still lived there. Alone and trembling, I walked up the driveway and knocked on the open screen door. Suddenly, I was face to face with my maternal biological grandparents. It was scary, but exhilarating. They put me in the car and took me to meet my birth mother. For the first time, I found someone who looked like me. I thought meeting my biological family, finding out I had a brother, and discovering my family history would finally make me feel whole. But it didn't. Nothing was enough to fill the black hole of rejection and longing within me. Although I made it through university, by the time I knelt on my Meme's floor, I just couldn't do it anymore. I was sick and tired of being sick and tired. The quest to be "perfect" so as not to let anyone down had depleted and drained me to an all-time low. I was exhausted in body, soul and spirit.

And my heart kept crying ...

Notice me.

Love me.

See me.

MY VICTORY

So there I was, curled up on my Meme's mint-green carpet, crying out for something to change.

And then it did. Just like that.

One minute I wanted to die: the constant and overwhelming pain had culminated and spiraled out of control to the extent I saw no other option but to quiet the hopelessness within; the next moment, I found myself sitting up and gluing my eyes to the TV screen . God suddenly invaded my life through televangelist Pat Robertson's *700 Club* and the show's co-host, singer Sheila Walsh. Sheila seemed to look right through the TV screen straight at me and said, "If you're empty, hurting, broken, if you've tried everything, if you've run from God, He's right there waiting. His arms are open."

It was like she knew me intimately, like she had read my mail. I could feel God drawing me to Him, filling the hole in my heart like rain pounding on parched ground. Then Sheila began to sing a song, a beautiful song about a prodigal daughter. And when she got to the chorus, the words went like this:

> *"Jennifer, come home, We are waiting for you. Jennifer, come home, how we miss you."*

How much clearer could God be? In that instant, I knew my cries to be noticed, loved, and seen had always been heard. The Lord was always there. He called me by name. He wanted me to come home to Him. I fell into the arms of Jesus, who turned my rejection into acceptance. He took the shattered pieces of my self-esteem and tenderly wove them into a tapestry of grace and love. Today, I am the mother of five sons, married to my best friend, and have many opportunities to minister to the down-and-out and the rich-and-famous.

My journey home continues. God keeps growing me through seasons of peace, prosperity and provision. Then, He pops another pocket of pain and there is a season of struggle, of operating in survival mode. But instead of it taking me away, spiraling me down into that dark place of despair, I see it as a chance to grip tighter to God. I lean on Him, and He helps me to reach out to others.

I am noticed.

I am loved.

I am seen.

I am no longer rejected but accepted. That's true God Crazy Freedom!

DEVOTION: DAY ONE
NEVER DOWN FOR THE COUNT

*A bruised reed he will not break, and a faintly burning wick he
will not quench; he will faithfully bring forth justice.*
ISAIAH 42:3 (ENGLISH STANDARD VERSION)

When you barely have the strength to hold on, when you are hanging
on by a thread, God will not let you go. You might be bruised and battered,
you may think you don't have anything left in you that can shine, but He
will not let your light go out. When I felt so damaged that I thought if I
got one more blow I would go down for the count, this scripture gave me
victory. God blocked the "three" in Satan's "one-two-three" punches every
time.

Sweet sisters, even on the days when we are hemorrhaging misery,
hurting and bleeding profusely, we can stand firm in the knowledge that we
will not die from the emotional pain we are processing. It will be a lifetime
process, worth every step in the journey. Life is not fair, but God brings us
justice. It won't be exactly when we want it. In fact, it may be when we least
expect it. Long after we walk through and work through something deeply
painful, the Lord finally reveals to us the purpose behind the pain.

Our pain then transforms into our testimony. God uses what the
enemy meant for evil to bring about something beautiful – reconciliation,
restoration, renewal. Remember, God never wastes a pain. Pain can
actually be our friend.

DEVOTION: DAY TWO
LETTING IT ALL HANG OUT

As soon as Joseph saw his brothers, he recognized them, but he
pretended to be a stranger and spoke harshly to them.
GENESIS 42:7 (NIV)

Then Joseph could no longer control himself … And he wept so
loudly that the Egyptians heard him, and Pharaoh's household
heard about it. GENESIS 45:1-2 (NIV)

As a teen, Joseph was sold off by his ten jealous older brothers. He ended up in Egypt, where the Lord used him to save the land from famine. Years after getting rid of him, Joseph's brothers end up in Egypt trying to get food so they won't starve. Joseph forgives them and saves the very people who cast him out. It sounds so simple and has a "happily ever after" ending.

What we don't dwell on in this story is Joseph's agony, the emotions he wrestled with when his brothers reappeared. They had utterly rejected him, even thought about killing him. Now their lives are in his hands, and at first he manipulates, lies, and fights an internal war that wants revenge. His emotions are unrestrained and all over the place before he finally forges his way to forgiveness.

Joseph had made peace with God over what his brothers had done to him, but when those ten guys got in his face, his feelings didn't line up with his decision. What a comfort to know that all our feelings – the good, the bad, and the ugly – are covered by God's grace and goodness. We can decide to forgive and move forward, even when our flesh wants to fight to the finish.

In the middle of the messiness of transformation and spiritual maturity, God vindicates, heals, helps, and creates His desired outcomes and endings.

DEVOTION: DAY THREE
PRESS IN TO YOUR PAIN

He heals the brokenhearted and binds up their wounds [curing their pains and their sorrows]. PSALM 147:3 (AMPLIFIED)

Just when you think you are completely healed from your past feelings of rejection, the Lord will reveal another area of your heart that He needs to mend. You may feel strong and invincible one minute – "I am woman of God; hear me roar!" – and like a sobbing little girl with skinned knees the next.

When you stumble across another sore spot, run straight into the arms of your Papa God, your Abba (Daddy) Father. Then you will become aware of the hints of hope He gives you in your pockets of pain. As He lovingly, tenderly cleans out our old wounds and peels away the scar tissue, He develops in us the ability to lean on Him. It still hurts, but that's okay. Not fun, but necessary for us to grow and move forward, accomplishing the good works God prepared ahead of time for us to do. (See Ephesians 2:10.)

So instead of avoiding it, running from it, or escaping into something other than the Lord, press in to your pain and ask the Holy Spirit what He wants to teach you through it. When you fall in His arms and raise your pain-filled eyes to His, you will see your true identity reflected there. You begin and end in Him. That's who you really are. You are created in His image. Accepted, amazing and absolutely adorable!

DEVOTION: DAY FOUR
GETTING A DO-OVER

In place of your fathers will be your sons; You shall make them princes in all the earth. PSALM 45:16 (NASB)

Do you remember when you were a kid and you made a mistake during a sport or game, which you followed quickly and loudly with the announcement, "Do-Over"? You didn't mean to throw the ball over the fence. You thought you should get another chance to get it right.

As a young woman, Psalm 45:16 promised me that I could look to my future and what He was going to give me, not stay stuck in my pitiful past. I wasn't married and didn't have children when I found this verse, but I felt like God was telling me to put my hope and trust in what He was going to give me.

If you grew up without a dad, or you had one but he wasn't present or active, the Lord will restore what you lost or never had. We don't have to dwell on the shortcomings of our fathers, grandfathers, or other male figures in our lives. Instead, we can look forward to the day when he gives our families a do-over. For me, the fulfillment of Psalm 45:16 has been in raising five sons, fostering eleven boys, and now enjoying two grandsons. Talk about restoration!

DEVOTION: DAY FIVE
ADOPTED AND ACCEPTED

He hath chosen us in Him before the foundation of the world …
having predestined us to be His own adopted children by Jesus
Christ … wherein He hath made us accepted in His Beloved.
EPHESIANS 1:4-6 (21ST CENTURY KJV)

In my life, putting the words "adopted" and "accepted" together seemed like an oxymoron. How could someone be both given up and wanted? It just didn't compute. Because I felt rejection so strongly, I believe I attracted more rejection. Think of it this way: you go to a friend's party convinced nobody really wants you there. You stand in the corner looking miserable, hoping someone will notice. But it's a party. Everyone is having a good time. They don't want to hang out with someone who doesn't look like she is having fun. Rejection becomes a self-fulfilling prophecy.

If we think rejection is what we deserve, we go directly against the gospel of Christ, which states that we are more than accepted – we are amazing. What have you been attracting to your life? Healthy relationships or sick ones? Confusion and chaos or peace and power? We look at ourselves in the mirror and see damaged goods. But 1 Corinthians 13:12 tells us the party isn't over yet: "For now we see in a mirror dimly, but then face to face; now I know in part, but then I will know fully just as I also have been fully known." In other words, if the back was stripped off the mirror and you could see through it, you would see only God reflecting back on you. You bear His mark, His fingerprints. You are adopted and accepted. You are His Beloved and favorite child. He adores you and has memorized you. He has chosen you!

GOD CRAZY FREEDOM CHALLENGE

Do we really wake up in the morning and remember how exquisitely and uniquely we are made? How gloriously we are loved? Probably not, what with morning breath and bed head! We strive for acceptance and approval, when we are already the warrior-princess daughters of the King of Kings. It's not about what we do; it's simply who we are.

So here's your challenge, Sister: today, make time to drape yourself in a gorgeous dress. Grab a tiara and put it on. (Go get one if you don't have one. Every girl should have a tiara!). Stand in front of your mirror as you dress up for your king and speak His words of truth over yourself as you get ready for the rest of your life. We get dressed up for date nights. Why not for our groom? We are His bride, and we need to speak His life over ourselves.

Words like Song of Solomon 2:14, which beckons us:

Oh, get up, dear friend, my fair and beautiful lover—come to me! Come, my shy and modest dove— leave your seclusion, come out in the open. Let me see your face, let me hear your voice. For your voice is soothing and your face is ravishing. (The Message)

That's right – you're ravishing. Say it right now. Tell that mirror, "My God thinks I'm ravishing!"

How about Zephaniah 3:17:

The Lord your God is with you; the mighty One will save you. He will rejoice over you. You will rest in his love; he will sing and be joyful about you. (New Century Version)

He is rejoicing over you and singing over you right now! It doesn't matter where or how you started or even where you are right now. It matters where you end. You matter to God. He more than accepts you. He adores you. He died for you and wants to spend eternity with you. Look in the mirror and let the Lord unleash His power to heal the little girl in you. He will help that little girl dream and hope again.

GOD CRAZY FREEDOM PRAYER

Holy Spirit, I invite you to come in and pop all my pockets of pain. I know this will be a process that isn't easy and won't be fun, but, Father, I want to be healed. Help me to see myself as your masterpiece, to remember that you sing and rejoice over me. Let me keep the picture of a princess in mind when I feel damaged and rejected. I know that if I don't go with you to the deep crevices and caverns of my soul where I have stuffed my hurts and wounds, I won't be able to shine the light of your love and truth on those around me. Expose every lie that the enemy has used to trick me into thinking I am less than uniquely beautiful, gifted, and ready to be used by you to reach others and bring you glory. Help me to know to the very depths of my soul that I am accepted by the one who matters most, that my face is lovely and my voice is sweet to you. I believe by faith that I am chosen by you and for you, that I am ravishing to you, my groom. You have cared for me all along my journey, even when I didn't know you or feel your presence. Please use my story to bring hope and healing to others. I set my heart to continue to renew my mind in order to always remember who I am in you, no matter what my circumstances. Thank you for loving me just the way you made me. In Jesus' precious name, Amen.

EMPTINESS TO INTIMACY

by Punky Tolson

Once upon a time there was a young girl who dreamed of a handsome prince who would rescue her from all her troubles and fears, and carry her away on a white horse to his kingdom far away to live ... happily ever after.

Isn't that every young girl's dream? And every not-so-young woman's dream, too? The thought, the hope, that there really is that someone who could rescue us, faithfully love us and, yes, make all our dreams come true. That has certainly been my dream and maybe your dream too. But is that really just a dream? Is it just a fairy tale, fantasy, or fiction? Or could it possibly be a downright fact that's meant to be realized in your very own life?

What if we're actually hardwired not only to dream that dream, but also to experience that dream for real? Could it be ... might it just be ... that we've been created by our Creator with that very dream divinely and eternally planted into our mind and heart? Is His dream too good not to be true? Selah (pause and calmly think about that).

As a young woman, I had two "great ambitions" (grin). I wanted to be an actress and to fall in love, get married and live the happily-ever-after life I'd read about in romance novels, and seen on countless soap operas and epic love stories on the silver screen. Have you ever noticed that nearly all of the great love stories of our time esteem unhealthy male-female romances? From *Gone with the Wind*, *Casablanca*, and *Camelot* to *The Bridges of Madison County*, *The Thorn Birds*, *Dr. Zhivago*, *Pretty Woman*, and many more, all include some form of "forbidden fruit" cocktail in the mix of tormented souls looking for true love that lies just beyond reach. There are always casualties, a trail of victims-of-lust in the wake of unrequited love. Art does indeed imitate life, and that's what the world offers as "true love." But that's not God's final word. After all, He created True Love to fill up a love-empty heart.

Those victims of lust I saw and read became my teachers, and in striving to fill up the cavernous, love-hungry hole in my heart, I followed their lead and found myself also looking for love in all the wrong places, and making poor choices for all the wrong reasons. Shocker, I know. Ironically, I could spot an idiot-girl in the movies but could not recognize her in my own bathroom mirror. Choosing men who were emotionally, spiritually, and socially unavailable created a deep insecurity within me that made me believe I simply was not enough of anything. I was not good enough, lovable enough, pretty enough, smart enough, worthy enough, etc.

Sadly, that became a mental mantra that would chant to me for decades - *You're just not enough.* With each passing year of my life, and as the fourth finger of my left hand remained bare at twenty-five, thirty, thirty-five years old and so on, I worried I'd never find true love. Well-meaning friends joined my destructive mantra with sympathies like, *Why aren't you married? You're just too picky ... What's wrong?* which only reinforced my false beliefs that something was wrong with me, that God was punishing me or had forgotten me altogether.

The vicious cycle continued: pick the wrong guy to satisfy myself with human love, get heart trampled, beg God to help me get "him" back. Broken and empty, I would stagger back to God. Then temptation would strike and the roller coaster ride would start all over again ... and again.

Thinking back on that season of my life, I'm stunned that God did not give me what I absolutely, desperately and shamelessly begged and pleaded with Him for. But there was a divine reason why He didn't. You see, I belonged to Him. I'd made a decision about Christ in high school and received the salvation of my soul and the forgiveness of my sins – past, present and future.

God always kept His promises to me and always remained faithful. I'm the one who said "I do" to Him, then cheated on Him over and over again. My greatest sins were committed after I said "I do." *After* I was saved. *After* my eternity was secure in Christ. Read those words again because somebody out there needs to know this and stop beating up on themselves. God remains patient, faithful and true, yet He is not a fool or a liar (Numbers 23:19), and He will not be mocked (Galatians 6:7). He will permit His child to make foolish choices and experience the earthly consequences of those choices. But His love is unfailing. He will not ... He *cannot* ... take back His promises in Christ Jesus (Deuteronomy 7:8-9, 2 Corinthians 1:20).

God is a faithful and jealous lover (Exodus 34:14); He is the Hound of Heaven who pursues His beloved bride. He was relentless with me, and His relentless love is one of the characteristics I've come to cherish most about the Lord. He allowed heartbreak after miserable heartbreak, and each one brought me closer to the end of myself, the place where I would finally surrender to Him and receive the full measure of His love.

I was thirty-six, devastated and depressed from the last of the great heartbreaks. At a dear friend's encouragement, I began attending a Bible study at her church. One night I heard a woman talk about falling in love with Jesus. I thought it so odd to speak of a relationship with Jesus in those words. I mean, really? Could one really fall in love with Jesus? But I saw and heard in this woman's voice something quite different. She knew Jesus in more than just a personal relationship kind of way. She knew Him *intimately*. That was it! That was what I needed ... what I wanted. I was exhausted, empty and broken from living life my way. It simply was not working for me. My heart was tattered from unfaithful and unhealthy love.

Driving home from the study that night, I nearly bawled my eyes out. "I want that, Lord!" I cried. "Whatever she has, if it's real, I need it. I want it. I want to know You like that." Back home I continued to pour my heart out to God. I remember it like it was yesterday. Gripped by the Holy Spirit I lay prostrate, facedown on the hardwood floor of my bedroom, and cried out, "Jesus, if You are who You say You are, and You can be to me everything You say You can be, then I need You to be that now because I GIVE UP!"

MY VICTORY

"I give up" are the three words that saved my life. As I continued to cry to Him, pouring out my heart, I felt at that moment that He scooped me up and loved me into Himself in a way I'd never experienced or imagined before. I did not feel better instantly, but I knew something was different. Something had lost its grip on me and I felt *free*. At the end of myself, I found the beginning of God's freedom and His all-consuming, unfailing love.

Up to this point, my life of faith had consisted of religious routines. I attended church, served on committees and prayed repetitiously. It was a mechanical faith, not a *living* relationship. I didn't really know God or believe Him, and was really only seeking His hand (what God could do for me) instead of His face (who God is). My relationship with Jesus always included a "plus something else" rider. My security was Jesus *plus* money in the bank; my happiness was Jesus *plus* a husband; my identity was Jesus *plus* booking a great part in a feature film. In Colossians 3:4 the Apostle Paul writes, "... when Christ, who is your life ..." Jesus was an addition to my life, but I hadn't considered Him to actually be my life.

I began praying day and night, "Lord, I want to fall in love with You. I want to hunger and thirst for You." Again, not an immediate change, but rather a gradual, growing passion for Jesus and an increasing hunger for His Word. I couldn't wait to get home from work each evening to grab my Bible and spend time with Him. There were many nights I fell asleep with my head literally in the Word, using my Bible as my pillow. It felt like a spiritual honeymoon. My relationship grew from simply knowing about Jesus to knowing Him, from merely needing Him to wanting Him. Jesus was enough for me and over time I *"learned to be content whatever the circumstances"* (Philippians 3:11-13), whether I was married or single.

For the first time in my life I felt peace and joy. Not simply happiness, but supernatural joy that transcends one's circumstances. My prayer life became an authentic and continual dialogue with the Lord, an ongoing conversation about anything and everything. I began to hear Him speak to me through His Word, and I began to encourage my friends and family with real Truth that makes a difference. He gave me purpose, and I found that more and more of my friends were coming to me for encouragement and help. He set my heart on fire for His Word, and I found that I loved to share and teach everything I learned.

Over the next several years I grew deeper in my faith and love for Jesus. I found in Him everything I'd been seeking my whole life: Security, acceptance, worth, beauty, purpose and a love that is faithful and true. In my pursuit to know God, I nearly tripped and fell over John Tolson, a man who loves God with all his heart, the man who eventually became my husband.

We were married in 2001 when I was forty-three years old.

I would never have had eyes to see John had Jesus not first opened the eyes of my heart to His perfect love. We serve the Lord together in full-time ministry, making disciples for Jesus Christ (Matthew 28:19-20). Who but God could bring a ministry out of my messes? But that's precisely what He excels in.

Yes, we are wired by our Creator God not only to dream but to experience True Love; a love that is faithful and true, an everlasting love; a perfect love that drives out all fears; an eternal love that knows no bounds; a "love that is as strong as death ... and burns like blazing fire" (Song of Solomon 8:6). We are wired for Jesus, who is faithful and true, and His love fills us and satisfies us as nothing else ever can or ever will. HE IS ENOUGH!

As for living happily ever after ...

I saw heaven standing open and there before me was a white horse, whose rider is called Faithful and True ... His eyes are like blazing fire, and on his head are many crowns ... He is dressed in a robe dipped in blood, and his name is the Word of God. The armies of heaven were following him, riding on white horses and dressed in fine linen, white and clean. Out of his mouth comes a sharp sword with which to strike down the nations. "He will rule them with an iron scepter." He treads the winepress of the fury of the wrath of God Almighty. On his robe and on his thigh he has this name written:

KING OF KINGS AND LORD OF LORDS.
(REVELATION 19:11-16 NIV84)

He's coming back for you and for me, sister. Oh, is He ever coming back ... and He's bringing an entire heavenly army with Him. That, my friend, ain't no fairy tale!

DEVOTION: DAY ONE
BELIEVE THAT GOD CREATED YOU

*Listen to the Lord who created you, the one who formed you says,
"Do not be afraid, for I have ransomed you. I have called you by
name: you are Mine."* ISAIAH 43:1 (NEW LIVING TRANSLATION)

Salvation in Christ is a gift, but satisfaction is found as we pursue God to know Him better. God wants us to know Him, not just know about Him but to believe the Truth about who He is. He wants us to know His character – what He's like, what He thinks and how He feels about you and me. As we pursue Him, we grow to believe Him more and more.

Believing God is life-changing because it's mind-changing! What we believe about God matters tremendously because it alters the way we think about, and the way we see, ourselves. Understanding our believe system is critical to our walk in victory because the way we think greatly affects the way we live. A faulty belief system preaches lies to us that we're not enough and makes us doubt our real worth.

We've got to form new thoughts by replacing the lies with God-given Truth that says, *YOU are God's beautiful and highly valued masterpiece* (Ephesians 2:10 paraphrase). When we replace lies with Truth, we "... capture rebellious thoughts and teach them to obey Christ" (2 Corinthians 10:3-5 The Message). God's Truth trumps the lie every single time and the results will show up in the way you live, the way you speak and the things you do. If you change your mind, you'll change your heart, which will change your life.

Belief #1: Believe that God created you: You are His masterpiece!

What do you think about yourself? Are your thoughts in line with the way God thinks of you?

Scripture reading: Psalm 139

Use the following statement to begin a study of yourself ... the way that God made you.

And God said, "I will make _____(*your name*), and I will make her
_____ and _____,
with a love for _____, a talent for
_____ and an interest in_____
_____. " (*fill these blanks in with characteristics about you*).
And after He finished, God looked and saw that what He had created was
very good! (Genesis 1:26-31 paraphrased)

Sister, believe that God has exquisitely and uniquely created you to
be you. Will you pray, thanking God for how He's made you and for the
beautiful creation that you are? He loves you so, sweet friend. In fact, He's
absolutely head-over-heels about you!

DEVOTION: DAY TWO
BELIEVE THAT GOD LOVES YOU

I am convinced that nothing can ever separate us from God's love
... in Christ Jesus our Lord.
ROMANS 8:39-39 (NEW LIVING TRANSLATION)

God loves you! Whether you feel it or not, He loves you and it's a fact
because it's the reality of who God is. Love is His personality, His character.
Love is not just what God does, love is *who God is* (1 John 4:8).

God loves you, but do you really believe it? Head knowledge is one
thing, but to embrace that truth and believe it down into the fiber of your
being is altogether different. The Apostle Paul urgently prayed that we
might know and *believe* the love God has for us to the fullest measure of
full power, full-throttle owning it. (Ephesians 8:38-39, my paraphrase).

When the fact that He loves us, *no matter what*, makes the eighteen-
inch drop from our head to our heart, it becomes a belief that transforms
us, of that I am sure! I couldn't always say that with certainty. Though I'd
been a believing Christian for decades and even taught the Word of God
for a dozen years, I had not always embraced the fact that God loves me.
Junk from the past, hurtful words spoken over me, lies I believed ... all

served to perpetuate a faulty belief system that made me think God must have conditions on His love and I just wasn't lovable.

The truth is that God's love is *unconditional*. No strings. He simply loves you and me. And sister, you will never be more greatly loved than when you're loved by God. He will never love you any more or any less than He loves you right this very minute. Pray and believe this critical, foundational Truth until it becomes your reality and the bedrock of your belief system, until you, like the Apostle John, can define yourself as "The one that Jesus loved" (John 13:23). Go ahead. Give it a try:

"I am _____(*your name*); the one whom Jesus loves"... no matter what!

Belief #2: Believe that God loves you—no matter what!

What prevents you from believing that God loves you no matter what?

Scripture reading: Romans 5:8; Ephesians 3:14-21

DEVOTION: DAY THREE
BELIEVE THAT CHRIST DIED FOR YOU:
YOU'VE BEEN RESURRECTED

See, I am doing a new thing! Now it springs up; do you not perceive it? I am making a way in the desert and streams in the wasteland. ISAIAH 43:19-20 (NIV84)

There is perhaps no greater fundamental truth more critical to our faith than this: *Jesus Christ considered you worth dying for.* That's right, you! Jesus Christ considered you worth being nailed to a cross and shedding His blood for because "God so loved _____(*your name*).

Let those words wash over you as you imagine Him singling you out, looking you in the eye and saying, "For you, child, I will do this for *you*." And He did. Then, three days later He did the unthinkable, unimaginable, never-to-be-repeated again: He got up from the grave. The glory of the Gospel is that Jesus didn't remain on the cross or in the tomb, but that He got up and lived again.

Resurrected ... alive forever. That fact means everything to Christ-Followers. It gives us hope beyond this life, peace in this life, and victory over the trials of this life. The Gospel is about Him, but it is for us! Because He lives a resurrected life, we do, too.

Resurrection means to "rise up from the dead." Christ took the penalty of death for your sins and mine. But Christ also got up from the dead with a new life so that we could live a new life, an abundant life (John 10:10). So, why do we keep going back to our old way of dead living? Because we still live by our old ways of dead thinking, thinking with the limitations of the grave rather than with the resurrected mind of Christ who "is able to do exceedingly abundantly above all that we ask or think, according to His power at work in us" (Ephesians 3:20).

Behold, He is doing a new thing in you and in me, Sister. Give Him the old in exchange for the new, abundant, victorious resurrected life. Oh, how we are in need of a Savior! Oh, how we are in need of resurrection!

Belief #3: Believe Christ died for you.

Where are you in need of a "resurrection" in your life?

Scripture reading: Isaiah 61

DEVOTION: DAY FOUR
BELIEVE THAT GOD HAS GIFTED YOU FOR A PURPOSE

God has given each of you a gift from his great variety of spiritual gifts. Use them well to serve one another. 1 PETER 4:10 (NLT)

Every woman has a desire to do something that's beyond her wildest dreams. What's your dream? If you could do anything you wanted to do, if money were not a problem and if you knew you absolutely would not fail, what would you do? Somewhere in the answer to that question lies your God-given passion. Your passion is divinely connected to your God-given purpose, and your purpose flourishes as you stay connected to Him.

God has perfectly gifted you with certain qualities that are perfectly suited to the wonderful life and purposes He has planned for you, plans that bring you into His eternal business. God can totally do His job all by Himself. But He chose not to do it without you, one-of-a-kind, dearly loved, worth-the-sacrifice, perfectly-gifted YOU!

He has endowed you with a unique package of qualities combined with natural talents and abilities for a specific, significant and profoundly effective purpose in His service. Choose to believe that. Yes, choose to believe that God has gifted you, Sister, and use those gifts for His glory.

Jesus said, "I am the Vine; you are the branches. If a man remains in me and I in him, he will bear much fruit; apart from me you can do nothing" (John 15:5).

His purpose *is* your passion!

Belief #4: Believe God has gifted you.

What's keeping you from dreaming and pursuing your dreams? Is your dream in line with God's eternal purpose?

Scripture reading: Romans 12:4-8; 2 Corinthians 3:4-5

DEVOTION: DAY FIVE
BELIEVE THAT GOD HAS A PLAN AND A PROFOUND PURPOSE YOUR LIFE

"For I know the plans I have for you," declares the Lord, "plans to prosper you and not to harm you, plans to give you hope and a future." JEREMIAH 29:11 (NIV84)

Every woman desires to have a real purpose in life, to leave a legacy that says, "I was here, I made a difference, and I mattered." That's a God-given desire in every individual that has ever lived because "God ... has planted eternity in the human heart ..." (Ecclesiastes 3:11, NLT). He's divinely wired us to do something that will last *forever*.

According to Scripture, there are only two things in all of God's creation that will last forever: *God's Truth* (Isaiah 40:8) and people (John 6:51, 1 John 2:17). Worldly efforts, even charitable pursuits, simply will not matter in eternity no matter how much "good" they did. There is a little saying that bears committing to memory, and it is this: "Only one life, 'twill soon be past. Only what's done for Christ will last."

Therefore, the focus of making a lasting difference with our lives must be connected first and foremost to those things that will surely last forever and be centered on the mission of Jesus Christ, or the Great Commission, which is to "go and make disciples of all the nations ..." (Matthew 28:19-20 NIV84).

Practically speaking, bearing fruit that lasts is to raise up some spiritual young 'uns, helping them to grow up in the ways of the Lord and teaching them to do the same for another for the rest of your life.

Psalm 92:12-14 says, *"The righteous will flourish like a palm tree, they will grow like a cedar of Lebanon; planted in the house of the Lord, they will flourish in the courts of our God. They will still bear fruit in old age; they will stay fresh and green."*

I don't know about you, but I'm all for staying *fresh and green!*

Belief #5: Believe that God has a plan and a profound purpose for your life.

What are you doing with your life and your time that is making a difference now and will matter forever? What are you intentionally doing to invest the Truths of God in the next generation?

Scripture reading: Psalm 78; Jeremiah 29:11

God Crazy Freedom Challenge

Women. We really are the "Total Package," are we not? And that package comes wired by God with essential needs that can only be truly satisfied in Him. Needs like security, purpose, beauty, identity and worth.

In my preceding testimony I described my relationship with Jesus in terms of "Jesus plus something else." Let's look at it as an equation:

Jesus + _____ = my _____.

How would you fill in those blanks? Let me ask that another way. Is Jesus alone enough for you? Is He your source of peace, purpose, worth or beauty? Or is there something else that when added to Him fulfills you, satisfies you, or brings you contentment?

Give the following statement some serious thought and prayer, and be as honest as you can with your answers:

If I could only have _____ *(person, place or thing) then I would be/feel* _____ *(loved, safe, peace, secure, like I belong, beautiful, valued, like I'm appreciated, have purpose, fruitful, fulfilled).*

So, what's your "plus"? Beloved, the Lord wants you to believe Him, and believe Him about how greatly and dearly He loves you. Over the next week or months or for as long as it takes, I ask that you take the following Scriptures and pray them through daily until the Truth permeates your soul and saturates every fiber of your being to the point that you can confidently say, "I am my Beloved's, and His desire is for me!" (Song of Songs 7:10).

My Beloved _____*(your name),*

You are precious and honored in my sight, and I love you. See, I am doing a new thing! Now it springs up; do you not perceive it? I am making a way in the desert and streams in the wasteland. • You are a crown of splendor in My hand. • You are altogether beautiful, my darling; there is no flaw in you. • Therefore, I am now going to allure you; I will lead you into the desert and speak tenderly to you. • Let Me satisfy you in the morning with My unfailing love, that you may sing for joy and be glad all your days. • I am enthralled by your beauty; honor Me, for I am your Lord. • Give all your worries and cares to Me, for I care about you. • Above all else, guard your heart, for it determines the course of your life. • I am your God, your refuge and strength, an ever-present help in trouble. • My way is perfect. All My promises prove true. I will be your shield, when you look to Me for protection. • Never will I leave you; never will I forsake you.

(Is. 43:4; 19; Is. 62:3; Song of Sol. 4:7; Hos. 2:14; Ps. 90:14; Ps. 45:11; 1 Pet. 5:7; Prov. 4:23; Ps. 46:1; 2 Sam. 22:31; Heb. 13:5)

GOD CRAZY FREEDOM PRAYER

Dear sister, I'm grateful for this short time I've had to spend with you and I pray that the Lord has used it to make a difference in the way you see your beautiful self. In closing I'd like to pray for you, but ask that you also turn this into a personal prayer to talk through with the Lord in the days to come.

Gracious and Merciful Lord, Creator of Heaven and Earth, perfect in wisdom, power and love!

Oh, Sovereign and All-sufficient God who fills everything in every way, by Your grace and in Your love bless my sister from the exceedingly abundant treasury of glorious riches in Christ Jesus!

Satisfy the deepest longings of her heart with your unfailing love that she may sing for joy and be glad all the days of her life.

Mend every broken place within her by Your gentle touch.

Fill every empty place in her with the spring of Living Water her soul thirsts for.

Give her an insatiable appetite for Your Word that takes her into deeper intimacy with You.

Keep her eyes so fixed on You that she sees her true beauty reflected there.

Crown her with strength and dignity.

May she find in You her true identity and may she always remember that out of all of this world, You have chosen her to be Your very own.

Lead her, Father, with cords of kindness and bands of love, and speak tenderly to her.

Help her to trust You to guide her and direct her into all of the good plans and purposes You've scripted for her life.

Give her courage to put the past behind her and step into the "new thing" that You're doing.

By the power of Your beautiful Holy Spirit, fill her, equip her and empower her to be more than a conqueror in Christ Jesus.

Give her confidence to fulfill her calling in You, and make her to become every measure of the woman of God that You created her to be, a woman who so strongly resembles Your Son, Jesus.

Now, Lord, put a new song in my sister's sweet mouth and let the testimony of her life bring many to know and believe the same wondrous love, this Redeeming Love, that she has found in You. May she confidently believe and never, ever forget the she is greatly and dearly loved by You, her King!

For Your name and fame, Lord God, I ask all this for my sister in the glorious, strong and saving name of the One who is Life to us, Jesus. In His all-powerful name I pray, Amen and Amen!

DIVORCE TO WHOLENESS

by Sharon Ball-Dale

$\mathscr{I}$always believed life was kind of like the ocean, and I was a surfer. All I had to do was pick the right wave, stay balanced and I would experience the ride of my life, all the while heading toward a beautiful destination. What I chose to ignore was the fact that storms can come without warning over the ocean, and lurking beneath the beautiful blue-green surface are sharks, stingrays, poisonous jellyfish and other dangers that want to take you down.

I grew up determined to be a good girl. If I did everything right, that was like catching the right wave. As long as I didn't rock my board, I'd stay on top of life's waves. My life would be smooth surfing, and anything dangerous would stay far beneath me. Skies would stay blue and filled only with puffy, marshmallow-white clouds, and I would glide straight into my happily ever after. Those were my dreams, but I was to learn that dreams you don't surrender to the Lord sometimes become your biggest nightmare.

My dream, like many other girls, was to get married, have children, and maintain a career. Pretty normal, right? I was an American woman. I was taught that I could have it all. At an early age, I began to believe that if I just followed the rules, kept on being good, and did things the right way, I would get what I wanted. I was a rule-follower and a goal-setter.

Goal No. 1: Marry Mr. Right.
Goal No. 2: Have three beautiful children.
Goal No. 3: Set up a thriving psychotherapy practice.

My focus on being good and following the rules worked at first. I received praise for being good, I liked the success that came with hard work, and I easily adapted to other's expectations. I began to define myself by my dreams and by how other people saw me, instead of seeking the will of my Father and desiring His approval of me.

On the surface, everything was going just fine. Goal No. 1: Check. Goals 2 and 3: Check and double-check. What I didn't realize until it was too late was that storm clouds were gathering on the horizon of my happily ever after, and sharks were circling just beneath the surfboard of my life. I was surfing in circles, not getting anywhere near the beautiful beaches ahead.

I was good at ignoring the whitecaps I began bouncing over, but my marriage was not smooth sailing. We almost divorced when I was pregnant with our third child, but I rode the wave of focusing on my marriage at all costs. I was teetering, but I was determined. I took a year off from work, my husband quit touring, and I kept riding the waves.

I clung to my board even when the waves became tsunami-sized. I refused to give up as Denial jumped on to ride with me. I could not, would not give up my dream. What would other people think? Good girls, Christians, overachievers like me did not get divorced. I was a psychotherapist, for goodness' sake. Couldn't I get to the bottom of the issues in my own marriage and fix them?

I couldn't, but I couldn't let go either. I grasped and clawed, even as I slipped and my head went under the water again and again. I'd climb back on top and hold fast as the waves pulverized me and the storm unleashed its full fury all around. Even through the pain, I believed that if I could just ride out the storm, I'd end up at that beautiful, peaceful destination. But the longer I hung on, the closer I came to drowning and disappearing.

Finally, I hit the beach, but it wasn't paradise. Denial jumped off as we landed on the dry sand of divorce. Papers in hand, attorneys present, and my children's tears finally jolted me out of my dreams and made me realize I stood shaking in the middle of my worst nightmare. No happily ever after anymore. I thought I had lost it all: my marriage, my children's innocence, my chance for love. All gone. All washed up.

I had no idea that as my husband walked out the door for the last time, it was actually the beginning of God's happily ever after for me. I could no longer surf under my own strength. He was going to have to ride with me on the sea of desolation until the waves calmed and I could see the God who provides, protects, and heals. My surfboard (my plans, goals and dreams) had washed right out from underneath me, but now my Savior could teach me to walk on water with Him.

When my despair could go no deeper, I surrendered. I could not make my marriage work. I could not fix the heartache my children were going through. I had to stop fighting the waves, roll over on my back and float onto that dry land of despair. When I finally did, I was weak and shaken to the core, but in my weakness He became strong. My trust had to be in Him. I felt like I had nothing else left.

It wasn't instant or easy. As I grieved over the next year, God slowly showed me how to be kind and gentle to myself. I grieved deeply over my shattered dreams, yet He began to reveal the high cost my soul had paid for clinging to what I desired instead of asking my Savior what His plans were for me. I wanted the special man, kids and career, and maybe God wanted that for me too. But not on my own strength. Not on my terms. Not when I based my success and self-worth on the approval of everyone but Him.

Tenderly, Jesus showed me that I had limits and wounds. My wounds needed to be tended to, but accepting that I was wounded was hard. I saw wounds as failure, and failure deserves punishment. Over time, God taught me through His Word, prayer, and wise counsel how to grieve my losses without taking them out on myself. I slowly learned to accept that bad things do happen to good people and my value is not measured by my failures or wounds.

Like I said, becoming a student of surrender was not easy. On many days, Jesus and I were not on good terms. I remember my spiritual director asking me to close my eyes and tell her where I pictured Jesus. Was he in the room with me or outside the door?

Weeping, I responded that I saw Jesus on a boat in the ocean, leaving me as I sat on the beach. That was where I saw Jesus in my life. I rode those fierce waves to shore, nearly drowned along the way, and arrived on the spiritually deserted island of divorce. It wasn't fair. I had tried to do everything "right." How could He let it all go wrong? In my heart, Jesus had bailed on me. He left me in my darkest hours. He left me because I my "right" wasn't good enough for Him. I wasn't good enough for Him.

What I longed for deep in my soul was Jesus to be on that shore with me. I wanted Him to hold me and whisper to me that I was still lovable. Most of all, I didn't want Him to leave like my husband had.

MY VICTORY

God's journey of grief for me started out as my enemy but grew to be my closest friend. Grief took me to dark places I feared, but then God show me He was strong enough to handle it. Grief stripped me of all my "right" ways of doing life so I could learn to let Him do it His way.

Through this surrender, I could finally see that Jesus had not abandoned me. He was waiting on the waves, watching over me, giving me space to come to the end of myself. During many dark nights, He watched over me. When I called to Him, he would quickly come ashore and join me on the desolate beach. I would rest my weary head in His lap, and He would whisper the kindest words to me:

"You are loved, you are beautiful, you are wanted." He told me again and again. He told me to rest in Him. He called me His "good and faithful daughter." He would whisper, "I have your back. I will not leave you. I will take care of you and your children. I will provide." He would sternly tell me, "Let it go. Let me carry this for you." Jesus knew exactly what I needed to hear.

Eventually, my wounds began to heal. Yes, they left scars, but those scars are good reminders that I don't ever want to surf under my own strength again. They are also evidence of the newfound strength I have in Him. The strength to be weak. The strength to give up everything so I can have it all. The strength to lose my life so I could gain it. That's the paradox of the gospel, isn't it? When we come to the end of ourselves, when we are washed up on the dry beach of desolation, He is always just offshore, ready to comfort, ready to heal, ready to reach out His mighty hand and pull you gently back out to sea.

Grief capsized me on the beach of divorce. But Jesus would never leave me there. Once I looked to Him, He led me back down to the water's edge. And as long as I stepped out humbly and let Him lead the way, this time I would walk on waves of living water. My steps were tentative. It's tough to be humble, but I learned to call my deacon for help when I needed groceries. I learned to reach out to my dad at three o'clock in the morning and be vulnerable enough to just weep over the phone, sometimes unable to articulate anything. In my weakness, He was made strong in me.

When I let go of my dreams, I experienced a reawakening of my soul. I even became grateful for those tsunami-sized waves (although truthfully I'd prefer not to be battered by them again) that tried to take me down to the depths. Because now I know that even when storms come and sharks circle, as long as I keep looking into the eyes of Jesus, we'll keep walking on water … straight into the real "happily ever after."

DEVOTION: DAY ONE

"Give sorrow words; the grief that does not speak whispers the o'er-fraught heart and bids it break." – WILLIAM SHAKESPEARE

Hear my cry, O God; listen to my prayer. From the ends of the earth I call to you, I call as my heart grows faint; lead me to the rock that is higher than I. PSALM 61:1-2

Grief, sorrow and despair are emotions that reflect something you have lost. When you go through a divorce, it is like your arm being cut off. Think of it like a soldier who comes back from war missing a limb. She looks at where her arm existed only to see nothing. Phantom pain makes it feel like it is still there, but she can see that it is gone. She remembers using it to touch. She has pictures to prove it existed, but now there is nothing. Her arm is not coming back, but there are so many memories of it that she still engages with the idea of it on a daily basis.

Grieve your divorce and the losses, and allow God to enter into that grief. Invite Him into your sadness, anger, disappointment, disillusionment, despair, frustration, loneliness, fear, and hopelessness. Cry out to Him today to carry you through your grief. You will not fall apart because you allow yourself to grieve. It may feel like you will, but you are actually learning to trust yourself with these emotions. These emotions are normal and okay, because they are reflections and remembrances of how much you cared about your partner, your family, and your marriage.

My choices:

I will choose to be kind and gentle with myself today.

I will choose to invite Jesus into my grief today.

I will choose to call a friend and invite her into my grief today.

Devotion: Day Two

"This is a good sign, having a broken heart. It means we have tried for something." – Elizabeth Gilbert

Make your face shine on your servant; save me in your steadfast love! Psalm 31:16

Divorce tears up every part of a human being, whether the divorce has biblical "grounds" or not. You experience a rejection that cuts to the very core of your heart. This kind of rejection is not a feeling that we are prepared for in life. Rejection crosses all boundaries: cultural, educational, racial, gender and age. You are not immune to this kind of pain. You will feel rejection at all levels; however, today you need to block the lies that you are not worthy and listen to what you know to be true: God has not rejected you!

Allow your gaze to be on His definition of you. Allow your heart to hear what He says about you. You are the daughter of the King, and you are loved. He created you for a purpose: to enjoy Him and glorify Him forever. Remind yourself that when you allow man to define you, man then defines your purpose and when that happens, you cannot enjoy Him or glorify Him.

DEVOTION: DAY THREE

"There is a sacredness in tears. They are not the mark of weakness, but of power. They speak more eloquently than ten thousand tongues. They are messengers of overwhelming grief ... and unspeakable love." – WASHINGTON IRVING

The Lord is close to the brokenhearted and saves those who are crushed in spirit. PSALM 34:18

You are not alone in your grief, but there will be days like today where you have to meet grief alone. Everyone's journey with grief is different, and sometimes other people just will not understand. That is okay. You will be okay. It will be hard, but Jesus is with you. He has not left you. He is watching over you. He values your tears, He knows what you are going through. He knows.

DEVOTION: DAY FOUR

"There were many ways of breaking a heart. Stories were full of hearts being broken by love, but what really broke a heart was taking away its dream—whatever the dream might be."
– PEARL BUCK

In the same way the Spirit also helps our weakness; for we do not know how to pray as we should, but the Spirit Himself intercedes for us with groaning too deep for words. ROMANS 8:26

Dreams, hopes and desires are lost during divorce. What you once knew no longer exists. What you once hoped for ceases to be a possibility. Your future as you desired comes to a halt. You will grieve events that did not even happen in life, but that you wanted to happen. Life will feel disoriented and confusing. That's normal. It should be confusing; the loss is great. There may be days when you don't know what to even pray for. Your desire to hope, dream and even pray may come to a halt. When we have no words, the Holy Spirit will intercede if we just ask.

DEVOTION: DAY FIVE

"With the new day comes new strength and new thoughts."
– ELEANOR ROOSEVELT

Everything on earth has its own time and its own season. There is a time for birth and death, planting and reaping, for killing and healing, destroying and building, for crying and laughing, weeping and dancing, for throwing stones and gathering stones,

embracing and parting. There is a time for finding and losing,
keeping and giving, for tearing and sewing, listening and
speaking. There is also a time for love and hate, for war and
peace. ECCLESIASTES 3:3-8

The days seem so long, dark and hard. Hard in a way that you have never experienced before. Your soul is weary and tired. You long for the day when the tears stop flowing with ease, as if they have become a habit that just reminds you of your loss. Your heart aches for good things, longs for reprieve ... your time will come. He has made a promise to never leave you. Although in this moment you may not feel His presence, you must rely on your knowledge of what the scripture says. This is a difficult task, so do not give way to the lie that you have been forgotten. He has not forgotten you! He will never leave you or forsake you.

GOD CRAZY FREEDOM CHALLENGE

Here are some challenges for you to take steps toward healing after divorce. You can do several all at once, or spread them out as you go. Each is designed to draw you closer to the Lord and one step further along your faith journey until you are confidently walking on water with your Savior leading the way.

1. Make friends with your grief. "She" will be around for a while, and the better you understand her the easier it will be to go through it.
2. Be kind and gentle to yourself. If all you do today is make sure you and your children are taken care of - good. Now rest.
3. Ask yourself where you see Jesus with you right now. Is he in the room with you? Outside the door? Where is your Jesus as you grieve this day? Where do you want Him to be? Ask Him to reveal His location to you.
4. Share with one person that your heart is breaking and ask for prayer. Do not hold your grief so tightly that others cannot minister to you.
5. Write down how you feel your divorce defines you. Now, write down how Jesus defines you.

6. Invite Jesus to grieve the wounds of rejection with you, and ask Him to give you the strength to be defined only by Him. Acknowledge your need for the Spirit to intercede on your behalf.

7. Acknowledge your weariness and lack of desire to hope, and enter into prayer willing to receive the Holy Spirit's groaning on your behalf.

8. Call a friend today and ask that friend to pray for you. Better yet, ask her to pray with you. Be authentic and let her know that you don't even know what she can be praying for. You just need prayer.

9. Give words to your tears during your divorce journey. Write down the losses you feel they represent. Allow yourself to enter into your grief, in spite of feeling alone.

10. Remind yourself that you are not alone; God is with you. He will give you strength to overcome.

11. Now identify one step forward that you have made. It can be small, for even a small step is a step.

12. Start a hope list. Name three desires you have for yourself and your children. Begin praying fervently that your desires will line up with God's desires for you, and that you will see His mighty hand revealed.

13. Pray for the change of seasons in your life. Identify your favorite season and allow your heart to look forward to it, in spite of not knowing when it will come about.

14. Call a friend today and ask her to contend on your behalf for the new season to come. Share with her one of your hopes, and ask her to remind you of your future!

God Crazy Freedom Prayer

Jesus, I am weary and tired. I feel like trash that has been put on the side of the road that even the trash man will not pick up. I don't believe that I could ever be loved again or that I am worth loving. My heart aches from this wound of rejection. I ask you to give me strength to believe what is true, that I have value because you made me. Give me strength to believe my value is found in You. This is such a lonely journey. The tears will not stop coming and I am growing weary of them. There are days when I'm not sure I can do this anymore. This place in life is too much for me to bear. This is not the way I dreamed it would be. This is not what I wanted.

Give me strength to see the value in my tears and to know that you will catch my tears. Hold me tight right now, for I am exhausted. Show me, Lord, that you are near. Put your hand on my head at night and take all of the thoughts that drive me into darkness. Give me strength to get up in the morning and be there for the precious gifts that you have given me. Encourage my heart that it may overflow into my children. And when the grief hits me once again like a tidal wave, give me the grace to embrace it and ride the wave knowing that this is part of the healing journey. In Jesus' name, Amen.

SINGLENESS TO UNITY

by Barbara J. Pruitt

I always knew as a little girl that God had His hand on me in a special way. I wasn't like a normal little girl who would play with dolls, dress them up, and pretend to have a family. I would get my parents' devotional book and read chapters on the love of God, His power to forgive, and letting go of the past. Then I would look up all the scripture verses that addressed each topic. Once I had an understanding of the scriptures in my heart, I would stand up and look in my little dresser mirror and preach to an imaginary crowd of thousands. I would teach with passion and power as if they were all really there. I would be so moved that I would actually weep and experience the love of God so strongly over the invisible, "hurting" people. After I released my word from God over them, I would dry my tears, move to the next topic and do it all again.

This passion for people has never left my heart. When I was just sixteen years old, I had a job that was downtown in the city I lived in, and I would have to drive through a rough area every day to get there. As I was driving, I would imagine picking up a young prostitute off the streets. I would share how much Jesus loves her, and then I would sneak her away from her pimp and give her a safe place to live and new clothes to wear. I then imagined her in my church, standing and worshipping God in total freedom with a brand-new start in life!

When I was seventeen years old, I actually helped one of my high school classmates escape from a cult that took her away from her family. I saw her safely reunited. I ran into her years later, and she recognized me in the grocery store where she was working. She thanked me over and over. She explained how her life was changed forever. She was now happily married with children.

I have such a deep longing and desire for you to understand the power of God's love and His ability to change and transform your life, no matter what you've been through. Ephesians 3:17-19 says, *"that Christ may dwell in your hearts through faith; that you, being rooted and grounded in love, may be able to comprehend with all the saints what is the width and length and depth and height— to know the love of Christ which passes knowledge; that you may be filled with all the fullness of God."*

This is a fulfillment that comes by experiencing His love that nothing else on earth can replace.

In my journey of twenty years in ministry, I have experienced every up and down and all the in-betweens I ever could. Some things took my breath away, and I wondered how I was ever going to survive. Some hard places stole my joy, my hope, my peace and some friends. Trials drove me into a cave of shame that I didn't know how to come out of. You, too, may have suffered life's trials so deeply that you wonder how you could ever have joy in life again, but I promise you that His love can fill you so deeply that you heal from the inside out.

God captured my heart at eighteen years old, and there was no turning back. I made a commitment to serve the Lord for the rest of my life, no matter what came my way. I have wanted to run away a few times, but my commitment to trust Him kept me anchored to Him. I am united to Him.

In my prayer time with the Lord, He called me to be single. He said, *When the right one comes, you will know it.* He set me apart for His purposes, and I knew it. He never told me I wouldn't marry, but I never knew for sure that anyone was the right one, either. Never did I imagine that at forty-three years old, I would find myself single but still having a deep, heartfelt desire to be married.

I didn't understand my journey, but all I could do is trust God even when I couldn't see God, when I didn't understand God, and when others in my life began to raise the eyebrow of disbelief.

I wasn't always faithful to Him. At thirty-nine, I grew very tired of waiting on God. I didn't want to believe Him anymore. I thought my life was passing me by, even though I was doing great things for the Lord. I didn't want to be alone anymore, and I was done waiting.

I said, "The next man who comes into my life, I will marry."

A man did come into my life, and I started dating him. It was a very exposed relationship, because I was an executive pastor on staff at a large church. Everyone was so excited for me; Barb was finally going to be married. I wanted this relationship to be right; I wanted it to be God's pick for me; but I felt this constant nudge that it wasn't. Ignoring that still, small voice in me, I went ahead with this relationship and began planning a wedding.

Let me back up a minute here. At eighteen years old, I had faced severe loneliness. I had stopped dating for a year, and I ached with loneliness. Everywhere I looked, everyone had someone. Driving in the car, I saw couples - on billboards, walking out of church together, hanging out in the park. I almost saw birds tweeting in circles around their heads and heard music playing.

After work one day, I went home, grabbed my Bible, hugged it close to my chest and said, "God, I don't know how to be single. All I know is you told me to do it. I don't know the Word on it, and I'm hurting so badly, God. I need YOU to help me." In that moment, I heard the still, small voice inside me, and it said: *"I desire to meet all your needs according to my riches in glory."*

At that moment, I knew there wasn't anything wrong with feeling lonely or with my desire to feel pretty, to be romanced and feel loved. I realized that God had to meet all those desires first. There was nothing and no one else He was going to allow to fill my void.

As I was hugging my Bible tightly in desperation, I felt the presence of Lord standing behind me like a strong man. He wrapped His loving arms around me, and I heard Him say, "I am going to fill you with my unconditional love." Then, this most amazing presence filled me so deeply and so lovingly. We were in unity, Christ and I. I never suffered with that degree of loneliness again until I was thirty-nine and decided to take matters into my own hand. I decided it was time for me to marry.

But I couldn't get rid of the feeling that something was wrong. We had planned everything, from the wedding dress to the honeymoon, but the longing to obey God at every cost and trust Him was screaming in me, even though I wanted to be married. One day before the wedding, I called it off. It literally threw my world into a tailspin. I was thrown into the horrific cave of shame and humiliation. Some people judged me; some simply didn't understand. Why didn't I do it sooner? What was it in me that had allowed it to go as far as it did? I hurt so many people, including myself. Many told me it was courageous, but I could only feel humiliation.

MY VICTORY

A friend that mentored me through my healing asked me a very tough question two weeks later. She asked, "What was in you that allowed you to have this relationship as long as you did?"

At first I was mad. *Are you kidding me? I could give you a scroll of reasons why!* But I didn't allow myself to go there. Instead, I sat back and came to the realization that I hadn't wanted to trust God anymore.

I had lost sight of that young girl who had such a passion for God, His love, and her trust in Him. I remembered once again that He had showed me I was never going to be that girl with the white picket fence and the *Leave-it-to-Beaver* life. God had separated me, even as a little girl, and called me for something specific that He knew would be complete joy to me.

He also knew that if and when He planned to connect me to a man, it would be a man who is very strong, one with the same calling, so we could run the race of faith together. I do things in my life, in ministry, and for God that I would have never been able to do if I had married by my own choice. I would have become very unhappy and also hurt someone if I had united with one God had said 'no' about. I knew it was better to obey God than to destroy our lives down the road.

I now have been serving God for more than twenty years because at eighteen years old, I experienced the fullness of God's love. It is the core of who I am, and He wants you to experience the same fulfillment. Not only knowing His love, but also experiencing the intimacy of His kisses. That intimate love for Him will get you through every disappointment, mistake, failure, rejection, and hurt. When you discover His love deeply, intimately, you will never be the same. He will heal your deepest, darkest pain through the power of His love and free you to a journey of freedom and liberty like you have never experienced before. That's what he did for me. I am changed forever!

DEVOTION: DAY ONE
SLOW DOWN

"Slow down and everything you are chasing will come around and catch you." – JOHN DE PAOLA

And on the seventh day God finished his word that He had done, and He rested on the seventh day from all His work that He had done. GENESIS 2:2-3

Read: Psalm 37:7, Philippians 4:6-7, Matthew 11:25-29

There's an old song that says, "Slow down, Baby, you're moving too fast." It goes on to describe someone who is pressing on the gas while holding her hands in the air, running from her past.

It is so easy to stay so busy in life that literally weeks will go by before we realize that we have not had any quiet time with the Lord. No word or worship time. It is in the quiet times with the Lord that He encourages us. He fills us with hope and promise and gives us a refreshing that only He can give.

I have learned in my very busy schedule that if I do not make my time with God intentional, it will never happen. We can have a heart and desire to spend time with the Lord, but that isn't enough. We have to plan our time with God. I have to look at my schedule every week to see where I can get my God time in. I have to be intentional! There may be mornings where you get up a half-hour early or take time on your lunch break. I have to prepare mentally each night when I go to bed and envision it in my day or it will not happen. Every time I do, it happens.

My Choices

I choose to make my relationship with God intentional.

I choose to set my schedule to have my God time and discipline myself to follow through.

DEVOTION: DAY TWO
TIME IN HIS WORD

"When you read God's Word, you must constantly be saying to yourself, 'It is talking to me, and about me'."
– SOREN KIERKEGAARD

Read: Psalm 119:105, Hebrews 4:12, Psalm 119:11, Isaiah 55:11, Genesis 1

John 1:1 says, *"In the beginning was the Word, the Word was with God and the Word was God."* The written Word of God is powerful, because it is the reflection of who we are, not what we see in the natural mirror but the reflection of our inner man, the part of us that was created in the image and likeness of God.

As you read the Word of God daily, you will begin to see God for who He really is, and you will see yourself the way that God truly sees you. All of the distorted perceptions of yourself: the past, the mistakes, and the hurts will grow dim as you light or illuminate your heart and life with the Word of God that doesn't return void, but accomplishes that to which it was sent. It's powerful, active and sharper than any two-edged sword. As you read the Word, it is going to tear out the residue that your life experiences have placed on you and begin to mold you and shape you into your true image – a beautiful, powerful, overcoming woman who is completely loved by her God!

As you read the Word of God, seeds of life are being planted in you; they will take root and grow deep inside you. When you find yourself in a hard situation, that Word in you will find its way to produce hope and joy. That Word gives you the peace that passes all understanding.

My Choices

I choose to die to my flesh daily and commit to read the Word of God.

I choose to believe what God's Word says about me and my life.

I choose to journal every day and reflect on His precious promises.

DEVOTION: DAY THREE
TIME IN WORSHIP

"The whole person, with all his senses, with both mind and body, needs to be involved in genuine worship." – JERRY KERNS

Read: Psalm 95:6, Psalm 99:5, Psalm 100:4, Psalm 150

The Bible says to enter into His gates with thanksgiving and into His courts with praise. There is something so amazing that happens when we open up our mouths and hearts to worship Him with a heart of thanksgiving instead of frustration and requests.

Imagine if someone you loved complained about their life, cried, and acted disappointed every time you saw them or talked to them. How much time would you really want to spend with together? I know when I get with my girlfriends, I want to laugh, have a great time and make the best memories.

Now, God loves you unconditionally, and any way you come to Him is just fine, but there is power released in your life when you begin to worship him with a thankful heart. Setting time aside to spend with Him, turning on worship music and lifting up His amazing name will do you great good. Faith will begin to rise up in your heart, the promises of God will flood in, His hope and joy will be stirred and activated in your life.

The situation may not have changed yet, but your heart has been changed by your lover. I was believing God to be healed of asthma, and I would ask Him to heal me and quote healing scriptures for years; but it wasn't until I began to thank Him every day for what He had already done, according to His Word, that I was completely healed. I have been asthma-free for over three years now. There's power in your worship and in having a thankful heart!

My Choice:

I choose to set time aside and not allow any distractions or excuses to take away my time to worship God. I will be intentional with Him and my worship.

DEVOTION: DAY FOUR
THE GREAT EXCHANGE

"You leave old habits behind by starting out with the thought, 'I release the need for this in my life'." – WAYNE DYAR

Read: 1 Peter 5:7, Job 23:10, Proverbs 25:4

I love this part of my relationship with God because His desire is to heal you of the brokenness and disappointment of your past and release you into your purpose. We need to "Cast all our cares upon Him, because He cares for us," learning to give Him everything. The Word of God says that He refines us like silver or gold. As the silver is heated up by the fire, the impurities that are found within will surface to the top; this is called dross. The silversmith is not disgusted or surprised by the dross; he expects it. He will simply reach in and remove all the dross until the silver is pure and at its most valuable state. God knows we have impurities in us brought on by life, and He is like a silversmith, purifying us for His use.

Here is how the great exchange works: As you read your Word and spend time with the Lord, it will be like a refiner's fire. He will begin to show you the impurities (hurts/pains) that He is simply trying to heal. It's not for you to embrace and relive; it's to lift it up to God and give it to Him. After you give Him your pain, you reach up and exchange it for the unconditional power of the love of God. His love is the only exchange you need to fill that empty void in your life. Receive His love and allow it to go deep inside the empty places of your heart.

My Choices:

I will, by faith, let go of the things in my past that hold me back from the love of God.

I will not pick them up again and embrace them as my own.

I will be excited about my future, because God has made it amazing.

DEVOTION: DAY FIVE
LOVER OF YOUR SOUL

"Too much of anything is dangerous unless it's God's Love."
– ANONYMOUS

Read: 1 John 4:9-11, Ephesians 2:4-5, Zephaniah 3:17, 1 John 4:7-8

Talking about the Love of God is my favorite topic because He truly loves you so much! Do you know that we were God's idea? Not man's, but God's. He saw Adam and said, "It's good, but let's make a woman so she can light up this world, be an encouragement, be a force to be reckoned with!"

You were created to have a relationship with Him. Love relationships work like this: give, receive, give. Your love relationship with your Creator is not a selfish, one-way relationship. Loving Him and serving Him is not enough. We need to take time to let Him love us back in return. His love fills the voids, brokenness and pain. But if we don't see His love or experience His love, we are missing the joy of our relationship.

Do you truly understand the love of God, not through knowledge (your head) or emotions (your heart) but through a deep, heartfelt "knowing"? Are you comparing His love with the broken and flawed love of a natural person? It is so easy for us to filter His love through our life experiences, but His love never ceases and never changes. He loves so much He sent His only son, Jesus, not just for the forgiveness of our sin, but to ensure you the security of knowing, no matter what life brings or what choices you make, that He never stops loving you.

My Choices:

To forgive others who have hurt me or abandoned me.

To change the way I view God's love for me.

To never let the broken and disappointing natural-love relationships I've had determine how I see and receive God's love in my life.

GOD CRAZY FREEDOM CHALLENGE

1. Add fifteen minutes of God-time every day to your schedule. Use it to talk to Him and to listen for His voice in return. You will be surprised at how easy it becomes to make that time, and you'll be so blessed by it too. Add fifteen more minutes in to read His Word. Take your Bible, a notebook and a pen. As you read, journal the words that speak to your heart so you can reflect on them later. After a week, look back at your journal and review all the wonderful blessings God spoke and ministered to you through His written Word.

2. Every day, think of one thing you can be thankful for in your life and write a small paragraph about it. Do this during the time that you have set apart to spend with Him.

3. Reflect on the past few days. See if there is any dross that has been coming up in your heart that maybe, instead of making the great exchange, you have embraced and relived again. Once the Lord shows it to you, then make a fist and imagine that pain in your hand. When you are ready, let it go. Lift it up to heaven, open your hand and release it to God. Now ask the Lord for His unconditional love, and pull that same hand down to your heart. Allow His love to flow deep inside you.

4. Put on some worship music and lift your hands to the Lord. Allow His presence to cover you and saturate you. Allow your heart to hear His words whisper, "I love you, and I will never stop loving you. There is nothing you could do to change my love; there is nothing to be ashamed or fearful of. My heart beats for you, and I desire your future to be bright and full of joy and precious promises."

GOD CRAZY FREEDOM PRAYER

Father, I thank you for every day that I make time to spend with you and be in your presence. Thank you that you fill me with your joy and peace each and every day. I thank you in advance that each day will be intentional and purposeful in slowing down and setting time aside just for you. Give me a heart and desire for your Word. As I read every day, I pray you fill my heart with revelation and truth. I don't want to read just words on pages; I desire to have insight into your precious promises and to see myself the way you see me. Thank you for all you are going to show me.

Forgive me, God, for the areas of my life where I have only been complaining. I commit today to begin to be thankful for all the good things you have given me. I surrender my hurts and fears to you. I desire to come before your presence and worship you for the loving savior that you are. I open my heart for the great exchange in my life. I pray that you give me the strength to let go of my past and trust you. I give the dross of my life as an exchange for your love. I thank you for all you are doing inside me and the courage you have given me to let it go. Please reach inside my heart and remove any false image of love that I am comparing your love to. I desire to know and experience your presence in my heart. Please fill any brokenness, unforgiveness, or pain. I desire to know your love so I can love others to the fullest who need to know your love. Amen.

OUTCAST TO BELOVED

by Bonnie Keen

GRACE ON THE FRINGE

"Jesus comes not for the super-spiritual but for the wobbly and the weak-kneed who know they don't have it all together, and who are not too proud to accept the handout of amazin' grace. As we glance up we are astonished to find the eyes of Jesus open with wonder, deep with understanding, and gentle with compassion."
– BRENNAN MANNING, THE RAGAMUFFIN GOSPEL

There was a 'certain woman' living on the fringe when Jesus the God-Man entered Galilee like a rock star. News of his power – miraculous healings, eating with sinners, hanging out with losers, speaking words of life like new wine – preceded him, catching fire through the hills of Israel. In stark contrast to his resume, the carpenter's son from nowhere Nazareth was a homeless prophet with no place to lay his head.

One certain day in Galilee, this broken woman dared to touch the fringe of His robe. She had been bleeding for twelve years. In her culture, she was perpetually unclean. A social leper, barred from the synagogue, condemned.

Truth be told, she smelled. She was repulsive. She was a card-carrying fringe dweller. Excluded. Uninvited. Undone. Orphaned by her circumstances.

Over twenty years ago, a 'certain woman' living in Tennessee was living on the fringe when Jesus the God-Man entered her mangled world. She was divorced, a single mom, a victim of date rape and clinical depression. She was bleeding out in her soul.

I am that certain woman.

There were rumors about my divorce, friends who stopped speaking to me, a sense that my upside-down life made people uncomfortable. Publicly, I wore a brave face.

In the mirror I saw a fringe dweller, stamped with disapproval, another child of Abba living on the edge.

The woman in Galilee was bankrupt, body and spirit. Everyone wanted a piece of Jesus. She wanted only a touch. Falling from behind him, she reached out like a drowning child. He felt healing power leave his body and pour into hers. Amid the eyes of a crowd repelled by the stains on her tattered gown, she made a profession of healing and faith. Her physical body was healed. But Jesus went one better. He would not leave until her dignity had been restored too. In the presence of the people she did 'life' with, those who would be around after his exit from Galilee, Jesus made an intentional declaration of grace:

> *Daughter, your faith (your confidence and trust in Me) has made you well! Go (enter) into peace (untroubled, undisturbed well being).* (LUKE 8:48, AMPLIFIED BIBLE)

In the aftermath of my divorce, trembling at the challenges of being a single mom, pocketbook emptied, credit card debt on the rise, ten years of public ministry impaled by a highly publicized scandal, I descended into the black world of clinical depression. Desperate for Jesus, could I possibly hear the beloved word, "Daughter"?

I didn't know then what I have now learned. In the words of Pastor Scotty Smith, "What we do with the pain of our betrayals and abuse is more important than the wounds themselves."

You see, I'm a Southern girl, born and bred in Nashville. We do wear shoes (when necessary), speak English and have fairly nice teeth. It's as humid a place as you'll find this side of the Mississippi, which I'm told is kind to the skin. It's a good-earth place to live and call home.

The South is also one of those studded buckles of the Bible belt. There are more churches in one city block than mosquitoes on a lake in July. As a child, I was lashed to one of the most graceless churches imaginable. It was frightening to hear that no matter how tightly one clung to the robe of Jesus, there was no guarantee God would smile in your direction.

Migraines began when I was just six. I was often hit with belts and switches and raised on the verse, "Spare the rod and spoil the child." My church told me to be perfect as God is perfect. I absorbed the burden like a sponge.

Maybe my church lived under these words by C.S. Lewis in *God in the Dark*: "If you think of this world as a place intended simply for our happiness, you find it quite intolerable; think of it as a place of training and correction and it's not so bad."

My church trained and corrected. The only music allowed in our church was singing of a cappella hymns. But God poured music into my soul from every direction. I reveled in classical piano, began to write songs, and found myself falling madly in love with theatre. As I grew, the Bible revealed a very different God from the terrorizing god of my youth.

Entering adulthood, generational chains of bondage continued to shatter. God graced me with an unlikely career as a recording artist— singing and writing about my faith with the trio First Call. Stunned by Dove awards and Grammy nominations, we sang at churches around the world, claiming Jesus as Lord.

Professionally successful, my private life also flourished. I was married and blessed with a daughter and son. The landscape in suburbia looked bright: A + B = C.

Eleven years into my marriage, a misplaced "Q" upended the equation.

Through the coming barren years Jesus whispered grace-drenched healing: "This is why I came to this fallen garden – for times when you can't breathe, can't pray, can't even find the strength to hope. Fall apart on me. Free fall into my arms. We will get to the other side." I railed, wept, gave up, shook my fists, took one step forward and five back, and nothing could separate me from His love.

"Is it possible," clinical psychologist Jim Finley asks, "that each time we stumble, fall and rise again, God can barely bear the bliss of it?"

As with the fringe dweller in Galilee, Jesus restored my dignity and healed my heart. Given a second-chance marriage and a platform as a solo artist and author, I offer His hope – revealing the underbelly of my life. Indeed, I hear Jesus call me "Daughter."

I love the way Ken Gire puts it in his book, *Moments with the Savior:* "With this tender word, he gives this orphan a new home within the family of God. He gives her healing. And he gives her back her dreams."

Still, I sometimes stumble over the word 'victory.' This side of heaven, battles rage. Satan lies. Angels and demons wage war in the unseen. Victory refuses to be boxed up, wrapped with a neat bow and put away on a shelf labeled 'Done.'

Until the icy shards of a conversation in the early morning hours of December 2010, my scalawag testimony seemed complete. Then ... another volcanic chapter.

Someone I love like life itself now struggles on the fringe. The church at large has yet to dialogue with those who weep silently in his terrain. Once it was easy to stand silently on the sidelines, watching the crowd throw stones. Now, the stones are directed at my child. One by one I feel them drop from my hands.

Who did Jesus reach out to touch? He embraced the fringe dwellers, the underdog, the sick, hurting, hopeless, lost, worn out, and beaten up, bedraggled ragamuffins on the edge.

Are we not called to live out this same love no matter the cost?

It will cost carrying the cross together trusting God is greater than our hearts.

It will require the honor of loving the unlovely, the faith of a mustard seed.

It will cause mountains to move, walls of hatred and prejudice to collapse.

We will see suffering mix with Jesus' blood in the mystery of love that heals because He has overcome sin.

We can offer freedom to the fringe dwellers through God the Redeemer, Jesus the Light, Spirit the Truth.

In *One Thousand Gifts,* Ann Voskamp puts it this way, "Grace that chooses to bear the cross of suffering overcomes that suffering."

Today, I continue to write, sing, record, and find myself cast in theatrical productions, the stuff of daily life.

Victory of the spirit is choosing to trust through chattering teeth, fear, sleepless nights and tears, insisting by faith that God has the final word.

A new generation of suffering fringe dwellers abound. Will we have the courage to love those whose choices carry a stench? We will reach out as Jesus did and touch the unclean?

As a former outcast, I know the healing robe of Jesus is offered to all who long for just one touch.

Victory is the ongoing choice to embrace those on the fringe, loving them as He loves.

Victory is a chain of joined hands clinging to the robe of Christ.

> *"Pray for the tears your enemy weeps*
> *Pray for the place the outcast sleeps*
> *Love is the key that will bring a soul peace*
> *Pray for the day your enemy's free*
> *Pray for the tears your enemy weeps"*
> – BONNIE KEEN, 2012

MY VICTORY

During a difficult conversation with my precious momma, an unexpected shaft of personal healing light broke through. Momma has her face in the Book every day. Still, tendrils of legalism threaten to choke out the beautiful victory on the page. She clings to ongoing lists of reasons why God's love is conditional.

I could barely believe my momma as she insisted that a missionary from her church had failed God. The saint-woman had returned from her travels, sick with pneumonia, and missed one morning of quiet time. Mom scolded the woman for not putting God first. Stunned by this works-bondage, we were both shocked when my arms flew up in an act of praise, my voice bursting like a child on Christmas morning, "Thank you God for Your Grace! For breaking the chain! For revealing Yourself!"

Looking over the landscape of my journey, littered with mistakes, failures, heartache and broken dreams, I cannot miss the miracle. I live as

God's girl, as His beloved.

His grace is freedom from impossible odds. Faith in His power is daily manna.

My son once looked at me, after pondering my past and said, "I honestly don't understand why you're not walking the streets as a crack whore!"

After a good laugh, I heard myself saying, "The grace of God…but for the grace of God."

DEVOTION: DAY ONE
COUNTLESS MORE

And there are also many other things which Jesus did.
If they should be all recorded one by one in detail,
I suppose that even the world itself could not contain
the books that would be written. JOHN 21:25

We're in this together, you and me, one girl of God holding hands with another, discovering healing and grace one day at a time.

For a few moments (or maybe more), let's soak in the implications of what we do *not* know about the life of Jesus.

The Gospels record numerous, astonishing miracles of Jesus. Yet the apostle John ends his book citing *countless more*. Here lies great comfort. Imagine the healings that went unrecorded.

There is no sin that was not nailed through His hands and feet to the cross. Have we dishonored the cost of Christ's suffering by delegating a wretched, hopeless few to live beyond the reach of His blood?

Surely Jesus, moved to tears by the funeral of a poor widow's son, the One who intentionally sat with a Samaritan loser in the midday heat to restore her sense of dignity, the Son of God who stepped in to diffuse the angry mob ready to stone an adulteress, was moved to heal all manner of human suffering.

Did God Incarnate not declare He came for the sick? The soul sick?

The woman who chose abortion.

The one who performed it.

The child molested and silenced by fear.

The homosexual, guarded and struggling.

How many *countless more* were healed?

DEVOTION: DAY TWO
FEED MY SHEEP

*"We know how God feels, because Jesus gave us a face, one
sometimes streaked with tears."* – PHILIP YANCEY, WHY PRAY?

Jesus is full of surprises. After His resurrection, He shows up to share
breakfast on the beach with Peter, John, James, Thomas and two other of
his beloved apostles (John 21). As best of friends they eat and fill the air
with laughter, sentences tumbling out, joyful embraces perhaps mixed with
tears – stunned by His love – from a cross to an empty tomb. There are no
more questions about who He is. Jesus, their friend and Savior, is God. He
who had been crucified now cooks fish with them – fully alive.

The conversation turns to love. If we love Him, we must love others as
ourselves – love even though tears fall hard. From tablets of stone given
to Israel to words of life spoken from God Incarnate, the message never
changes.

For God so loved the world that He gave ... (JOHN 3:16)

The word for love in this verse is the same word used by Abraham,
who so loved his son Isaac (Genesis 22:2). It is the strongest translation of
affection ever found in any Earth language. Isaac was not to be the sacrifice.
Another must bear the wounds. God assigned this act of love to His Son,
His Heart, Himself.

On the beach that morning, Jesus repeated the phrase three times:

"If you love me, feed my sheep."

Will we?

DEVOTION: DAY THREE
BEHIND THE SEEN

For the Lord sees not as man sees; the man looks on the outward appearance, but the Lord looks on the heart. 1 SAMUEL 16:7

Riding a subway in New York City brings out the best and worst in earthlings. One can quickly turn on iTunes and drown out the world. Forced into a small space teeming with people and their 'lives', the wisest choice may be to pull up the drawbridge of the heart and play it safe.

What assumptions are made by one guarded, sidelong glance?

Stephen Covey wrote of an interruption during a rare, quiet subway ride one Sunday morning. A man with several unruly children boarded the train and as he put it, "bedlam erupted. Stress became distress."

The father of the children seemed to have no control whatsoever. He did nothing to try and keep the children quiet so as not to disturb the other passengers. Frustration and disapproval increased by the minute.

Covey turned to the father and offered kind advice. "Perhaps you could restore order here by telling your children to come back and sit down."

"I know I should do something," the father replied. "We just came from the hospital. Their mother died an hour ago. I just don't know what to do."

We are most like Jesus when we foster compassion. Many a ship is sinking from icebergs that rip into lives.

Open the eyes of our hearts, Lord. Give us Your sight.

DEVOTION: DAY FOUR
DARING TO ASK

*"We are asked to bring to God our hopes for the future as well as
the hunger we have right now; we are asked to bring yesterday's
failures as well as tomorrow's fears."* – KEN GIRE

This new mountain I face is staring me down. I can't take a pickax to
its rocky slope. That strength will come in time. However, I am hungry
enough this day to ask God for hope. Hope for right now, hope that only
He gives, and then maybe I can take the next first step. Regardless of how I
feel, I'm choosing to believe what Mary believed.

> *For with God nothing is ever impossible ... Let it be done to me
> according to what you have said.* (LUKE 1: 37-38)

Let it be done unto me. God has allowed this situation to be done.
My beloved child is embracing a lifestyle that could destroy his body and
agonize his soul. I know he is God's child first.

Is God not ever present?

Is He not able to work in the bars of San Francisco as well as the church
halls of Iowa? Can He not shatter the darkest lies and strengthen the reaches
of the faithful heart? Are both places not HIS? Today, this I know: I AM
is everywhere and more than able to conquer any darkness and bring the
light of hope to any heart in desperate need.

So I dare to ask.

Because He Is.

DEVOTION: DAY FIVE
PRAISE PRECEDES MIRACLE

"Will You touch me deep where I weep and mourn
Will You touch me, touch me deep
Will You touch me deep where my hopes are born
O You touch me, touch me deep"
– BONNIE KEEN, "COVER ME"

I've heard that Orthodox Jews will offer thanks to God before and after a meal. How beautiful to thank God on all sides for His provision. It's easy to thank Him when the table overflows and the day smiles long. What happens when cupboards of heart and hope run dry and there looms a dark night of the soul?

Job praised God while scraping boils, through the loss of family and even when his life was ripped away. "The Lord gives and the Lord takes away, blessed be the name of the Lord," he said. Did the words choke out through sobs or song?

Faith in God's sovereignty means I will praise Him in the light or the dark, in famine or abundance, in confusion or understanding. Only then do I battle the enemy in places unseen when I insist my God is holy, holy, holy – when it costs me everything.

"The real problem for me," writes Ann Voskamp in *One Thousand Gifts*, "is lack of thanksgiving. The table is set. There is enough and more than. Though I be tried and sore tested."

When I can praise in every circumstance, maybe I have begun to believe I am truly His daughter and He is a trustworthy Father.

Such faith moves mountains.

GOD CRAZY FREEDOM CHALLENGE
DARE TO BE LOVED

"Quit keeping score altogether and surrender yourself with all your sinfulness to God who sees neither the score nor the scorekeeper but only his child redeemed by Christ."
– JAMES FINLEY, MERTON'S PALACE OF NOWHERE

I dare you and me to actually believe God is crazy in love with us. It's a huge dare this one. No more instant replays from the past. No more regrets in the present or fear of the future.

What seismic changes might occur if we actually live as daughters of God? What walls would crumble and what peace abound? How much of a threat could we be if we stopped trying to please everyone but God? What if we take Him at His word and lay our most private dreams willingly in His hands? What if we truly trust and believe His Spirit will guide us into obedience?

What if we fail? Of course, we will! It's guaranteed. Why not try to strip off the orphan mentality and imagine ourselves as *being loved*?

It's the least we can do after He's gone to such creative lengths to make us in His image, die for our sin and promise us eternal life.

A taste of authentic freedom thrills at such a thought.

Let's do this thing. Dare to believe we are His beloved, forever.

For I am persuaded beyond doubt that neither death nor life, nor angels nor principalities, nor things impending and threatening nor things to come, nor powers, nor height nor depth, nor anything else in all creation will be able to separate us from the love of God which is in Christ Jesus our Lord. (ROMANS 8:38-39)

GOD CRAZY FREEDOM PRAYER
TEARS AND HOLY FOOLISHNESS

When I came across this prayer, it rang like a bell in my soul. These words written so long ago, inspired a song of a cappella vocals when I recorded this prayer on my third solo CD.

This powerful benediction is for all of us who are crazy enough to follow hard after God. Truly may our faces streak with tears for the things that move God's heart. May our hearts open like a child's, fearless and brave, willing to risk. May we be fools in a world calling those who bend their knee to worship Jesus, 'unenlightened'. Let it be so!

In His name, together bonded forever, most beloved girls of the risen Christ.

A Franciscan Benediction

May God bless you with discomfort
At easy answers, half-truths, and superficial relationships
So that you may live deep within your heart.

May God bless you with anger
At injustice, oppression, and exploitation of people,
So that you may work for justice, freedom and peace.

May God bless you with tears
To shed for those who suffer pain, rejection, hunger and war,
So that you may reach out your hand to comfort them and
To turn their pain into joy.

And may God bless you with enough foolishness
To believe that you can make a difference in this world.
So that you can do what others claim cannot be done
To bring justice and kindness to all our children and to the poor.

Amen

www.leeellison.com/franciscan.hmtl

CONTROL TO SURRENDER

by Natalie Gillespie

When I was two years old, my mom lost me in the grocery store. She was frantic and rushed from aisle to aisle, searching for me and listening for the wails of fright she was sure she'd soon hear. None came. A few minutes later, she saw me at the end of an aisle. I was standing still, calmly looking around. When she revealed herself, I simply said, "There you are, Mommy. I thought you were lost."

Evidently, I knew right where I was. It was my silly mother who had gotten misplaced.

Mom laughed at my precociousness whenever she used this story as an example of how self-assured, how independent her firstborn was from the get-go. I was scary smart, with a strong will and personality to match, and my innately shy and meek mother didn't really know what to do with me. She loved me immensely, but she had very little experience with children before she had me, and she honestly believed that I was pretty capable of taking care of myself from a very young age. By the time I was six years old, I had three younger siblings; and my self-sufficiency made it easier for her to manage the three younger ones.

For years, running my own show seemed to work out pretty well for everybody. I was always voted into student government, managed to get top grades, and received my weight in achievement certificates, ribbons, and medals. I was named a National Merit finalist and offered scholarships to any university I wanted to attend. I sang boldly in church choir from the age of three and performed solos on stage. I participated in youth group and school clubs.

In short, I was the star, and I knew it. I liked to do things "right," and the accolades that came my way felt great.

My faith and family rounded out the perfect picture. My strong Christian parents brought me up in a Spirit-filled environment of true vibrant faith in action, helping to open a Christian coffeehouse and hosting a Monday night prayer group that met for years. I witnessed lives transformed and bodies healed. I asked Jesus into my heart when I was four years old, and I meant it. I tangibly felt God's presence and loved Him with all my innocent heart, even dubbing myself the "Jesus Kid" as my CB radio handle. (Okay, now I've just dated myself.)

When I was a kid, we were tight, Jesus and me. I knew He loved me. And I loved Him right back.

Until my capableness turned into a monster called "control."

Until my performance became an insatiable and unattainable drive for perfection.

Until my self-sufficiency became the façade to cover my low self-esteem.

By adolescence, I didn't think Jesus knew I existed anymore. By the time I was sixteen, I kinda hoped He'd just leave me alone to keep running the show my way.

I can see now that the roots of control were unwittingly planted in early childhood by the praises I received for my performance, and they grew firm and deep with blows to my self-esteem in middle school. I gained quite a bit of weight in preadolescence, and the popular girls at my little Christian school loved to tease (no, torture) me. I was a misfit – a fat teacher's pet, and mouthy to boot. I cried through most of eighth grade. I was a cheerleader, salutatorian of my class, and on my way to great academic achievements. But I was lonely and falling apart inside. I no longer heard the voice of Truth. All I could hear was that I was ugly and unlovable.

I began to develop the two-sided personality and double life that many

American Christians live. On the one hand, I felt terrible about myself. I knew I was far from perfect. I knew what I was hiding from the world. I was intimately acquainted with my flaws – my struggle to control my eating; my jealousy of the pretty, popular girls; my annoyance with younger siblings; the lies I told my parents to get my way. I knew I was a sinner and felt ashamed. On the other hand, I felt proud of the fact that I was a "good girl," not nearly as bad as my culture or many of my peers. I wasn't using drugs, smoking cigarettes or skipping school. I didn't get drunk on the weekends or yell at my parents. I was capable, determined, motivated, and smart. Almost everybody said so.

So why did I feel like such a fake and failure?

As Americans we are taught that we can be anything, do anything, and achieve our dreams. We are to "pull ourselves up by our bootstraps" and "take only a hand up, not a handout." We are strong, independent people who are steeped in the lies that we "deserve" to be happy and "if it feels good, do it."

As Christians, we are to be weak, so He can be strong. We are to do nothing, so He can do everything through us. We are to lay aside our dreams, so He can provide our "hope and a future" (Jeremiah 29:11). We are to trade happiness and feeling good for peace and joy.

My split personality only grew worse throughout high school and into my young adult years. I had waited all my life to get full control without parents, teachers, or anyone else telling me what to do. Now all I heard from my parents, pastor and youth group was that I was supposed to hand it all over – give up my hopes, my dreams, my happiness and my plans for His.

But I had no guarantees that He would give me back what I wanted.

For all my intelligence, I could not understand that surrender meant getting something better. I felt like a contestant on the old TV game show "Let's Make a Deal." I was convinced that if I traded my hard-won independence for what was behind God's Curtain No. 3, all I would get was a goat, a basket of fruit, or something else I would find utterly disappointing (like having to be a pastor, a missionary, or some kind of servant when I liked being a star). I had no idea that He loved me so absolutely that I was guaranteed the shiny new convertible (a life perfectly suited for me), the trip of a lifetime (and beyond).

Instead of wanting Jesus, I was desperate to be loved and accepted and held. I fell in love in high school for the first time. He was a football player. He was beautiful. And he was bad news. After nearly two years of dating, when I was a junior, I gave in to his pressure and gave all of myself. I knew better. But he was gorgeous and exciting, and for some reason he wanted me. I was addicted, emotionally and physically.

I knew my boyfriend wasn't faithful, and that just about killed me. I would do anything to keep him "reeled in." All the while, I felt guilty and ashamed. I couldn't tell anyone who loved me what was really going on. I couldn't let my parents down. Also, they might stop me. I hated what I was doing, but I hated even more the idea that he might be taken from me.

Then I discovered that my boyfriend was also sleeping with my best friend. My self-esteem dropped even further. How could the two people who claimed to be the closest to me – my boyfriend and my best friend since fourth grade – do this to me?

Instead of seeing their betrayal as their problem, I turned it on myself. What was wrong with me that they would want to do this to me? This was once again my need to control. After all, if it was my fault, I could fix it, right? Wrong. But I still tried.

Throughout my next relationships and into my first marriage, I tried desperately to "fix" the men I became involved with. If someone needed me, I could bring out the best in him. Then maybe he would appreciate me so much he wouldn't see my flaws and leave me. It never worked. Whenever I combined my emotional neediness and rock-bottom self-worth with a man steeped in dysfunction, we never "fixed" each other; instead, it always became dysfunctional squared.

My double life continued into my mid-twenties, when everything finally came to a crashing halt. On the outside, I still looked good: I had earned the degree with honors and was achieving small-town fame as a television news reporter and then as a newspaper reporter. I had a husband now and a beautiful baby girl. He was a paramedic, saving people's lives every day. We had friends. We were making it.

On the outside.

On the inside of our hearts and within the four walls of our apartment, it was a nightmare. He used alcohol and chemicals to numb his emotional pain. I wanted to "fix" him of these problems and fought with him constantly. He would lash out physically at me, and then feel so guilty that he'd turn back to the substances that numbed him. I would feel like I wasn't enough for him to give up what was clearly hurting us. I'd try to fix him again … and the cycle continued. We had no fellowship. We didn't attend church. I never prayed anymore. I loved him for who he could be (with my help, of course) and hated him because he wouldn't change.

Above all, I would not, could not, fail. I had never gotten a bad grade. How could I fail at marriage, the most important thing in life? Ultimately, I could not control the outcome.

My husband began having affairs, and admitted that he didn't want to be married. Unable to let go, I found him an apartment and helped him move out, believing that separating from me and his little girl would bring him to his senses. It didn't. We divorced a few months later, but I still wanted to fix it. We battled back and forth. My raging need for control did not produce the reconciliation I wanted, but it did leave me pregnant.

I was twenty-seven years old, alone except for my three-year-old daughter, and pregnant. My ex-husband was living across town with another woman. I was a Grade-A failure. With a capital "F."

Shortly after our son was born, one night while driving home from work I found myself tempted to jerk the steering wheel into the cement wall that bordered the highway. I wanted to be done – done hurting, done controlling, done failing. Only the thought of my kids being left without me kept me on the road. I raged at God in my car, begging to know why my ex-husband – the adulterous addict – had someone, while I – the "good girl" – was always alone. Then, I heard a voice that was so audible I looked around the car to see who was speaking. It said,

> *Where are you spending your time that you could meet the one*
> *I have for you? For you are my child, and I don't want to see you*
> *hurt like this again.*

I realized it was time to surrender. To real love. A love that never fails.

It didn't all come that night. It took time for the Lord to gently but firmly pull each root of control out of my stubborn heart. Some, He is still prying loose today. But that night was the first step on my journey home to Jesus.

My Victory

Soon after that night, I quit my job at the newspaper and moved with my children back to Florida, where all of my family lived. They loved on me, prayed for me, and helped gently lead me back to emotional health.

Where are you spending your time? echoed in my head as I began to pray. I began going to church for the first time in a long time. I needed to be where my Lord and Savior was and where other people who believed in Him met together. I could finally feel His presence again, and this time I welcomed it. He was not intruding on my life; He was life!

I went back to school for a master's degree and met a man at church who eventually became my husband. We married with our combined five children in attendance, and within two years added a son of our own. Fast-forward to today, and we have been married almost twenty years and have nine children, including three beautiful adopted daughters from China.

Our years together have not been easy, but they have been blessed. By daily surrendering my heart, my home, and my children to the God who created us, I give Him the freedom to do His healing work in us. Sometimes, I still forget and try to do things my way, tacking God onto my prayers, asking Him to "bless" my plans. But when those plans of mine take me places I didn't expect, He gently guides me back onto His path of grace and leads me home.

Devotion: Day One

Trust in the Lord with all your heart and lean not on your own understanding; in all your ways submit to him, and he will make your paths straight. Proverbs 3: 5-6

When I was a little girl, I did trust in the Lord with all my heart. I guess I was young enough to know that I didn't know much, so it was easy to put my little hand in His and let Him lead the way.

As I grew, I received praises and accolades for how much I understood, how much knowledge I had. I didn't know that knowledge is not the same as wisdom; intelligence is no match for experience. When I started making decisions according to my own understanding, I lost the ability to hear my Father's voice. My path veered in a direction He never intended for me, and Satan moved in to steal my self-worth, kill my relationships with authority, and destroy my future.

Surrender is toughest for those who have been told how capable they are, I think. That's probably most of us women. We tend to develop what I call the "Little Red Hen" syndrome. Like in the children's fable when no one would help the Little Red Hen, she just did it herself. And did it well. She leaned on her own understanding.

Is that where you are today? Relax into God's arms. They will never let you go.

DEVOTION: DAY TWO

*My dove in the clefts of the rock, in the hiding places on the
mountainside, show me your face, let me hear your voice; for
your voice is sweet, and your face is lovely.*
SONG OF SOLOMON 2:14

How many days do you feel like your voice is sweet and your face is lovely? Maybe not many. Satan loves to make us feel ugly, unlovable, unappreciated … simply *un*. But if you believe in the Bible, you have to believe it all. And Song of Solomon 2:14 clearly tells us that we are beautiful. No ifs, ands, or buts. Not only on good hair days, when our skin is clear, or when we've lost fifteen pounds. God finds us lovely, period! Adorable, drop-dead gorgeous, stunning.

He is so head-over-heels for you that He sings over you. Listen to Zephaniah 3:17:

*The Lord your God is with you, the Mighty Warrior who saves.
He will take great delight in you; in his love he will no longer*

rebuke you, but will rejoice over you with singing.

He rejoices over me. He rejoices over you! Determine once and for all to hear only the voice of truth about your body image, your self-esteem, your sense of worth and purpose. If you hear words in your head that condemn you, they are lies. If you hear words from others that damage, they are lies. God only speaks words that HEAL. His words are always Helpful, Encouraging, Affirming, and Loving. Remember Jeremiah 31:3, which says.

...I have loved you with an everlasting love; I have drawn you with unfailing kindness.

He loves you now and for eternity. He only speaks to you kindly. He couldn't talk any other way.

DEVOTION: DAY THREE

As long as Moses held up his hands, the Israelites were winning, but whenever he lowered his hands, the Amalekites were winning. When Moses' hands grew tired, they took a stone and put it under him and he sat on it. Aaron and Hur held his hands up— one on one side, one on the other—so that his hands remained steady till sunset. EXODUS 17:11-12

Another tool that Satan uses to destroy us and pull us away from the love of God is isolation. When we start relying on ourselves, we often pull away from other people who love us, know us and could speak wisdom to us. Sometimes we drop out of fellowship and community altogether. We don't go to church, don't call our Christian friends, and stop hanging out in places where we might meet someone who could convict us of our sin.

When we are isolated, we become vulnerable to the enemy's attacks, as vulnerable as a lone sheep is to a pack of wolves. Soon, all we can hear are the growls and snarls as he tells us how unlovable we are, how unforgivable our sin is, how miserable we are always going to be.

If you are out of fellowship, take a step today to get back into it. Go to church, call an old friend, or ask a close relative to forgive you for distancing yourself. Allow those who love God and love you to gently lead you back into the fold. They will hold your arms up when you are weary in battle, so God can win!

DEVOTION: DAY FOUR

This is God's Message, the God who made earth, made it livable and lasting, known everywhere as God: 'Call to me and I will answer you. I'll tell you marvelous and wondrous things that you could never figure out on your own.' JEREMIAH 33:3 THE MESSAGE

For a long time in my life, I stopped talking to God. I knew He was there, and I still loved Him (I thought). I just wanted Him to keep His distance. As our conversation dried up, I drifted farther and farther away from Him. When the bottom fell out of my life and the pain was so great I wanted to end it, I finally cried out to the Lord again. My first cry was not one of humble repentance. Rather, it was raging anger at the injustice of being alone while the man who had betrayed me found new relationships. It wasn't fair, and I let God know it!

But when I called to Him, He answered me in such a loving way that my anger melted. My heart softened. I began to heal. And He showed me things I couldn't figure out on my own. He showed me that surrender was not about giving up but gaining more than I ever imagined. That peace, which used to sound boring to me, is far better than an emotional roller coaster. That His plans took me places that gave me lasting joy, not fleeting happiness.

Call to Him, and He will answer you. It's a promise. You may not hear His still, small voice at first. But keep calling. I guarantee His help will be on the way, and you will experience wondrous things!

Devotion: Day Five

Commit to the Lord whatever you do, and
he will establish your plans. Proverbs 16:3

When I surrendered my life back to the Lord after my divorce, He began to pull the weeds of control out of my heart. But I am still a work in progress even twenty years later. I have a big – no, huge – patch of control weeds.

Going into my second marriage, I often tried to control my husband and my new stepdaughters so we would look like a "normal" family, Christmas pictures and all. It never worked, and my stepdaughters resented it for years. I tried to control my career, but every time I pounded on doors looking for work, none came. I tried to control my body shape and instead had to fight an eating disorder for two decades.

Only when I let go can He do a great work in me. And when I do, I get to see His miracles. When I give up, He can move in mighty ways, dropping unexpected book projects into my Inbox, restoring my relationships, and freeing me from the chains of disorder.

The Lord constantly reveals new areas of my control addiction that He then gently "breaks." He reveals, and then I have to surrender. I surrender, and He can pull out the roots. He reveals something else, I surrender, He weeds, and so on.

When I remember to surrender to Him first, before I take the control, He can establish my plans. And there's a lot less weeding that has to be done! Ask God what His plans are for you, and be willing to drop yours for His.

GOD CRAZY FREEDOM CHALLENGE

Ask three people you trust who know Jesus well and who hear His voice to tell you about yourself. Ask them what they see as your top five strengths and your top three weaknesses. Be open to both the positive and the areas you can let God work on.

Pray with these trusted people about each of these areas on a regular basis. Find Bible verses that pertain to these character issues that encourage you and remind you to follow Christ where He wants you to go. Write these verses on cards or note paper and paste them where you will see them daily – on your bathroom mirror is a great place to start.

Meditate on these verses until you hear these voices of truth by heart, and then replace them with others. Ask God to reveal His plans in you, and get ready for the ride of your life!

GOD CRAZY FREEDOM PRAYER

Dear Jesus,

I thank you so much for this day, because no matter what I am going through, no matter how far I've gotten off Your path, Your mercies are new every morning. I pray that you will help me each day to forgive those who have hurt me, and to forgive myself. Help me to ask you what Your plans are for me today and every day instead of asking you to bless my plans. Help me to seek you first – in my relationships, my work, my finances, my ministry and in every area of my life. Keep leading me with Your love and stop me from racing ahead of You. I don't want to be in control anymore. I'm not the Little Red Hen. I don't have to do it all myself. I couldn't if I tried. This is Your show, and I am a small player in it. Help me to hear only Your voice of truth and to see myself through Your eyes – as the adorable, fun-loving, beautiful, sweet, God-Crazy lady you made me to be. Help me to walk in God Crazy Freedom with you. In Jesus' mighty name I pray, Amen.

FEAR TO COURAGE

by Kim Vastine

*For you have been my help, and in the shadow of your
wings I will SING for joy.* PSALM 63:7

The pounding of an impatient fist knocking on the wooden frame of our
front door sounded relentless. It was one of those beautiful California days
that had a tantalizing combination of warm sunshine and a cool breeze
from the nearby bay of the Pacific Ocean. My mother had left the front
door wide open so that the outside air could be welcomed in through the
locked, screen door.

"Hello, anyone home? Hel-lo, Kim, are you here? The relentless
knocking on the screen door jolted me out of my childhood afternoon
reverie. Curiosity prompted me to skip from the patio through the house
to see who was at the door. Upon reaching the front room, my eagerness
was quickly replaced with a sickening panic as I recognized the figure of
the man peering through the screen. He saw me, grinned from ear-to-ear,
and his tone changed immediately to a sweet, syrupy drawl. "Kim, honey,
how are you? Let me in, okay?"

Overwhelming feelings of dread grounded me to a frozen posture in the middle of the living room. Familiar fingers of fear began to tighten around my throat. I simply could not find my voice to utter a responsive word. My face felt hot and my stomach began to churn violently as the heat of shame surfaced. Sounding impatient now, Uncle Buck's voice grew a stronger, "Kim, honey, what's wrong? Come on now, let me in. I brought you something."

Then I heard the familiar sound behind me of my feisty little grandmother running from the garage. I felt the angry energy in her ample, yet agile, body as she raced around me to the front door. She began loudly berating the man whose face held no expression. "How dare you show up at this house, you sucker! Get out of here NOW or I will call the police! Don't you ever show your face here again."

Uncle Buck stood there stunned. He quickly regained his composure, and then looked past my Grandmother at me. "Kim, did you tell our special secret? How could you do that? You promised me ..."

"Uncle Buck" was a friendly distant relative in the family who occasionally stopped by to visit. I enjoyed the special attention and compliments he handed out to me like candy. It seemed that he really saw me. So when Uncle Buck had stopped by one day when mama was at work and I was alone, I was happy to see a familiar face. When he came inside the house and took me to my parents' room to ask for a personal favor, I began to sense that something was wrong. But I was just a little girl. A good little girl. I could not tell an adult "no."

I hated what he made me do with him. Not just that time, but on other occasions too. Afterwards, he would give me the change in his pocket because I was such a "good girl." I asked him to stop, but he ignored my tearful pleas and said he just could not help it. I came to despise being a good girl, but I also craved approval and attention.

After Uncle Buck started visiting me, my grandmother moved in with our family. She was my best friend, and my siblings and I thought we were the luckiest kids to have her with us for awhile. She was a retired nurse and took great care of our scratches and bumps with warm hugs and bandages. Her pies and cinnamon rolls were the talk of the family.

I was only seven years old, but I kept Uncle Buck's and my "secret." Like most children who are victims of abuse, I both admired and feared my abuser. I was ashamed and didn't want to get anyone in trouble. So when

Grandma had demanded to know why I kept displaying signs of physical pain and discomfort, I didn't admit a thing. She then marched me into the bedroom to see what was going on. It was obvious that I had been severely sexually abused. Terrified and confused, I confessed. I felt deep grief at exposing someone and was convinced it was my entire fault.

Suddenly, I had a lot of unwanted attention and my pelvic pain and sores became defined by trips to a doctor. As a child, the agony and torment inside my body and mind were relentless. How could I have been so untrustworthy as to betray Uncle Buck? I had promised him I would never share "our little secret." After my initial confession, my father reported it to the local District Attorney's office. I do not remember anyone ever asking me for full details about what occurred with Uncle Buck. As a young girl and later as a young woman, I certainly never offered to talk about it. Rather, our family pretended it never happened, even later when the sexually transmitted disease attacked my body. As bad as it was physically, emotionally it was worse. The cancerous tentacles of the secret were not excised and they found fertile soil to flourish in my heart and soul.

Our family life was a contradiction. There were days when we looked fairly normal. Other days, well, it felt like we lived in hell. Mama took us to church every Sunday morning. We also went on Sunday, Tuesday and Thursday nights, and attended endless revival meetings. Seasonally, my dad would come and go with us. Early on I discovered that I loved to sing, and people seemed to enjoy listening. Congregational and solo singing at church gave me a voice. It was a way for my heart to be heard and accepted. I sang soulfully and passionately. Music was a healing gateway; my voice gave me value. I sensed the Lord actually *heard* me and loved my "song voice."

I remember one special day in the tiny church prayer room when I literally poured out my plea for Jesus to come into my heart and save me. It was a wrenching, guttural cry for salvation and rescue on so many levels. That day, I felt His presence surround me in a way I had never known. A mountainous weight lifted off me, as wave after wave of His love washed over my spirit.

Soon, however, the weight returned. In those days, preaching from the pulpit produced an endless list of rules that qualified as sins. We were truly "sinners in the hands of an angry God" in our church. It was great training for me to become a judgmental "Pharisee" at a young age. At night, sleep became elusive until I was sure I had repented of every possible sin I had committed that day. The need for approval became an idol in my life.

My father struggled to know how to show healthy love. He was filled with volcanic rage and a voice that wielded damaging words like a machete. Explosions occurred with little notice. It seemed that the most inconspicuous events or movement could set off a series of actions that would leave us three children and our mother cowering, sobbing, or desperately striving to seem invisible.

One day, my dad began screaming and angrily dragging my mother by the hair of her head. He yanked her out our front door and down the front lawn for all the neighbors to see. Another time he pinned her down on the bed, waving a knife near her throat and screaming that he was going to kill her. We kids sat terrified and helpless at the kitchen table, trying to see the tuna sandwiches on our lunch plates through a puddle of tears.

Dad found solace in the garage by hand-carving wood into unique shapes to be used as paddles for our beatings. One time, my little sister and I watched in horror as he used heavy-duty rope to string up my brother by his arms to an old iron swing set with eight-foot poles. My father let him hang there as punishment for some wrongdoing. Any infraction called for punishment. If the garage light was left on, we would hear him scream our names to line up for the whippings until one of us confessed. We became great liars.

Dad finally left home permanently, divorcing my mom when I was ten. A later year, we were given scholarships to attend our church school. Hopelessness filled me the day my brother and I were sent to the pastor's office to receive disciplinary swats for saying the forbidden, slang word "wow." Bitter anger and fear silenced me as his swats hit their mark. We were in familiar territory. In my world, only men had power. God, whose love and acceptance I had felt so clearly in my little-girl cry for salvation, now seemed silent and still. My voice was silent, but my heart cried out for justice. The abuse I received and witnessed throughout my early years left their mark through adolescence and long into adulthood. Did God really love me? Where was He when life was unfair? I buried these questions deep down in my heart and soul. I was good at pretending bad things weren't there. But anger, abuse, disappointment, unforgiveness and sadness won't stay buried forever. Like splinters under your skin, eventually they become infected, painfully working their way back to the surface. My emotional pain and anger stayed buried under a mask of service and striving – until the infection started leaking out into my "perfect Christian" life.

My Victory

By the age of twenty-five, I had been married for six years and had a precious three-year-old daughter. I should have been on top of the world, but the internal need to be the perfect Christian, wife, mother, daughter, servant and businesswoman was crushing me. My identity was found in serving the church rather than knowing my Redeemer, Jesus Christ. I wanted to know love, but crossing over a canyon of insignificance and anger (which manifested in road rage and general impatience with the world) only increased the unrelenting sadness.

The turning point began the day I drove home from work screaming and weeping profusely. "God, this anger and pain is making me crazy, and I'm desperately afraid my children will be hurt by it. I cannot do this anymore," I sobbed.

The Lord, my Refuge, met me once again. Like the joy and lightness I had experienced as a child inviting Him in for the first time, He once more led me to green pastures and still waters to restore my soul. Those waters have and continue to bring healing redemption. It's a divine exchange to daily choose to forgive and to replace the lies of the enemy with the truth that God declares over me.

The Lord sings over me and my responsive song is heard in the night. I am my Beloved's and He is mine. In that secret place, His perfect love is bringing freedom and I cannot keep silent. *"Open your mouth for the mute, for the rights of all who are destitute, open your mouth ... defend the rights of the poor and needy."* (Proverbs 31:8-9)

DEVOTION: DAY ONE
YOUR INVITATION

Come to me, all who labor and are heavy laden,
and I will give you rest. MATTHEW 11:28

Water wells were extremely important in ancient times. From earliest history, men dug wells by hand and civilizations were established where groundwater was available. Water was as precious as gold. The same is true today.

I don't know about you, but as the pace of technology accelerates it seems to easily overtake my personal bandwidth. Statistics prove we are increasingly experiencing a state of information overload. We are interrupted every three minutes during the course of the workday. Multi-tasking between email, cell phone, text messages, and four or five websites while listening to an iPod forces the brain to process more and more information at greater and greater speeds.

Are you weary of trying to be all things to all people? Or maybe you feel dry like a barren wilderness with little desire to rise up and meet the day? Do you want your relationship and journey with the Lord to possess you more completely?

You and I have an invitation every day to come to The Well, Jesus Christ, and drink from the definition of love. Just for today, ignore the tyranny of the urgent that beckons us to forget our greatest source of refreshment and strength. Join me today and come sit at His feet. Lay back against Him and receive rest.

Devotion: Day Two
The Kiss

*"Thirsty hearts are those whose longings have been wakened by
the touch of God within them."* – A.W. Tozer

I am a hopeless romantic. As a child I loved to read magical stories of the princess who was rescued by the prince, and they lived happily ever after. Even today, I do not need a child to join me in order to watch my favorite fairytale movie, *Beauty and the Beast*.

Many metaphors used in scripture define patterns of relationship with our God. He is our Shepherd, Father, Master, Friend and beloved Bridegroom King. Isaiah 62:5 says, "I will take delight in you, as a bridegroom rejoices over his bride, so I rejoice over you." Song of Solomon is full of explicit love language that applies to our covenant relationship with Jesus Christ. Song of Solomon 2:16 says, *"My beloved is mine, and I am his."* I believe this defines the highest area of growth in our relationship with Him and will one day be fully culminated with His return for his bride, the body of Christ … you and me.

Genuine worship is complete surrender of ourselves to Him. My greatest times of divine inner healing have been worshipping Him in the secret place of the Most High (Psalm 91). The kisses of His mouth are His Word that speaks truth that sets us free!

Today, release your fear and doubt. Listen to His whisper over your heart that you are His beloved.

Book Recommendation: *Song of Songs* by Jeanne Guyon

DEVOTION: DAY THREE
IT'S YOUR CHOICE

"The highest degree of courage is seen in the person who is most fearful but refuses to capitulate to it." – OSWALD CHAMBERS

Can we be real here? Let's just admit it. Life is not generally fair and the good gal/guy rarely wins. We have recently taken in a pastor, his wife and children to live with us until their financial circumstances change. They lived simply, aimed to serve the Lord by loving the people in their community, sacrificed and gave everything they knew to give. Now they find themselves feeling betrayed and wondering how they failed because they no longer have a home, a penny in their pockets, transportation, or a job.

I have experienced betrayal by dear friends, disillusionment with God and the bride of Christ, anger at doing the right thing, and suffering what seemed to be huge losses. How about you? Who are you finding it difficult to forgive? An unfaithful spouse or prodigal child? Often, the root of unforgiveness is fear. We want to know: why? Today, choose to give up your perceived right to know why and choose to give it to God. Then let Him fill your emptiness with His goodness and gentleness.

Freedom from pain can only be found in *choosing* to forgive (without waiting for the offender to repent). Scripture is clear that if we do not forgive, we will not be forgiven by our Heavenly Father.

Today, look in the mirror and speak out loud to forgive. Ask the Lord to enable you to see what He loves and declares over that individual. It will begin to set you free.

DEVOTION: DAY FOUR
WOMEN'S VALUE TO JESUS

Strength and dignity are her clothing,
and she smiles at the future ... PROVERBS 31:25

Do you know there is a spiritual war between heaven and earth for your heart and destiny? Since the Garden of Eden, when God told Satan that the seed of the woman would bruise his head, the devil has been viciously attacking women all over the world.

A few years ago my purse was stolen. Within forty-five minutes the thieves had spent over ten thousand dollars on my credit cards by assuming my identity. Two months earlier, my laptop was stolen. The sense of loss I felt in both of these situations was enormous. My identity, tools and resources were stripped away and I felt angry and grieved at having no control over these events. I could not see the goodness of God.

The statistical facts on abuse of women around the world are pandemic. Here are a few:

- In the United States, one in three girls is sexually abused before maturity.
- A girl is twice as likely not to be educated as a boy.
- Battery, rape, incest and other abuse occur in just about the same percentage of Christian homes as is found in the general population.

What if girls and women of every age could be set free to walk in the knowledge of God's love for them? What if they experienced healing and forgiveness so they can fulfill His purpose for their lives?

Today, He chooses you! Refuse to let others dictate your Kingdom identity. You are a joint heir with Christ and have power and authority.

DEVOTION: DAY FIVE
FIND YOUR VOICE

ARISE, shine, for your light has come, and the glory of the Lord has risen upon YOU. ISAIAH 60:1

Two-thirds of all Bible-believing Christians are women. World missionary Frederick Franson said, "If two-thirds of Christians are excluded from the work of the Kingdom, the loss for God's cause is so great that it can hardly be described."

Girls, our junk in the trunk has enormous capacity to distract and distort our purpose here on the earth, which is to glorify Him and make Him known. Your mission, should you choose to accept it, is to: *"Share the Message of good news to the poor, announce redeeming hope to prisoners and give vision to those who cannot see, to set free those who are oppressed, to proclaim that Jesus Christ has come to set them free"* (Luke 4:18-19). Jesus said we would do greater works than He!

Now is the time for the "Sistahs" to arise as God's ambassadors here on the earth. You have unique characteristics of God which no one else has. Your past does not disqualify you but rather gives you a platform with enormous potential to bring great glory to His name. Remember, the first woman evangelist actually had a scandalous history (see John, Chapter 4).

Today, my dear girlfriend and sister, get unstuck, clear your throat and put your walking shoes on! Make daily choices to get healed from your junk. Watch and participate to see His kingdom come on earth as it is in heaven. Find your voice!

God Crazy Freedom Challenge

I know that my story is not unusual and there are many that have been through far more devastating circumstances. For years, that frustration and anger from my pain seethed, then spewed like a geyser of hopelessness because I did not know how to give it up. Today, the healing I have received from my past pain has clearly defined issues in which I have become vocally passionate to make a difference. My hurt has become a determination to bring His hope to others.

James 5:16 says, *"Confess your sins to one another and pray for one another, that you may be healed ..."*

Someone wise said, "You are only as whole as the secrets you reveal."

My loving challenge to you is this:

1. Create some quiet time and ask the Holy Spirit to reveal the area where He wants to work healing in you.
   a. Is there unforgiveness in your heart toward any person or circumstance?
   b. Have idols of approval, comfort, power, or control taken root in your life?
   c. Are you so distracted by the cares of life that your intimacy with Jesus Christ is distant?
2. Find someone safe that has discretion and a vibrant relationship with Jesus. Schedule time to confess your need for healing and restoration. Allow that person to pray for healing to come into your life in that area.
3. Find your voice and share your story with someone within the next week. Sharing your truth will dig a deeper well of healing in your heart, as well as encourage the listener.
4. Watch the video, http://www.youtube.com/watch_popup?v=W5mbl dTkruM&feature=share

GOD CRAZY FREEDOM PRAYER

There is no fear in love, but perfect love casts out fear. For fear has to do with punishment, and whoever fears has not been perfected in love. 1 JOHN 4:18-19

Lord, I am so thankful for all the gifts you have given me in my life. I know You are as much at work in my life as You are in the people that have brought pain into my life. Your grace, mercy and love cover a multitude of sin. Today, I confess you as Lord over my life. I want to follow You, not lead. I choose to forgive (list names here of your offenders) and ask that you would heal their brokenness. Help me to see what you love about them and transform my heart. I want to spread your fragrance and light everywhere I go. Consume my being completely with Your love so that all fear is removed. Let my life radiate Your life and love in me. Shine in me so that every person I come into contact with may feel Your presence and healing power. May they see You in me. I pray for courage to take risks that cause me to confront my fears, for the sake of Your name.

May my life be a living sacrifice, which is true worship. Help me to love You and others with a radical, crazy love. Let your perfect love go deeper still in me to cast out all fear so that I am made whole in You. My bridegroom King, you have won my heart and I am Yours.

Be glorified through your body and bride, here on the earth as it is in heaven. Let me say with confidence, I am my Beloved's and You are mine. In Jesus' precious name, Amen.

ABORTION TO MERCY
by Marcie Schneider

My best friend, Sonja, went with me to confirm what I already knew. Hearing the words, "It's positive," stirred feelings inside of me that I'll never forget. I was sixteen and so scared. I worked up the courage to tell my parents, and the decision was made for me to have an abortion. It wasn't really my idea, but I sure didn't argue with it. The only person I really remember showing me any mercy or trying to discuss other options was my stepdad Jim. It's interesting now to look back at how I didn't think he cared at all about me. Nothing could have been further from the truth.

I wouldn't say I was neglected as a child, but I don't remember a lot of family time either. My parents divorced when I was four and my sister Michele was three. Mom and dad both remarried and added half-siblings to the mix. Michele and I lived with my mom, stepdad and half-sister Melinda. We went to my dad's house every other weekend until my stepdad was transferred to Colorado. I was nine years old when we moved, and until then my "happy place" was wherever my grandfather was. I loved spending time with him. When I was eleven, he died of a sudden heart attack. It was the saddest day of my life. Soon after his death, my mom moved us back to Texas so we could be closer to our family.

That's when the trouble began. In seventh grade, I started hanging out with an unhealthy group of friends. We drank alcohol when we could, and we definitely weren't concerned with sexual purity. We weren't actually having sex, but we were doing everything else. By the time I was fifteen, I lost my virginity at a party to a good friend who was also a virgin. Believe it or not, it was just a game. Everyone was cheering us on to "do it," so we did. I knew what I was doing was wrong, but I got attention for it. Sex made me feel loved and wanted. Just one year later, I was facing the consequences of my choices, leaving an abortion clinic literally empty inside.

Still, even the abortion didn't stop me from seeking love in the wrong ways. I continued to have sex and became pregnant for the second time less than six months later. This time I had a friend who was also pregnant, so we went to the abortion clinic together. This experience was very different from the first one. I remember everything about that day. I remember looking at the doctor's face, and I remember that he never spoke a word. I remember how it felt looking around the cold, impersonal recovery room and seeing the rows of beds occupied by women like me. I remember the nurse who went from bed to bed, making insensitive comments or jokes.

By this point, I had convinced myself that I was pretty much a loser. I wanted the "good life," and I wanted to start making the right choices, but in my mind I was so far gone that it was just too late. I knew the good kids would reject me, and even if some didn't, I would never fit into their group. I felt I was forever marked as a slut who had no chance of ever being accepted by the "good" people again. I felt dirty and worthless. I had become a Christian early in my life, and I knew that God loved me and could forgive me, but I also knew how other Christians my age treated people like me. I was not about to put myself through that humiliation. I decided to stay bad and learn to deal with it. I was only seventeen years old.

When I became a senior in high school, I reconnected with a guy who had graduated early, gotten a job, and now lived in his own apartment. I hated life at my house because I was grounded all the time and couldn't get through a day without fighting with my family. So I packed some clothes and moved in with him. When I didn't come home the first night, my mother called his apartment looking for me. I did not talk to her and I almost felt good about making her suffer. I wanted her to be sorry I was gone.

I finally called my mom several days later to tell her that I wasn't coming home because I had gotten married. This marriage wasn't about love, but it did feel like a fresh start.

Once I was married, it was okay to get pregnant. So I did and gave birth to my beautiful daughter Britni when I was eighteen. I wouldn't trade that day for anything in the world; however, my dream of creating the perfect little family was far from the reality I was living. After only a year of marriage, my parents paid for my divorce.

Britni spent a lot of time at my mom's house. I wasn't a terrible mom, but I wasn't the kind of mom Britni deserved either. I was still a teenager, still trying to figure out life and find love, and I put my selfish desires ahead of her so many times. I loved her very much, but I was desperately seeking a relationship that would make me feel complete. I wanted to be loved, accepted and adored by someone.

I had several relationships over the next few years. Some were serious and some not-so-serious, but most of them included sex. At the age of twenty-four, I once again headed for an abortion clinic. I remember sitting there, thinking to myself, "Is this really my third abortion? Maybe it's my fourth." I honestly could not wrap my mind around it. Each time I had an abortion, I buried the emotional pain deep in my soul. I also subconsciously buried the reality of what abortion was and that I was killing my own babies. Three of them now. This abortion has been the hardest to deal with, because the father of this child was Marc, the man I married when I was 27. We went many years without ever discussing this issue.

Soon after Marc and I married, we became pregnant again. We chose life and had a precious son, Brock. We bought our first home, started a new business and finally my life was good. It was just like I had always imagined. I had a great husband, a home, a daughter, a son, a dog and even a new minivan in the driveway. Marc accepted Christ as his savior a year into our marriage, and I rededicated my life and signed up to teach Vacation Bible School. Britni and Marc were baptized, and Brock was dedicated to the church. We had a church, a Sunday school class and Christian friends. You know, the kind who had perfect lives like mine, right? Not so much.

Over the next several years, God began to do a work in me that I did not see coming. I clearly heard God speak to me at a ladies' retreat when I wrote the word "anger" on a piece of paper and threw it away. I committed to get rid of my anger even though I had no idea where it was coming from. I really didn't recognize how deeply I had damaged my spirit in those teen years. God was so gentle in the way he led me down the path of post-abortion healing. Everything I had spent years trying to forget was all about to emerge, but God was faithful to hold my hand each step of the way.

Peeling back the years that covered a multitude of sins was extremely painful, but there was no way for me to completely heal without getting to the bottom of the pit. He showed me people in my life I needed to ask for forgiveness as well as those I needed to forgive. I was broken, truly repentant, and finally restored. Every now and then I still find a little leftover piece of some junk in my life. It still hurts to clean it out, and sometimes I'd rather start stuffing again, but then God reminds me of His faithfulness to forgive: *See, this has touched your lips; your guilt is taken away and your sin atoned for* (Isaiah 6:7). He also reminds me of His love for me: *May the Lord direct your hearts into God's love and Christ's perseverance* (2 Thessalonians 3:5).

My Victory

My past sin of abortion not only took the life of my unborn children, but also it took away parts of my own life. It killed my spirit as the depression and anger continued to build up over the years. Many other sins and strongholds got lodged in the cement I was forming around my heart to protect it from any more pain. God began to chisel away at my hardened heart, and I felt Him pour a peace into my soul that I had never felt before. God tugged at my heart for a long time before I finally started letting Him in. I had learned how to turn off my emotions when I needed to and mastered keeping anyone who triggered any emotion in me at an arm's-length distance, so what was the point? Since my healing process began, I have seen the point over and over again. I spent much time recently with my dad, Bill, as he went through chemotherapy and radiation for a very rare and aggressive cancer. I'm so thankful that God gave me the courage and strength to open my heart again in time to build a relationship with my dad. As I continue to allow God to renew a steadfast spirit within me, I know there will be many more victories in my life such as this one.

DEVOTION: DAY ONE

Before I allowed God to heal me from my past sin of abortion, I remember having so much anger inside of me. I would almost look for things to be angry about. I was a nice, Christian person to the world; however, my family saw a very different side of me. I think we tend to take out our frustrations on those we assume will always love us unconditionally. By the grace of God, my family was willing to stand by me as I walked through the healing process. They were patient and forgiving as God transformed my heart and allowed me to release all of the anger I had built up over the years.

Romans 12:2 says, *"Do not conform any longer to the pattern of this world, but be transformed by the renewing of your mind. Then you will be able to test and approve what God's will is — his good, pleasing and perfect will."* Is there a specific area that you need to completely release to God? If you are not sure, ask Him to reveal it to you in a way that rocks your world. I promise He will. The pain may seem unbearable at first, but as you release this heavy burden and hand it to God, you will feel as though He is wrapping His arms around you as He begins to renew your mind and transform your heart.

DEVOTION: DAY TWO

Has anyone ever told you how precious you are? What about when you were growing up? Did your family discuss sexual purity and how precious your virginity was? As a child I always felt like the ugly duckling who was just in the way. I don't think my parents intentionally wanted me to feel that way, there just wasn't much done or said to make me feel any different. I definitely wouldn't say I felt "precious." Sexual purity was never discussed, and all I was told about sex was that it was something I was going to hate doing when I was married. Wow! Our words are really powerful.

I often wonder what I've said to my children that they remember to this day or that will affect their marriage in the future. I pray God will take any hurtful or negative words I've said to my children, erase them from their minds, and replace them with His promises. Luke 12:7 says, "Indeed, the very hairs of your head are all numbered. Don't be afraid; you are worth more than many sparrows."

It amazes me to think that God really knows how many hairs are in my head! It also amazes me that he loves me enough to even care. Do you know you are precious to God? Ask Him to show you through His word what you mean to Him and to help you believe it.

DEVOTION: DAY THREE

Have you ever seen a child put his hands over his eyes, thinking if it's dark and he can't see you, then you can't see him either? I cover my eyes to some things in my life, hoping to keep them in the dark and hidden from God. Hebrews 4:13 says, "Nothing in all creation is hidden from God's sight. Everything is uncovered and laid bare before the eyes of him to whom we must give account."

For many years, I kept my sin of abortion in the dark. I felt shame and embarrassment when the subject was discussed. I definitely couldn't reveal my secret once I started to look like a "real" Christian, going to church every Sunday, volunteering for Vacation Bible School, signing up for every Bible study offered and sometimes even eating Wednesday night dinner in the Baptist church dining hall. What would everyone think if they knew? Yet the more I tried to avoid the subject, the more God put me right in the middle of it.

Is there a past sin in your life that God may want to use to heal someone else? Do you continue to stuff this memory deep down so that your Christian image isn't shattered? Ask God to gently begin to bring this to the surface. As He opens the door for you to share with others, you will feel His Spirit guide you. Most of the people I was afraid to share my deep dark secret with were keeping the same secret themselves.

DEVOTION: DAY FOUR

If you have personally experienced abortion, you know that while you were sitting in that waiting room, nothing about the experience made you feel like it was okay, whether you were a Christian or not. In an abortion clinic waiting room, no one talks to you. No one looks you in the eye. No one comforts you. There's just nothing good about it.

I remember the first time I actually thought about what I had done and admitted to myself how horrific it was. I had no doubt about God's ability to forgive, but that was just for lies I had told or for the time I stole a bottle of nail polish from the store when I was little. This sin was just way too big, and I felt like it was presumptuous to even ask for it to be forgiven.

God quickly humbled me by revealing that my attitude basically said that His son's death on the cross was just not good enough to cover my sin. Seeing it this way helped me realize how arrogant it was not to accept God's forgiveness. Ephesians 1:7 says, "In him we have redemption through his blood, the forgiveness of sins, in accordance with the riches of God's grace." Christ's death on the cross is enough!

Are you struggling to accept God's forgiveness? You must accept His forgiveness before you can start the healing process. Ask God to open your heart and help you understand that His desire is for you to be completely healed.

DEVOTION: DAY FIVE

During my healing process, I asked God to reveal certain things to me about my abortions. I wanted to know if my children were boys or girls. I had never thought of this before, probably because I had not acknowledged the fact that these were my children. I had only looked at it as a "condition" I was in and a "problem" that needed to be taken care of, not as a beautiful life that God had created. Jeremiah 1:5 says, "Before I formed you in the womb I knew you, before you were born I set you apart; I appointed you as a prophet to the nations."

There's no doubt that God knew each of my children before He formed them in my womb, including the two who are still living. I once read something that said to imagine which of your living children you would have chosen not to have. As painful as it was, I needed that visual to show me that my aborted babies were also my children.

I am comforted in knowing that I will see my children in heaven one day. I am also comforted in knowing that the blood of Christ covers me and my sins … all of them. Are there certain details you would like to know about the children you aborted? God is faithful to reveal the details as you ask Him to. He's also faithful to comfort you with His promises and His forgiveness.

GOD CRAZY FREEDOM CHALLENGE

As you begin to allow God to heal you, ask Him to reveal something specific you can do to help you move forward in the healing process. Some find it comforting to write a letter to their unborn child. Others name their child and hold a memorial service in their honor. God led me to write the following as He began to heal me:

I woke one day to hear your call,
Although it didn't sound like you at all.
The God I had known wouldn't do this to me.
He'd forgive me of my sin, and just let me be.
The God I had known wouldn't put this in my head,
"You committed a sin; now your babies are dead."
The God I had known wouldn't take me through these years,
And after all this time, dredge up all these tears.
As I slowly began to trust You completely,

Your Holy Spirit showered me with mercy.
Even though you'd forgiven me, you knew that it was time
To deal with this particular, so you brought it to my mind.
You allowed situations in my life to eventually make me see
That trusting you to help me heal would truly set me free.
You knew the tears I'd held so long,
Thinking I was being strong,
Putting my family through undeserved rage
While my true personality was locked in a cage.
Those tears I know I needed to cry.
My children, I never even said goodbye.
But now I hear you loud and clear.
You've said there's no room for shame here.
I pray you'll lead me day by day
And teach me how to walk in your way.
Saving the unborn is now my mission.
Oh, Heavenly Father, please give me a vision!
Thank you for appearing to me in a brand new light
Revealing Yourself to me day and night.
Father God, I'll give you all the glory
Each time I'm able to share my story!

God Crazy Freedom Prayer

God, I thank you for who you are. You have shown mercy in my life more times than I even remember. I pray that you will continue to mold me into exactly who you want me to be. I pray that you will help me see any distractions in my life that are keeping me from knowing you more. Your presence in my life has taught me so much about forgiveness, both given and received. I want to believe with all my heart that you sacrificed your only Son so that I would be saved. Help me to grasp what that means about how much you love me. Please remove any doubts about you that may enter my mind, and help me to replace them with your promises. Lead me to others who are suffering because of their past sin of abortion, and anoint my lips as

I tell them about you and your power to restore their lives. Please begin to prepare the hearts of the people around me who do not know my story, and especially the ones who do not know you. Help me to be sensitive to these people and open doors accordingly, so I may share your awesome truths with them. Please place your hedge of protection around my family as we continue to heal. In Jesus' perfect name, Amen.

ABANDONMENT TO FORGIVENESS

by Michelle Moore

*And forgive us our sins, for we also forgive everyone
who is indebted to us.*   LUKE 11:4 NKJV

*W*hen I was fourteen, my mother changed her identity and left me. I simply did not know if she was dead or alive for nearly eighteen years. This abandonment was the most painful thing that ever happened to me, and it left its mark for many, many years. Immediately after my mom left, I became a shell of the girl I used to be. Wrecked by pain, fear, and emptiness, I did not recognize my life at all. My mother and I had been so close. She and my dad were divorced, and mom was my best friend. Now she had left me. I couldn't call her. I couldn't write. I had no idea where she had gone or why. I couldn't even process it.

I would lie in bed and say to myself, *Just how awful am I? Even murderers and rapists have their mothers visit them in prison. My mother left me. Just up and left. How awful must I really be?* I would ponder over and over what I had done that could have been so bad, blaming myself for her decision. My self-esteem plummeted, and insecurities reared their ugly heads with a vengeance. My father wasn't much help. After my mother had gone, I asked if I could live with him. He told me that he had a new family now and asked if I could just stay where I was. My own parents didn't want me. How could anyone else?

Abandonment is ugly. It wasn't like I could just put that event in the back of my mind and act like it didn't matter or like it never happened. After all, there were so many constant reminders of what I was missing – Mother's Day, family holidays, and friends who all had their mothers. Moms were everywhere around me – except for mine.

The people around me weren't able to understand or relate to the deep, deep pain I carried. On the outside, I looked perfectly fine. On the inside, I was crying out for help. The feeling that no one understood what I was going through left me isolated and alone. I could be in a room filled with people but feel like the loneliest person in the world.

During the eighteen years that my mother was gone, I struggled to make sense of something that was so senseless. Eventually, I began to build my own life without her. I grew up, but every achievement, every milestone in my life carried the dark cloud of knowing that my mother wasn't there to witness it. High school graduation, wedding, even the births of my children were tainted by the absence that had become more like an abscess in my heart. When my youngest son Carson was born, I cried—not tears of joy from his arrival, but of despair because I wished my mother was there with me. Since she had simply disappeared from my life, I had no closure. The void in my life and hole in my heart remained a festering wound.

One night, like so many others, I found myself crying inconsolably to my husband about the injustices and hurts from my childhood and the pain of my parents abandoning me, while our own children played in the next room. When I realized what I was doing, I felt convicted. I was ashamed. I was crying about the past while my loving husband, our adorable children, and I were safe and healthy in our beautiful home. I couldn't help but wonder how many mothers pray for healthy children every day, or pray for loving husbands, or wish they had a safe place to live. Here I was, not enjoying what the Lord had blessed me with. I was letting life pass me by while I should have been busy enjoying all that He had given me. Still, I hurt. I cried. I couldn't get past my past.

I had spent many years searching for love, value, and hope from my earthly mother and earthly father. But due to their own issues, they were unable to provide those things for me. When I didn't find value and worth at home, I thought I could find it in business. However, regardless of the success, accolades, money, and material possessions, I still couldn't find or replace what had been missing in my earlier years.

That night as I cried and as my husband and I discussed all the things my mother and father didn't do for me as a child, everything came to a head. I finally realized that the reason my pain wouldn't heal was because I had not forgiven them. I was carrying the weight of the past because I had not let go. Finally, I was forced to face my past. I had to confront the pain in order for healing to happen.

That was the first step in my healing. I began to understand that God was with me at all times and that He was not going to leave me like my parents had. They may have abandoned me, but God had not. He was different. Upon realizing this fact, things began to change. I had felt like a puzzle that had been missing pieces for so long, but slowly those pieces were being found and put in their places. As my relationship grew with the Lord, my parents' shortcomings didn't matter so much. It wasn't the end of the world, as it had always felt like to me.

As I journeyed down the path, I slowly began to feel mercy, grace, and forgiveness in a way I never had before. I began to consider human nature and I realized that sometimes when people make poor decisions, they don't always know how deeply they wound others.

My mother might have told herself that even at a young age, I was better off without her being in my life. My father might have believed that it was best to keep his distance from everyone involved—including me—in order to avoid confrontations with other family members. Truth be told, I may never know their reasons. But I wouldn't be the person I am today if it weren't for the choices—good and bad—that my parents made.

I share all of this because I want to encourage anyone holding forgiveness hostage, so they will avoid making this same mistake. If we don't forgive others, it is impossible for us to heal. Although rewarding, forgiveness is a journey and it is one of the hardest things you will do in your life. It's not just something you say once and it's done; you have to commit to it and recommit to it often.

As Christians, we must forgive. It is not a choice; it is a command. Many of us withhold forgiveness until the person who has wronged us asks for it. That makes us feel in control of the situation. But the Bible doesn't say we get to forgive when we have decided that a person has suffered enough, according to us, to atone for their actions. It says we must forgive. No ifs, ands, or buts.

Forgiving doesn't mean the person has permission to hurt you again, nor does it mean you will forget. It doesn't even mean that they will be so moved by your graciousness that they will change their behavior. More than likely, the person who has offended you has no idea how hurt you are. They may not even realize they hurt you in the first place. While you wallow in your pain, that person has gone on with life, unaware of the damage they caused.

Forgiveness doesn't mean everything will be fixed and relationships will be miraculously restored. But it does mean that we choose not to seek revenge or reciprocity. And by the way, if we put conditions or expectations on our forgiveness of others, we set ourselves up to be hurt again and again.

If we were to take an inventory of the toll that not forgiving really does to us, we would be begging to forgive. I envision us saying something like this: "Please let me forgive you right here, right now. Please don't make me hold these grudges and continue to carry this pain, resentment, and bitterness. I don't want to dwell on the past. I want to glorify God by forgiving you as He has forgiven me."

Forgiveness is a choice only you can make. Not just once but over and over. To the man asking how many times he should forgive, Jesus said, "I do not say to you, up to seven times but, up to seventy times seven" (Matthew 18:22 NKJV). This shows that the depth of forgiveness Jesus taught is not about the size of numbers; it's about the size of your heart. Forgiveness is not always easy but the rewards are limitless.

You may have endured hours upon hours of anger, grief, horror, tears, fear, and suicidal depression. You might have been dragging around a bag filled with pain and bad memories since the nightmare started. But you cannot change what happened. The "what ifs" and "if onlys" are not productive and not healthy. Instead, take what happened and use it for good. When God moves in your life, share it with others. Stop focusing on yourself and focus your time and energy on helping other people.

Your head might be swimming with angry questions for God: "Why did this happen to me?" "Why did the other person get to move on?" "What am I supposed to do with all this hurt?" Life is full of difficult questions like these that we cannot possibly answer because we do not see all that God sees. But we can trust God's leading because He has promised to destroy all evil eventually. We know He will use our suffering to strengthen us and glorify Him. We just have to take the first step.

Make a commitment to not make the same choices that harmed you. My parents weren't around for me physically and emotionally. However, I choose to be the best mother I can possibly be. And I chose wisely when I married my husband. I saw his heart for children and knew I would be providing a great father for my future children. My husband says all the time how grateful he is that my childhood was the way it was. He says that he knows I am the great mother I am because of what I didn't have as a child.

Obedience to God begins with humility. We must believe that His way is better than our own. We may not always understand His ways of working, but by humbly obeying, we will receive His blessings. We must remember that God can use anything to accomplish His purposes.

When you can remember what happened and direct those emotions instead to doing something significant and positive today, you can declare yourself an overcomer.

Bank accounts will go up and down. Jobs will come and go. People will disappoint you over and over again. But if you are able to forgive and have hope that today, tomorrow, and everyday thereafter your best days are still to come, you have everything you need. You can do all things through Christ who strengthens you (Philippians 4:13 NKJV). That includes forgiveness.

You're probably wondering what happened when I discovered my mother, alive and well in a distant state after an eighteen year absence. One morning eight years ago, a voice on the phone that I didn't recognize announced herself as my mother. After some questioning to determine the authenticity of the call, my heart dared to hope that all would be well and I would get the answers I had longed for so long. After a face-to-face meeting and some interaction, I came to realize that my dreams of a sweet reunion, with everything lining up to fill the hole in my heart were not to be a reality. But, I had asked God for closure and He answered. For that, I am grateful; but the work of forgiveness continues.

MY VICTORY

This past Christmas Day, I was joyful. There wasn't any anxiety about the upcoming holiday with disappointing thoughts of another Christmas without my parents. No thinking, *Only five more days until the day I will be crushed yet again.* The ever-optimistic person I am, I always held out hope that each year would be different, all the while harboring this deep and dark feeling of knowing that they wouldn't come. This year there were no tears filled with feelings of sadness and emptiness. There was no longing for my parents and the childhood that had been stolen from me. Instead, I spent the day enjoying family and good food while thanking God that we were all together, happy, and healthy. Our home was filled with love, laughter, and joy. It wasn't until that evening, while cuddled up on the sofa with my boys, that I realized how happy I was . . . and just how happy I'd been all day.

You see, this year was different. This was the year that I chose to walk down the path marked forgiveness and learned how sweet it is . . . with Jesus holding the lantern to light the way.

DEVOTION: DAY ONE

"Repentance needs to be as loud as the sin was."
–JOHN MACARTHUR

Jesus began to preach, and to say, "Repent." MATTHEW 4:17 KJV

Choose to be open and repent from sin. To repent means to change one's mind. It's the act of turning from sin and turning to God. As we focus on the horrible things others have done, we lose sight of our own shortcomings. Those we do see we hide so no one will know just how in need we are. In order for change to occur, we need to risk becoming open about the struggles we are going through. We need to confess the sins we are committing. We have to stop hiding and open up. Openness gives an outlet to shame and stops its accumulation.

In the passage above, John the Baptist came crying, "Repent! Repent!" Jesus Christ began His ministry with a call to repentance. When we repent and turn to God for salvation, we must exercise or use our faith to receive salvation.

Turning from sin must be tied to action. Following Jesus means more than saying the right words; it means acting on what He says. Take full responsibility for all that you have done, admit you are wrong, and ask God to forgive you.

Many people want to add God and the benefits of Christianity to their lives without acknowledging their personal sin and guilt. But confession and repentance must come before receiving forgiveness.

DEVOTION: DAY TWO

"Forgiveness means letting go of the past." –GERALD JAMPOLSKY

Forgive and comfort him. 2 CORINTHIANS 2:7 NKJV

The forgiveness process includes yourself—forgiving yourself is a necessity. It can be deeply healing. Make the decision to forgive yourself. You must offer yourself the grace you give others and the grace God gives you.

Conduct a self-examination. Ask yourself what feelings you feel most. Are they fear, anger, guilt, or resentment? Where do you keep those hurt feelings? What's the cause of those emotions?

In the passage above, the Bible says, "Now instead, you ought to forgive and comfort him, so that he will not be overwhelmed by excessive sorrow." We can apply this to how we feel about ourselves. Until we forgive ourselves, we will focus on our pain, regret, sorrow, and shame, which give life to bitterness. By forgiving ourselves, we free ourselves to love and receive God's love. We also free ourselves to receive the love of others.

Whatever happened in the past is over and can't be changed. So turn your focus to the present. Forgiving yourself is the beginning of changing the future. Whatever happened, you can only use it as a conduit. Take the pain you lived through and direct the power of it into something significant—and positive—today. Today you are a survivor. Today you are living with many gifts, talents, and strengths. You must walk away from the past and wake up to the life you have now, focusing on the opportunities before you.

DEVOTION: DAY THREE

"To forgive is to set a prisoner free and discover
the prisoner was you." –UNKNOWN

Live peaceably with all men ... ROMANS 12:18–21 NKJV

Choose to forgive those who have hurt you. Life is full of choices and this particular choice is tough. However, do not underestimate how rewarding it can be for you and so many others. There is no moving on without forgiveness.

Forgiveness involves both actions and attitudes. Even when you don't feel forgiving toward someone who has hurt you, try to act forgiving. Many times you will discover that right actions lead to right feelings.

In the passage above, God didn't suggest we consider getting along with one another if we feel like it. He commanded that we are to put all we have into making peace with our enemies. Treat the one who has hurt you with the same measure of forgiveness you want to be treated with. Be an example. Look after his needs. If he's hungry, give him something to eat. By giving an enemy some bread, we're not excusing his misdeeds. We're recognizing him, forgiving him, and loving him in spite of his sins, just as Christ did for us. Even if your enemy never repents, forgiving him will free you of a heavy load of bitterness, allowing you to walk into your future with hope.

We must muster up the energy to deal with the pain of what people have done to us and then go through the additional pain of forgiving them for doing it. We have to forgive in order to free ourselves from the bondage from the trauma the perpetrator inflicted.

When you truly forgive, it will allow you to live free of the influence the evil has had on you. Letting go of the pain is letting go of the very thing that keeps you from love and hope.

DEVOTION: DAY FOUR

"Some of us think holding on makes us strong; but sometimes it is letting go." –HERMAN HESSE

Do not worry about your life. MATTHEW 6:25 NKJV

Choose to let the pains of yesterday go. For those of us used to being in control, letting go is never easy. Giving your life and will over to Him is a powerful act of faith. It is an open acknowledgement of your trust in God to take care of you when you turn it all over to Him. Let go and let out a big sigh of relief!

In the passage above, because of the ill effects of worry, Jesus tells us to "take no thought" about those needs that God promises to supply. The Bible teaches that the act of worrying can consume your thoughts, damage your health, negatively affect the way you treat others, and reduce your ability to trust in God.

By focusing on God's faithfulness in the past, we can face crises with confidence rather than with worry. Choose God's peace over stress and unrest.

DEVOTION: DAY FIVE

"Gratitude is not only the greatest of virtues,
but the parent of all the others." –CICERO

In everything. give thanks. 1 THESSALONIANS 5:18 NKJV

Give continual praise and thanks to God. Instead of keeping a record of wrongs to forgive, focus on counting your many blessings.

We celebrate the "Thanksgiving" holiday, a wonderful day focusing on all that we are grateful for, but giving thanks is something to be celebrated more than on just one day of the year. It should be an integral part of our lives.

In the passage above, Paul was teaching that we should thank God for everything that happens to us—everything. Evil does not come from God, so we should not thank Him for the presence of evil. But when evil strikes, we can still be thankful for God's faithfulness and for the good He will accomplish through the distress.

Sometimes we look at our life situations and think that there is not enough to be thankful for. Sometimes we survey our relationships or circumstances and think that giving thanks borders on the ridiculous. However, the Bible teaches that there are many ways we can be thankful.

Start by being thankful for God's provision for your needs, for God's character and wondrous works, for your brothers and sisters in Christ, or for God's blessings. Focusing on blessings will transform your life. God gave you a gift of 1,440 minutes today. Ask yourself, *Have I used one to say, "Thank You"?*

GOD CRAZY FREEDOM CHALLENGE:

1. Repenting and forgiving yourself as well as others for past hurts is only the beginning. Make the choice to show mercy and grace by being quick to forgive and moving on to love and hope.

2. Daily take the time to stop what you're doing for one or two minutes and quiet your mind. During this time, think of two or three things or events you are or ought to be grateful for. Feel how fortunate you are to have them. Write them down in a gratitude journal.

3. The Word of God is alive and powerful. Pick up your Bible and commit to getting the Word in you.

4. Every time you begin to have feelings of bitterness, or forgiving someone seems difficult, say the God Crazy Freedom prayer that follows this challenge and remember the Scriptures from this week.

GOD CRAZY FREEDOM PRAYER

Great and Mighty Lord, thank You for all that You are in my life. Thank You for Your abounding grace and everlasting faithfulness. May I be as quick to forgive others as You have forgiven me, Lord. I beg pardon of everyone, for I have inflicted hurt. Thank You, Jesus, that I am being freed from the burden I have been carrying for so long of not forgiving others. May bitterness and pain leave my body and may Your Holy Spirit fill me with light and let every dark area of my mind be enlightened. May everything I do and say glorify Your name. In Jesus' name, I pray. Amen.

ABUSE TO FAVOR

by Jo Ann Aleman

"When we are no longer able to change a situation, we are challenged to change ourselves." – VIKTOR FRANKL

As children we make vows to ourselves, promises about who we want to be, what we want to have, and how we will live our lives when we grow up, without realizing the impact they will have on our futures. For me, those vows were shaped out of a childhood that was far from normal. Although abuse was my family's normal, my momma's normal, in my little heart I knew it wasn't normal at all. Even though we are all somewhat conditioned by our surroundings, something deep inside of us reveals the truth.

Growing up, I knew things my eyes saw were not what most kids in my class were exposed to. There were many nights I would lay awake believing that I was uttering prayers to God for change, only to discover later in life that I had actually been making vows (oaths, promises) to myself. Oaths like, "I will never live like this when I grow up," "I will never let a man treat me this way," and "I will never depend on anyone else to take care of me." My heart cried out for someone to sweep in and rescue me from all that I knew. So I made my vows to myself that I would be different. The image

I had of the perfect life did not include abuse of any kind. I would look for someone who would love me and love the Lord, not hurt me or our family. Little did I know what I truly needed was the King of Kings, not Prince Charming. It would take many years of heartache and failure before I finally left abuse behind and found the favor of my true Savior.

Although my father was very loving to his children and an incredible provider, he was at times, very abusive to my mom. Consequently, our weekends consisted of fear. We would quickly gather our clothes, just enough for the night, in an attempt to escape an environment of rage. My childhood involved leaving most weekends for a few days, enrolling in new schools only to withdraw from them and come back home to promises that life would be better. Unfortunately, the abusive cycle of chaos would continue for many years. In spite of her abuse, my mother was determined to keep her family intact. She was faithful to her own childhood vows. As a little girl, my sweet momma had uttered prayers of her own, not realizing that those prayers were oaths born out of her own abusive childhood. She promised herself never to allow her children to grow up with a stepfather; therefore, she kept her marriage vows to my daddy and remained in the home. We didn't have a stepfather, yet she did not escape the pattern of abuse that had been set for her.

The image of how a man treats a woman and how a woman responds was formed in me by what I saw in my parents. I didn't like it, my heart knew something was wrong, but abuse was my "normal." And despite my childhood vows, it set the stage for me to be destined for heartache. Many times we think of abuse as only physical; however, abuse takes on many forms. Sexual abuse, verbal abuse, emotional abuse – even neglect – are all perversions of real, unconditional love. But they are sometimes hard to recognize. As the victim, we are inclined to excuse the abuser because of our love for them. As a child, even if we are not the one being physically abused, we are still scarred by the experience of watching someone we love go through the process. Although it would take years to surface, for me the damage had been done.

When I grew up and started searching for "Mr. Right," the lasting effect of my parents' abuse cycle would take center stage in my own life. Without thinking about the consequences, I married for the first time at the age of seventeen. Everything appeared to be just as I had promised myself:

a man who loved God and a family who was very involved in ministry. Alas, that equation included me. I was free on the surface, yet broken and wounded deeply inside. I so desperately longed for someone to rescue me that I jumped on the first train to freedom. We were very young and from very different worlds, different cultures. After just six months of marriage, I became pregnant with my first and only biological child. Chelsi Marie Gentry brought hope for a little while to an already shaky foundation. Sadly, shortly after I had my daughter I became very ill and spent the next two years in and out of hospitals. Eventually, I had to have a hysterectomy, taking away my chances of bearing any more children. I was barely into my twenties, and now felt like even less of a woman. I felt worthless. My marriage faltered, and after four short years, we were divorced.

There were many things that led to my first marriage failing, but I believe that ultimately it had to do with the vows I made as a child. I still longed for love, for the perfect marriage and family, but I had absolutely no idea how to find, create or sustain what my heart desired. Nonetheless, that didn't stop me from forging ahead. Just thirty days after my divorce was final, I made the decision to get married again. Maybe I did not know how to be on my own. Maybe I was afraid to go home. Whatever the root causes, at just twenty-one years old, I married a man ten years my senior. This time, I was determined to make it work. The next six years sent me spiraling into a life of abuse much like the home I had left. Not only did I endure physical abuse, but also emotional abuse.

My husband refused to work and was always out. Many nights I was awakened by his fists pummeling my face. Luckily, my daughter was not with me when my husband would come home after a night of drinking. He would get so drunk that he would black out, and the next morning he would wake up to a house that looked like a tornado had run right through it. Every picture on the wall would be broken, every plant turned over. He put holes in the walls, bent on complete destruction. I would come home from a night of sleeping in my car at the park to find everything destroyed, and then spend the next several hours cleaning it all up. It was a vicious cycle that I couldn't break. My heart was not prepared to admit that I had made another mistake.

My parents lived across the street, and by this time my father was a changed man. He was no longer abusive. Still, I never ran home for safety. I could not bear to break their hearts. During those years my daughter spent more time in my parents' home than she did in mine. It broke my heart, but I knew she was in a safe place. I financially supported my husband and endured his abuse for six years before he decided he no longer wanted to married. He packed my daughter's and my belongings, set them out on the front yard, and told me to get out of his house. Devastated by the fact that I had failed once again at the one thing I wanted most in life, I filed for divorce for the second time.

Still, the life I longed to have as a young girl continued to tug at my heart, and I jumped right into the arms of another man in my search for love. I needed to feel worthy. My actions were foolish and completely selfish. I blindly fell into a trap without thinking about how this would affect my daughter. After only a few weeks of knowing him, my daughter and I moved in with the man who would become husband number three. He was a widower with a seven-year-old daughter, and his life was as broken as mine. Still, after several months of living together we decided to get married. Little did I know that the next twelve years of my life would center around intimidation and fear.

Within a year of marrying, I rededicated my life to God but I was still broken. What I needed was not a savior but *the* Savior. I knew about Jesus. I even thought I had a relationship with Him. But I never understood my value to Him. Religion, not real relationship, guided my decisions. So when the abuse cycle began again, I felt I could not leave this third marriage. I had made vows before God (and those early vows to myself); I could not break them again. In his brokenness, my husband lashed out physically, emotionally, sexually and verbally. His words had a way of cutting me to the core. I already felt like a failure. I already felt worthless. His words confirmed my feelings. They shaped me, took root in my heart, and I believed the things he said. "You will never amount to anything," or "You're a mutt and no one will ever want you," were venomous phrases that echoed in my heart.

For over a decade, I lived on a roller coaster of sexual, verbal, and physical abuse. Not only was my heart shattered and scarred, but also my body now bore the visible scars of physical abuse. In addition, my daughter suffered a great deal of emotional abuse. But if I gave up on my marriage, I felt I would be letting the Lord down. I stayed, but the marriage still ended.

In October, 2004, I found myself once again broken and alone, my fairytale vows shattered. Would I ever find my happily ever after?

My Victory

After my third divorce, I determined to find healing. Many believers think that being whole takes place in an instant. One good cry at an altar and behold, all things are new. The truth is that the healing process is just that – a process. Don't get me wrong. I believe God's Word is true: *"If anyone is in Christ, he is a new creation; the old has gone, the new has come!"* (2 Corinthians 5:17, NIV) However, this passage speaks of reconciliation, not instant healing. The healing process has been ongoing for me over the past eight years.

I have had many victories in my life and know that I have overcome abuse. I now feel like everywhere I go, His shield of favor follows me. During the past eight years, I have earned both a Bachelor's and Master's degree. I do not boast about such accomplishments because they were mine, but I revel in the goodness of God for surrounding me with grace not only to set goals but also to meet them. Because of God's Word, I am able to see myself in a different light that has forever changed my life. God has given me clarity and has revealed the truth that I am His, and I have been created in His image – beautiful. I have His favor. He is better than Prince Charming. I am the beloved daughter of the King of Kings. His Word has given me newfound hope. My failures have led me to the cross. They forced me to face my childhood vows and refute them with words of life. In doing so, God has granted me life and favor (Job 10:12).

Devotion: Day One

"Words once spoken can never be recall'd."
– Wentworth Dillon

Our words create our future. James 3:2-5

As human beings created in the image of God, we have been given authority to speak words that can affect our future. In James we are taught that the tongue is like fire. Although it is a small thing, it can spark big things, good and bad. We should never underestimate the use and power of our words on ourselves or others. Words spoken are like feathers in the wind; you can never take them back. The moment those words leave your mouth, they begin to produce fruit. Your future is impacted by the words you speak. Not only do your words shape your future, but also they impact and shape the futures of those around you. We do not often think about the impact our words have on the generations to come.

We must be mindful of the words we speak, because listening ears will also be impacted, whether they belong to your children, siblings, family, or friends. We must train ourselves to use words that are in line with God's plan for our lives. It is important to speak love and truth, to ask for forgiveness when we make mistakes (because we will). The enemy's plan is to get us to speak against the plan God has for our lives, in order to change the course of our future. Even the enemy knows that our words direct our actions. But we have been given a weapon to use against the enemy – God's Word. Therefore, choose to speak God's words because they remain eternal.

DEVOTION: DAY TWO

"The prayer that prevails is not the work of lips and fingertips.
It is the cry of a broken heart and the travail of a stricken soul."
– SAMUEL CHADWICK

In brokenness we can rejoice. PSALM 51:7-9

We are all broken, sometimes by our own hands, our own decisions, and other times by the tender hand of God as an act of mercy. In this scripture, David had come to the end of himself. Aware of his sin and need for a Savior, he pleaded with God for mercy, forgiveness, and cleansing. By this time, David had known much sorrow and his heart longed for joy and gladness once again. David was confident in one thing, that the One who crushed his bones was able to restore them. After all, David was known as a man after God's own heart.

How is it that in our season of brokenness, when our heart can barely utter words, we feel God the most? It's simply because our innermost being cries out to the one who formed us, pleading to be mended and for life to flow again. God, out of mercy, hears our cry; He wants our hearts to be right with Him and stands ready to rescue us. In brokenness we can rejoice, but it takes faith to call on God. What is keeping you from crying out? Is it pride? Is it fear? Whatever the obstacle, reach deep within and cry out for mercy. God will never let you down. Like a parent who runs to hold their little one who has fallen, so is it with the Defender of our soul. He will run to His own and shower them with love, restoring that which has been crushed.

DEVOTION: DAY THREE

"The heart is the only broken instrument that works."
– T. E. KALEM

Rend your hearts. JOEL 2:13

Webster's Dictionary defines the word rend as: to separate into parts with force or violence. To tear apart, split or divide. To pull or tear violently.

In the Old Testament, the rending of clothes was often an outward expression of extraordinary, uncontrollable emotion or grief. There are many examples in the Bible where deep remorse was often shown by the tearing of one's clothes. But God looks at the heart for deep repentance. He is not interested in an outward show. Joel teaches us that when one truly seeks to repent of sin, she must start with the inmost parts. It is in these moments of sincere brokenness that God promises to return grace and compassion. The Bible tells us that God is slow to anger, abounding in love. God loves His people back to a place of redemption and restores what has been broken.

It is not always easy to dig deep. As a matter of fact, it can be quite painful. Not just emotionally, but also physically. Still, if we really want to be free of sin and find forgiveness, we must be willing to separate our hearts into parts in order to bring about real change. That is far better than letting the world change us, or not changing at all. The good news is that God is willing and able to help us through this difficult process. If we allow God to help us with this inward display of grief over our sins, we will never be the same.

DEVOTION: DAY FOUR

"As we hunger and thirst for God, we come into deepening levels of relationship with Him." – SMITH WIGGLESWORTH

For they will be filled. MATTHEW 5:6

Water and food are essential for survival. Studies show that a human body can survive eight to fourteen days without water depending on the person and how fast sweat, urine, and tears are leaving the body and up to four weeks without food depending on conditions like weight, temperature and exertion. But if the human body exceeds these time limits, death is certain.

In the book of Matthew we uncover a wonderful promise from God: *"Blessed are those who hunger and thirst for righteousness, for they will be filled."* Righteousness in the Greek is simply defined as: *what is right, justice, the act of doing what is in agreement with God's standards, the state of being in proper relationship with God.*

How could any follower of Christ survive without being in proper relationship with God? The Bible promises us that those who hunger and thirst to be in proper relationship with God shall be filled. Filled with what exactly? LIFE! Along with life, those who hunger and thirst for righteousness shall also be filled with the benefits of God (Proverbs 3) such as love, faithfulness, favor, a good name in the sight of God and man, wealth, joy, peace, longsuffering, and much more.

God longs to give good gifts to His people. What He desires most is to have proper relationship with His children, righteousness. It is just as essential for our spiritual survival as water and food are for our physical survival. Unfortunately, we do not always recognize the gnawing sensation we often wrestle with from deep within, but it's there. Take time to seek God and eat and drink of His goodness.

DEVOTION: DAY FIVE

"Our 'safe place' is not where we live; it is in whom we live."
– TOM WHITE

Shielded with Favor PSALM 5:11-12

The Psalmist understood that the favor of God was equivalent to that of a shield or protection. Many times David found himself in deep trouble because of his enemies. This did not stop David from seeking God for justice and protection. Everywhere David went, the favor of God followed him. The Bible reveals that the righteous of God will surrounded with His favor. We can rest in the assurance that God's promises are the same today. We can take refuge in the Lord, knowing that He will spread His protection over us at all times.

During some of the darkest hours in my life, when I was afraid for my life, God's presence would sweep in and overtake me. I remember one day while in my office, I pleaded with the Lord to draw near to me. I asked Him to let me feel His presence. A few moments passed and my co-worker, who was also a believer, asked me, "Do you feel His presence?" As tears rolled down my face, I answered, "Yes, I do. I asked Him to come." I knew that the Lord's favor was over me like a shield. He had come into that office to protect me from the fear that gripped my heart. I have never forgotten that demonstration of love. I want to encourage you today to be glad and sing for joy, righteous one, for the Lord's favor surrounds you like a shield. Allow Him to be your "safe place" and do not be afraid of the circumstances that you find yourself in today.

GOD CRAZY FREEDOM CHALLENGE

As you walk out this journey for healing, you need to understand your purpose. And in order to understand your purpose, you must first go through the discovery phase. Here is an exercise to take you through the discovery process. Take your time going through these steps. Be honest with yourself and remember that you do not have to walk through this alone. God will help you.

Discovery Challenge:

1. Pray before making decisions.
   a. Make choices that will better your life.
   b. Never make choices when you are upset.
   c. Take your time and do not rush when making choices.
2. Make meaningful connections with individuals that will add value to your life.
   a. Acquire a mentor.
   b. Become accountable to someone.
   c. Surround yourself with positive people.
3. Make a list of promises that God has given you. (If you do not remember, ask the Lord to bring back promises He has given you in the past. Whether it is through prophecy, the Bible, a dream, etc.)
4. Take some three-by-five or four-by-six cards and begin to write out those promises. Add scriptures to these flash cards that align with the promises.
5. Clarify what is important in your life by discovering more about yourself. Take a short personality assessment like this one: http://www.humanmetrics.com/cgi-win/jtypes2.asp
6. Set short-term goals.
7. Create a personal five-year plan for your life.
8. Do something that is out of your comfort zone. (i.e., enroll in school, learn a new language, pick up a new hobby, take a dance lesson, learn to play an instrument, etc.)
9. Use your gifts and talents to make your world a better place.

GOD CRAZY FREEDOM PRAYER

Dear Lord, thank you for all that you are in my life. Without you, life would be unbearable, but you make everything better. Father, I ask that you open my eyes so that I might see myself as you see me. Help me grasp the wonderful truth that I was created in your image, with a purpose and a future. Surround me with protection and let your favor shield me. I take joy in knowing that you can restore these crushed bones. Help walk out my healing and help me stand firm on your Word throughout the process. And when I am afraid, listen to my cry for help. I want to overcome, I want to be free.

Right now, I ask that you cleanse me. Create in me a clean heart and renew a right spirit within me. You know me like no other. LORD, I hunger and thirst after your righteousness. Show me your ways. Let my words be pleasing to you. I speak life to those dreams that lay dry within me. Revive what is dead. Awaken me, and redo me, so that I can be all that you want me to be. Reveal unto me what I was created for. I ask that you never let me forget how much you love me. Thank you for the gift of your blood on Calvary. Thank you LORD, for being concerned with my life. I love you LORD, with all my heart. I praise you for all you have done for me. You are good! In Jesus' name, Amen.

CONDEMNED TO FREE

by Chanda M. Crutcher

ℐarly in the morning of July 6, 2010, I had a nightmare that could have changed my life forever. Later that same day, my nightmare came true … but the dream turned out to be only the beginning of a series of events, orchestrated by God to set me free.

Let me explain.

Earlier that spring, I had given birth to our fourth child, a bouncing baby boy we named Ckingston. He was a delight, but by the summer of that year our marriage of almost nine years definitely was not. My husband Darrell and I could not seem to get on the same page anymore. Our ability and desire to communicate effectively lived on opposite sides of a busy street. No conversation ended well. The only things we knew we still held in common during this time were our selfless love for our children, our faith in God, and the agreement that it would take a miracle of God to save our marriage.

Then came the nightmare. At three o'clock in the morning, I sat bolt upright in bed. Lying beside me, Darrell jolted out of sleep as I startled. In my nightmare I had been arrested for murder, and it was as if Darrell and

I had both awakened to the sound of a prison cell door slamming shut in our bedroom.

"What's wrong with you?" Darrell asked, visibly shaken and a little annoyed.

"I had a bad dream," I replied, trying to sound like I was dismissing his inquiry as nothing, although my heart was pounding through my chest.

"What about?" he asked.

My mind responded initially with a bitter, *As if he cared*, but my mouth utilized more wisdom and mumbled the words, "I was arrested."

"For what?" Darrell volleyed back.

"For murder." That got his full attention.

"Who did you murder?" he asked, just a tad sarcastically.

Even though I would normally engage in the verbal sparring, perhaps that night I was too shaken. I was troubled as I said from a place of total exhaustion, "I don't know." The not knowing was driving me crazy, yet I did not really want to try to fall back into that nightmare. Little did I know that a few hours later, I would get my answer.

The following morning, Darrell headed off to the high school where he is an assistant football coach, his normal summer routine. Some of my work could be done at home, so I stayed home with the kids in the mornings. When Darrell would return at noon, it would be my turn to go into the office. This was starting out to be a typical summer day in the Crutcher household.

My assistant only booked summer appointments for me after two o'clock, so that I would have plenty of time to get Darrell situated with the kids and head into work. That Tuesday afternoon, I had a two o'clock appointment with a professional colleague named Jason and an unscheduled "walk-in" with an eighty-five-year-old client. By noon I was switching gears from stay-at-home mom to professional, waiting impatiently to hear the sound of Darrell's car in the driveway.

That day, Darrell ran late. He didn't get home until well after one-thirty. It was 1:44 PM, in fact, according to the clock on our kitchen stove. One forty-four, meaning that I had just fifteen minutes to get out the door, drive to the office, and greet my team and the visitors in the office who would inevitably be standing there when I arrived. I was angry, very angry. Seething.

I heard Darrel's car pull into the driveway and couldn't get out the door fast enough. Within minutes I was in my car, on my cell phone, and backing out of my driveway. I arrived at work about twenty minutes later and, sure enough, found both clients waiting. I jumped out of the car and ran in to get started, feeling like I was already outnumbered as I hustled in the office door.

I found Jason in the reception area, while my other client and a concerned neighbor were in the conference room. I hugged Jason, more a friend and prayer partner than professional contact, and explained that I would be right back. I hurried into the conference room to tackle the first business of the day. About forty minutes later, I walked out and invited Jason upstairs to the classroom. I was still on the staircase when it suddenly hit me … my baby … my precious Ckingston … was still in my car! In my haste and anger, I had left my four-month-old son strapped in his car seat … in July … in the 90-degree summer heat … with the windows up!

Murderer! rang in my head. My nightmare flashed before my eyes again. Heart plunging, I knew my answer without a doubt. I just *knew*. Suddenly, I was turning in circles. Panicked and shaking, I held my head and prepared to go outside. My insides felt like they were physically ripping apart. *I had killed my baby.* I yelled back at Jason to pray for my baby as I ran toward the door, steeling myself to move toward the car, prepared to see the lifeless body of my son inside. I knew that Ckingston was gone. And it was all my fault.

But it was all just a dream. Yes, I had really had a nightmare about being arrested for murder. Yes, I had really left Ckingston in the overheated car. But my baby was not gone. Everything faded around me, and all I could see and feel was the presence of God. No matter what I discovered in the car, a supernatural peace was washing over me. Then Ckingston's gurgle broke the silence. *My son was alive!* Although my natural instinct was to want to strip off his clothes and run on foot the few blocks from my office to the children's hospital, God's peace continued to flood my spirit. I picked up my son and hugged him close to my chest, then held him away from me so I could inspect his tiny body from his sweaty little head to his miraculous feet.

I told Jason I needed to take Ckingston to the emergency room to make sure that he was really okay. When I entered the hospital with Ckingston in my arms, I had to repeat my story again and again. I left my baby in the car too long. As I said the words, the peace I had felt dissipated until I tumbled into a dark well of humiliation and guilt. I had just experienced an encounter with the Lord unlike anything I had ever known. Ckingston was alive! Now I felt ashamed and isolated, even though there were people milling all around me. *I left my baby in the car, I left my baby in the car, I left my baby in the car* ... I sank into a dark place that I before that day I did not know existed within me.

Jason arrived in the emergency room as the doctor was questioning just how long Ckingston had been in the car. When I told him, he thought I must have overestimated. But I knew exactly how long my son had been out there. I knew exactly what time I had stomped out of the house in my anger and exactly how long it had taken me to finish my first appointment. Puzzled, the doctor shook his head. All of Ckingston's vital signs were within normal limits. He had no elevated temperature, and he actually laughed as the nurses poked and prodded him. When I stood in my office parking lot expecting the worst, I had witnessed the miracle of God's mercy and His peace. I knew that Jesus had saved my baby's life, but now I couldn't open my mouth. The doctor stood, puzzled, when Jason said casually, "That's God."

My Victory

The police came then, as they had in my nightmare. But they did not arrest me. Ckingston was not dead by my hands, thanks to my loving Savior. I was not a murderer. That July 6 miraculous event changed everything for me and for Darrell. Whereas we had just spent months at each other's throats, now he understood that he had to get my back. Darrell loved me through it all. He stood by me and protected me from the enemy's attempt to get me to focus on self-destructive thoughts, and because he did I fell in love with him all over again. Satan wanted to speak words of condemnation to my heart; God wanted me to be set free. Instead of losing my son, I found the glory of God. He allowed me to witness his touch, and now I can serve Him set free.

Today, I continuously reflect back with amazement on that day, from the nightmare that began it to the miracle that ended it. One seemingly mundane summer day, in less than an hour, became a supernatural experience that has forever transformed my life, my marriage, and my commitment to serve God with all my heart, with all my mind, with all my strength. I will serve Him with all my being and all my 'doings.' I am not a murderer because my Savior comes that I might have life and have it more abundantly (John 10:10).

DEVOTION: DAY ONE

Jesus Christ, the same yesterday, today, and forever!
HEBREWS 13:8

Jesus has observed the challenges faced by humanity since the beginning of time. He set the standard for living a life of purpose so that we would know that we can overcome trials and know how to do it.

The Message version of the Bible tells us in 1 Peter 2:21-25 that, "This is the kind of life you've been invited into, the kind of life Christ lived. He suffered everything that came his way so that you would know that it could be done, and also know how to do it, step-by-step." We don't have to figure God out; we just have to pursue Him.

How many times have you found yourself in a hopeless situation that man's wisdom could not explain or reconcile? It's times like those that we must recognize the restoration power of the God of our Creation.

If you are hurting; go to Him. If you are whole, give someone else directions to the throne of grace. If you don't know where you are in regards to your spiritual and emotional wellness, don't assume you've already got it down pat. Instead, pray and invite God to search you. For it's on the other side of redemption and restoration that revelation shines the brightest. Keep in mind that revelation is not the objective; revelation is the roadmap that aligns us with God's will.

Ask yourself today: "Do I have a relationship with Jesus or is He just a friend of a friend?"

DEVOTION: DAY TWO

The Lord grant that you may find rest,
each in the house of her husband. RUTH 1:9

So often our priorities don't line up with the things that matter most. As powerful women of God we must deliberately take care not to allow our families to take a back seat to the other demands of life. These precious ones have been given to us by God to steward. My mother reminds me of this when she says, "Take care of home and home will take care of you."

The biblical character Ruth was committed to the family ties that she had with her mother-in-law Naomi even though she would have been totally justified to cut the ties and leave Naomi behind. Ruth's husband, Naomi's son, had died. Ruth could have returned to her family to start again. Instead, she stuck by her mother-in-law's side.

In John 16:23 Jesus says, "Whatever you ask the Father in My name He will give it." If you are struggling with managing all that is on your plate today, pray and ask God to equip you with the tools you need to organize your world. I have found that when things seem to spiral out of control, I must cling to the word of God in order to see my to-do list line up with the things that will have eternal impact. Everything else falls into place when I seek Him first.

Are you tired and thirsty? Rest is real and can be a reality for you. Jesus will direct your paths. Are you leaning on your own understanding of how you should manage your life? Invite His still, small voice to calm your chaos today.

DEVOTION: DAY THREE

Give us this day our daily bread. MATTHEW 6:11

As long as I can remember, I have been able to recite the words Jesus spoke as an example of prayer in the gospels. We call it the "Lord's Prayer," and I know it by heart; yet if I really focus on the words, they never become routine. Life experience and Godly revelation can shed brand new insight into things that we thought were very familiar.

How do you prioritize Jesus in your routine? As the mother of four I can tell you that my husband and I do more before eight o'clock in the morning than most people do all day. However, I have learned that in order to walk in the place of peace that surpasses all understanding, I must invite the presence of God to orchestrate my day.

When God saved my son, I promised that I would never just go through the motions again. I became intent on making the behavioral changes necessary for my life to be a witness to the fact that God can use me to do great things. The good news is that He can use you too!

I Peter 2:9 says, "But you are a chosen generation, a royal priesthood, a holy nation, His own special people, that you may proclaim the praises of Him who called you out of darkness into His marvelous light."

The word of God is our instruction manual whether we are intent on transforming the world or just surviving in it. Our bodies need nutrition to perform the physical demands of each day. The word of God is like manna from heaven, spiritual nutrition for each day. Remember, it really is true, "You are what you eat!" What have you eaten today?

Devotion: Day Four

*And it shall come to pass in the last days, God declares, that I will
pour out of My Spirit upon all mankind, and your sons and your
daughters shall prophesy and your young men shall see visions,
and your old men shall dream dreams.* ACTS 2:17

I have never been a big dreamer. Usually by the time I get to go to bed
I am so tired that I am not aware of my existence until morning comes.
However, the more I seek God for direction, the more I have begun to dream
what I believe to be divinely inspired dreams with tangible significance for
my life.

I prayed a few years ago and asked God to teach me how to hear His
voice because I did not feel that He was speaking directly to me. What I
have learned is that God speaks daily. My personal problem was that I had
not learned how to listen.

If you feel like you have been forgotten and that your situation is lost
on God, I challenge you to turn your ear toward Him. The process is a
relatively simple one. First, commit to spending time daily with the Lord,
not just talking to him but "resting" in His presence. Second, forgive and be
forgiven. Forgiveness can be the key to unlock the lines of communication.
Finally, get to know the Holy Spirit who desires to abide in each of us.

Visions and dreams combat complacency. If you feel stuck, step out and
watch God meet you where you are. What excuses are you making so you
won't permit God's spirit to lead and guide you into your Promised Land?

DEVOTION: DAY FIVE

My joy has been made full! And there is no
condemnation in Jesus. ROMANS 8:1

Some days I wake up not feeling like I can raise my head off the pillow. July 7, 2010, was one of those days. It was the day after my nightmare, and the day after my dream come true. My emotions were swirling, caught on a roller coaster of His mercy and my shame. Even though I knew God was in control and that the drama in my life had not caught Him by surprise, my heart was heavy.

Condemnation is defined as: "A statement or expression of very strong and definite criticism or disapproval." I believe Condemnation has a big sister named Fear. When Condemnation can't beat us down alone, Fear always backs her up.

Know today that the word of God says in 1 Peter 3:13-18:

> *If with heart and soul you are doing good, do you think you can*
> *be stopped? Even if you suffer for it, you are better off. Don't*
> *give the opposition a second thought. Through thick and thin,*
> *keep your hearts at attention, in adoration before Christ, your*
> *Master ... That's what Christ did definitively: suffered because of*
> *others' sins, the Righteous One for the unrighteous ones. He went*
> *through it all - He was put to death and then made alive – to*
> *bring us to God.* (THE MESSAGE)

You are not condemned. You are free. Your joy is made full. Now run and tell that! Greater is He that's in you than He that is in this world. So whose report are you believing? Will you walk out today based on what you feel in this moment or based upon what you know in your heart?

GOD CRAZY FREEDOM CHALLENGE

Acknowledge to yourself and to God that your life is not your own. If you have never accepted Christ as your Savior, now is the perfect time to do so. John 3:16 says, "For God so loved the world that he gave his one and only Son, that whoever believes in him shall not perish but have eternal life." It doesn't require anything but surrender. Love yourself enough to entrust your soul to the Creator of the Universe.

If you know Jesus as your personal Savior, ask yourself whether you are truly involved in an intimate relationship with Him. God desires to engage our lives. Worship is a lifestyle, the word of God is a compass, and the Holy Spirit is jealous for more of you. *"Remain in me, as I also remain in you. No branch can bear fruit by itself; it must remain in the vine. Neither can you bear fruit unless you remain in me."* (John 15:4)

If your life is lacking the fruit that you were created to produce, commit the area of concern to Christ. Complacency can be an adversary of spiritual growth. Love is what love does. Find new ways to serve Christ.

If you know Christ as your Savior and have learned to sit at His feet, walk in His truth. As it says in Habakkuk 2:2, *"Write the vision and make it plain."* Today, write your personal mission statement and use it as a guide for your commitments. When in doubt, recognize that there can be just as much power in a "no" as there is in saying "yes" in order to stay in alignment with God's plan.

GOD CRAZY FREEDOM PRAYER

Lord, I love you and I thank you for the influence that you give to each of us. Allow us to appreciate more and more each day the call that You have had on our lives since we were yet in our mother's womb. Lord, I pray that You will reveal Your plan for every woman who forsakes herself to follow You.

Jesus, I acknowledge that You are the Son of God. I appreciate Your willingness to take on the body of man to come to earth to save my soul. I believe that You were persecuted. I believe that You were verbally and physically abused. I believe, Lord, that You saw levels of dysfunction all around You. I believe that a sinful world crucified You, a sinless man. I know, Lord, that You conquered death and the grave when You rose again on the third day and that the Holy Sprit desires to abide in us and flow through us.

God, I ask for Your forgiveness in any area where I am not producing fruit. Lord, I ask for forgiveness in any area that I have experienced a missed opportunity to support the growth and development of others around me.

Lord, I pray for _____ and _____ because you have laid them on my heart. I pray that You will restore their souls and speak peace to their hearts.

I thank You, Jesus, for all that You are, for all that You have done, and for all that You have yet to do in my life! In Jesus' name, Amen.

FALLEN TO RESTORED

by Julie Terwilliger

"You are no daughter of mine," he said, his words cutting into my heart like a knife. I tried to let them roll off my back and pretend I was okay. I can't even remember what I did to make him mad; I just remember that this time, my dad turned his back on me and it seemed like once and for all. As mean, harsh and abusive as he was, I still loved him. All I wanted to do was make him happy and proud of his little girl. I longed and ached for his big arms to hold me, keep me safe and tell me it was okay.

But at some point, the hugs and kisses had stopped. Even as I watched him turn away this time, I wondered if I should try to go and give him a good-night hug. Maybe even give him a kiss? Would he reject me, stiffen up and make me feel foolish for wanting that affirmation now that I was older and not a little girl? I decided he would. I said, "Good night, Dad," and ran up the stairs to bed.

I so easily forgave my dad every time he hurt me, my sisters or my mom. Each time, I hoped he would see what a gem I was, hoped he would have an epiphany and finally recognize my sparkling joy and appreciate what a pretty girl he had. Nope. Quite the contrary, he despised the very precious qualities God had given me, and my resilience to his abuse only seemed to infuriate him further.

My father refused to love or bless me. When I met the love of my life, my husband Keith, my dad refused to bless our marriage. He would not walk me down the aisle or even attend our wedding. He convinced the rest of my family not to attend or be part of it either. Even then, I kept telling myself, *Forgive, forgive. It's okay, he will come around eventually.*

Eventually, my parents divorced; and my dad promptly married a very, very young woman, a woman who was very similar to me, the daughter he had rejected all these years. His new wife was bubbly, joyful, happy, pretty and all I could think was, *Wait a minute, Dad, you've had a girl like this in your life all along. I've been right here!* Then my dad moved far overseas, and slowly I began to feel what I had been pushing back all my life ... the rejection and abandonment of my father.

That's when a man I'll call "The Counterfeit" slipped into my life. He was a strong man, a powerful man, like my dad. He was also a spiritual man, a man to be respected. Unlike my father, at first he was a source of affirmation and encouragement. He scared me at times, like Dad had, but if I made him happy he was a safe man.

The Counterfeit sowed into me and encouraged me. Only later did I discover his careful attention was only given to win my loyalty. First, he encouraged. Then he humiliated me and confused me. He kept me off balance by reminding me that I was nothing until he found me and helped me become something of worth. Still, when he was happy with me, we would talk and laugh and do life together. There were no better times than those. This man was my pastor, my boss, and now he was giving me the attention my father never had. Never mind that he threw in a little verbal or emotional abuse from time to time. I was used to that, and like any victim of abuse, I felt like I had to take it from him. The Counterfeit and I worked together and battled in our codependency, all the while building his successful ministry. This man was there for some of my biggest, proudest moments and the lowest moments of my young adult life: my parents' divorce, my first time recording for a live CD, and the birth of my husband's and my child.

Others fought for The Counterfeit's approval, so being part of his inner circle made the humiliating manipulation seem not so bad. But the man I admired so much now drew my little family in so close that we began to become isolated from our families and friends. He did not want anyone to be a greater influence on us than himself, and in our naïve foolishness we clung to every word he said. It was an honor to be on the 'inside' and spend time with him, even our weekends, our evenings and our holidays. What he said influenced our every move, from who we hung out with to what car we bought. He even imposed his opinion on my hair cuts and the shoes I liked. One word from him and we skittered around to make it happen.

Over time, Keith and I began having some trouble in our marriage from the abuse and abandonment I had suffered from my dad. The Counterfeit sat me down one day and told me that the issues that I was having were because I didn't have a dad. Then he told me me that he wanted to be my dad and said that he would heal my wounds. At first, this seemed almost exciting. *He* wanted to be my dad? He would step in and give me what I had been denied – the love of a father? Still, a very faint, quiet voice in my spirit raised a red flag, whispering, "He can't heal your wounds. Only I can."

I argued with the voice: *But God, surely this must be from You. You know my every need. Thank you, Jesus, for sending me this blessing.* The faint voice was silenced with my own reasoning.

He began our daddy/daughter relationship by praying over me, saying that he received me as his daughter. All the while, he rubbed my back, his breathing getting a little bit heavier. Then came our first daddy/daughter 'date.' I was thrilled! I asked him to take me out for pie. On the way there he held my hand and and rubbed it too. Then his wife sent a text to his phone asking where he was. His reply said he was on the road, when we were actually at the lake. I questioned him and he responded breezily, "Well, we *are* about to get back on the road." I began to wonder if his wife knew he was with me. Still, I ignored the signs that something was not right.

As our daddy/daughter relationship progressed, The Counterfeit would hug me. I would run to him arms, his big strong arms that I had once dreamed of as a child, and he would hold me. I felt so safe, like a hurricane could come and as long as I was with my 'daddy' it would be okay. Then the hugs became longer, and I would also give him innocent kisses. But he would abruptly let go of me if someone saw us. I was hurt and frustrated.

"Why? They know you are my daddy now," I would protest.

"They won't understand," he told me.

I wanted to shout from the rooftops that I finally had a loving daddy, but he wanted to hide it. As quickly as the red flags popped up, I would bop them down with a little plastic hammer of reasoning. I was quick to defend him even in his dishonesty. He made a few feeble attempts to point me to the real Father. However, I think he enjoyed 'saving' this poor, pathetic girl from her daddy wounds too much to let God get the glory. "I think God brought you into my life more for me than for you," he said. I wanted more of him – more time, more snuggles, more hugs, more kisses.

Then one day he kissed me inappropriately and asked me how I liked it. I froze, mortified and disgusted. I couldn't believe what had just happened. I was in shock. Then I didn't know what to say. I didn't want to tell him how I really felt because I didn't want to crush him or make him upset. So I didn't answer at all, and our relationship changed. Now our relationship became even more inappropriate with other physical overtures. I kept telling him I did not want that, yet I didn't stop him either. I even began to enjoy it. A few times I tried to end it, but then he would shut off from me emotionally and that would hurt so badly that I wouldn't follow through. I needed the texts, the hugs and the affirmation, but he wanted my body. We plunged right into the dark, swirling pool of sin, the trap the enemy had waiting the whole time.

A dark cloud hung over me everywhere I went. My brightness dimmed. I was sick to my stomach and tired of everything. I became nervous and irritable, a fractured egg ready to spill. I remember thinking that if only someone would ask me what was going on, I would tell it all.

My Victory:

Too scared to come forward, too fearful of The Counterfeit, I suddenly realized I could ask God for help. I cried out to Him and asked him to stop everything since I was too scared to end it. My God, my Savior heard me. In one fell swoop, it all ended. It was ugly, but it was over. I felt relief at last. It wasn't easy. We lost everything, our ministry jobs, our ministry 'friends,' our 'Dad,' our safety net and six years of our life.

Then came the healing process as I broke the soul ties that had formed. I threw away the beautiful necklace he had bought me. I physically felt an amputation by renouncing the ties; it felt like part of my heart was being torn away.

The Counterfeit never admitted to anything. His cowardice, his lack of taking responsibility dumped buckets of guilt and condemnation on my already broken and feeble heart. Not only would I still have to heal from the old father wounds and now the freshly inflicted abuse, but also I would somehow have to come through that thick dark cloud of deception to see clearly enough to shed this new unrighteous burden I had taken on.

My counselor kept telling me I was abused. I could barely believe or hear her as I could only hear the loud voice of guilt and the accuser.

Then one day a new (and now very dear) friend of our family passed along some teachings on CD about healing from spiritual abuse. I had never even heard of spiritual abuse! Tears streaming down my face, I sat and listened and identified with every single symptom.

I attended Freedom Ministry. The once professional and paid minister who was trained to have all the right answers was now humbled, vulnerable and being ministered to. As words of life were being spoken into me, I clung to them.

My husband and I pursued and found more truth; we began to see through the fog, realizing the horror of what had truly happened. Walking from deception and abuse into freedom and light took more than seeing clearly, it took hearing Jesus' voice and believing it. Every time a negative voice crept in I referred back to His words. They were life and healing.

But my Savior redeemed what the locusts had eaten. Over the next two years, He lovingly brought restoration to every area of my life. He restored us to our families. He restored our marriage and continues to help it bloom. He gave us new and greater opportunities. He blessed us with financial increase and new friendships. The greatest victory of all is that He restored Himself to His rightful position in my heart as my Abba Father, my one true Daddy. He has won my heart and the victory!

DEVOTION: DAY ONE
COUNTERFEITS

Have you ever seen a piece of fake money or a fake replica of something valuable? I grew up in the jewelry business and was trained to spot fake diamonds. However, as technology advances the fakes become harder to spot. We need a tester to read the thermal index to tell us whether it's real or not.

Counterfeits in our life are much the same. Sometimes you may not recognize one right away. The cunning plot of the enemy is to present us with something that will lead us away from the Father and disguise it as good or as a blessing so that you never even bother testing it to see if it's real.

The way to test a counterfeit is by the Holy Spirit. He is our tester, but you have to be connected to Him first. Are you listening to the voice of the one holding the diamond or to the tester? Do not gaze too intently at the enticing sparkle or you may forget to test it because it appears so good and beautiful. When you allow the Holy Spirit to be your litmus test, you will become tuned in to hearing His voice constantly. As you tune in, your awareness of Him will grow. Jesus promises us in John 16:13: "*When the Spirit of truth comes, he will guide you into all the truth.*" So when something seems too good to be true, stop and listen to the still small voice before rushing to receive it.

DEVOTION: DAY TWO
SPIRITUAL ABUSE

Leadership. Submit. Authority. What do these words mean to you?

If you feel anger, guilt, fear or confusion as you read any of the above words, or if you experience pressure to perform, paranoia, lack of balance, or feel like there are unspoken rules in any situation in your life, chances are you have been (or are being) spiritually abused. Spiritual abuse occurs when a leader in a position of spiritual authority controls or dominates by weakening, decreasing or undermining those under him. Spiritual abuse is manipulation.

Jesus came to expose this system. In Mark 10:42-43, He says, "... you know that those who are considered rulers of the Gentiles lord it over them, and their great ones exercise authority over them. But it shall not be so among you."

An abusive leader lies and makes bold promises to gain trust to relax you into a 'safe' place to then get what he (or she) wants. Abusive leaders present themselves as the source of knowledge, direction and authority. They demand 'respect' while appearing to be cloaked in humility.

My goal in helping you recognize if you have been abused is to point you to the next steps to getting help. The biggest step first is realizing any relationship is out of line or off balance. Once the recognition comes, healing can begin so that you can learn to forgive. It is important also to get professional counsel outside of the organization. There are many books and teachings on this subject, but ultimately, your goal is to place Jesus in His rightful position in your life as Lord and King. Ask Him to show you what righteous covering and leadership looks like and to heal every wound and wrong.

DEVOTION: DAY THREE
HEALING

Confession brings forth healing, both spiritual and physical. There are scientific ties to un-repented wrongs or motives and physical illness. Our bodies and spirits were never meant to carry such a burden. Confession is for healing. *"Therefore, confess your sins to one another and pray for one another that you may be healed"* (James 5:16).

I always thought confessing sin was a way to humiliate, then condemn and shame me back into shape so I wouldn't sin again. What an icky definition that is! Let's replace that lie with truth. *Sin*, as defined in *Strong's Concordance*, means: "missing the mark" and "to not have a share in the prize." *Healed* in Greek is "to make whole, to bring about salvation." In other words, God wants to make you whole from when you've missed the mark so that you have a share in the prize. It is His kindness that leads us to repentance (Romans 2:4) because He wants us to have a share in His treasure. He does not aim to condemn, humiliate or shame. He wants to forgive us, make us whole and bring about our salvation, deliverance. He means *didomi*: "to minister, bestow a gift, give something to." Confession will empty you of your yuck, fill the void and also send you off with a gift —a share in the prize. You will not walk away empty-handed but filled and rewarded.

Devotion: Day Four
Stolen Treasure

The thief comes only to steal and kill and destroy. JOHN 10:10

The trap the enemy sets is not just to cause us to fall, but ultimately to derail us and keep us from fulfilling our calling and destiny. He wants to rob you and leave you thinking that you will never fully recover. He wants to make you feel inadequate, unworthy and not just unqualified but disqualified.

Do not let this put fear into you, because the end of John 10:10 redeems what the thief tries to do, when it says: "... I came that they may have life and have it abundantly."

Abundance! Not just normal, but superior, extraordinary, remarkable, more excellent, exceeding measure.

What has the thief stolen from you? Your joy? Purity? Finances? Hope? Family? Time? Calling? It's time to reclaim what is yours and take it back. Take some time today to write down what has been stolen from you. If we have the ability to curse with our words then we surely have the ability to bless. Start speaking and claiming and praising God for those things. Speak scripture over each item. As you see it come to fruition, check it off the list. It may take years or only days. I've even seen it happen in minutes!

"So shall my word be that goes out from my mouth; it shall not return to me empty, but it shall accomplish that which I purpose, and shall succeed in the thing for which I sent it" (Isaiah 55:11).

DEVOTION: DAY FIVE
KEEPING YOUR FREEDOM

It would be a sad thing to see a great work of God happen in your life only to go back into the same chains of imprisonment. *"Where the spirit of the Lord is, there is freedom"* (2 Corinthians 3:17). Freedom is not just the absence of sin but the presence of God.

Each time we go back to our bondage, it becomes worse: *"When the unclean spirit has gone out of a person, it passes through waterless places seeking rest, and finding none it says, 'I will return to my house from which I came.' And when it comes, it finds the house swept and put in order. Then it goes and brings seven other spirits more evil than itself, and they enter and dwell there. And the last state of that person is worse than the first"* (Luke 11:24-26).

Saturation in His presence daily is our protection, defense and antibody. It doesn't take hours of soaking to get filled with His presence. When you wake up, simply ask Him what He wants to say to you. Be still, so you can hear His voice. If you are not used to His gentle promptings, you may think it's your head making it up. No, it is Jesus! He has so much to tell you. It is exciting and addicting to wonder what He will say next. Talk to Him and feed on His Word. It's your provision for each day's need.

GOD CRAZY FREEDOM CHALLENGE

You may have heard the term 'soul ties.' This essentially means 'cleaving.' *"Therefore shall a man leave his father and his mother, and shall cleave unto his wife: and they shall be one flesh"* (Genesis 2:24). To cleave is to pursue closely or cling to, and anytime you join yourself to a person or thing you develop a soul tie.

There can be soul ties not only to other people but also to objects or substances, such as food, cars, drugs and electronics. Anything or anyone that consumes your mind, life and body will be something that you have cleaved to and given a part of yourself to. Like Genesis 2:24, "... *and they shall be one flesh*." When you form this bond and then move on, you lose a part of yourself. From relationship to relationship, you end up feeling ragged and empty.

The only Biblical examples where this is healthy are to tie yourself to spouse and to God: "... *love the Lord your God with all your heart and with all your soul,*" says Mark 12:30.

Ask the Holy Spirit to point out any unhealthy soul ties you have. Those ties need to be broken so that you can have wholeness and have your heart back. Renounce each tie and break down the altars that were built to these idols by throwing away or burning items of significance. Now, offer that portion of your heart that you recovered to God.

GOD CRAZY FREEDOM PRAYER

Daddy God,

Thank You for Your kindness, Thank You for Your love. Thank You for rescuing me as I cry for help in time of need. I repent for allowing counterfeits into my life that could never take the place of You, the Almighty, the Eternal One. Jesus, I forgive those who have harmed me and abused me and used me. Show me what Your true leadership and authority look like. I place You as Lord and King in every area of my life. Shine Your light into every dark place and corner, expose where I have missed the mark so that I can be restored and receive the prize.

Heal me, make me whole and minister to me. Please fill me to overflowing. Any gift You see fit to give me, I receive. Lord, I claim and speak Your word into existence in my life, that You came for me to have life in abundance.

Fight for me, Lord, and help me claim back what is mine. Restore every area that has been robbed. And now, fill my life new and fresh every morning with Your precious mercy and Your sweet presence. What do You have to say to me for this day? Speak, and I will listen. Say, and I will do. Let Your kingdom be made real in my life. I love you. In Jesus' mighty name, Amen. Let it be so!

BROKEN TO BEAUTIFUL

by Alison Stevens

"*Is* there someone else?"

I was sitting on the bed in the guest room, and he was sitting on a chair across the room. Our 'conversation' had gone the usual route – me talking, ranting, being angry, and him just sitting there, stoically silent. It's a well-known fact that men naturally have fewer words than women. My husband was a man of even fewer words than most men. But my husband was not the kind of man to stray. Anyone would tell you that. My question was intended as a sarcastic jab, thrown out as a joke to provoke him, an attempt to get a rise out of him, to get him to say *something*.

The silence that followed was deafening, oppressive, telling …

Our conversation had started in a Starbucks. I told him we needed to talk because life could not go on as it had been. We weren't headed anywhere relationally, spiritually, financially, as a family. We needed to make some changes. We needed a plan.

Sitting in silence for quite some time, nursing our lattes as people watched, I remember thinking, *Oh my gosh, we're one of those couples.* The kind we would see when we were newly married and thought were so sad, sitting silently for an entire meal. We vowed we would never let that happen to us. And yet, there we sat. Completely silent. Awkward. Avoiding. He broke our silent standoff at Starbucks with the words, "I'm not happy," and I stood up and walked out. I could feel the anger welling up inside me. The hurt I'd been burying for months. No, this conversation was not happening in a public place.

The year was 2005, and it was one day before our sixteenth anniversary.

Before I go on, I need to tell you my story is not about an affair and what happened to me, although that event has been a catalyst for much growth in my journey. If you are expecting a list of crimes committed against me and how I survived, you needn't read any further, because if all this journey of life is about is what happens to me, what a sad story that would be.

Life is a journey of overcoming. Think about it – what don't we need to overcome? Pride, jealousy, insecurity, trust issues … conditions of the soul, the things that happen *in us*. In *all of us*. The events in our lives – whether they happen by our choices or someone else's choices—are the catalysts that bring those soul issues to the surface.

In my journey, I have come to realize that there is a difference between a defining moment and being defined by a moment. Read that again. A defining moment in your journey rather than being defined by a moment. I've learned this truth: Nothing – no event, no person, no moment – should define me more than the Jesus people see in me.

Let that one sink in. *The defining factor in my life, first and foremost, should be Jesus.*

A connection exists between defining moments and being defined by the work of Jesus Christ in me. That connection involves a choice. Ultimately, I will be faced with this choice, and the path I choose will determine what defines me – the event, or the work of Jesus in me.

The choice? To embrace the process of being broken or resist it.

There are situations, choices, sins, and circumstances beyond our control that can leave us ripped open to the core of our being, feeling as if our soul has been torn in two and the tear has no end. Honestly, sometimes I think I heard an audible rip after I asked that question and the silence ushered in reality. I experienced physical pain even though there was no outward injury. I remember the feeling of falling and wondering if I would ever find the bottom. I remember thinking at one point, *I had no idea the soul went so deep.* The vulnerability I felt was unlike any I have ever known. At times, I felt as if I was naked inside and out in front of the whole world, all my deepest darkest secrets laid out and exposed, every flaw in my physical and spiritual being on display for everyone to examine, scrutinize, evaluate and judge.

I was being broken.

I wouldn't have used that word at the time. Scared, hurt, betrayed, angry, even abandoned – those are the words that I would have used. And that's where Jesus met me. He didn't rebuke. He didn't lecture. He didn't placate or patronize. He didn't even tell me to forgive – at least, not at first. In the middle of my hurt and fear, shattered and broken, He simply wrapped His loving arms around me and spoke truth through His word.

God's word is living and active. I believe this with all my heart. I'm continually amazed how passages of scripture I have read countless times, even committed to memory, can suddenly have new, deeper meaning and purpose in my life. Two such verses – ones I had learned as a teenager – came alive for me during this time and gave me the strength and hope I could not find on my own. One is a promise, and the other holds great truth.

Romans 8:28 promises us:

> *And we know that in all things God works for the good of those who love Him, who have been called according to his purpose.*

Look at those first few words. *In all things ...*

Not just some things. Not just the things that the world or society deem acceptable or worthy of redemption. Not limited to your own definitions of forgivable or overcome-able. *All things.*

During the days and weeks that followed that conversation with my husband, I found myself overcome with shame. I felt less than worthy, less than lovable ... just *less than.* Sunday after Sunday I would slink into church with my sunglasses on and head for the back row. Yes, I wore my sunglasses in the building. The one who was usually on stage, up front, always visible, always available, was hiding behind sunglasses in the back row.

Why? To avoid making eye contact. Because eye contact might lead to conversation. And conversation might lead to truth. And this truth, this thing by my definition was ugly, humiliating, shameful, *less than.* Less than redeemable. Less than lovable. Less than forgivable.

But not by God's definition. He tells us right here in Scripture *in all things … God works for the good …*

The Creator of the Universe. The great I Am. Alpha and Omega, the Almighty, the Author of Life. He works. God works. Understand this: in every situation that seems in our limited vision to be ugly, humiliating, shameful … less than … He is working for us.

He is working for *you.*

The God who created the world and everything in it, who has no beginning and no end, who holds all the power of the universe in His hands, is working on *your* behalf *for good.* He will make something good, something wonderful, something beautiful *in you.* His love, mercy and grace will come in and transform you into something beautiful *no matter what your circumstances.* Our Lord desires to heal and change you. He desires to restore your joy.

Are you hearing the message?

The Creator of the Universe loves you, calls you, and is placing an opportunity before you. He desires for you to know His God Crazy love, mercy, healing and redemptive power in an amazing and life-changing way. He desires for you to be free.

Hear this as well: There is one whose sole purpose is to keep you in bondage, to keep you from being the God Crazy woman you were created to be. One who has constructed a web of lies to ensnare you along your journey. I became entangled in those lies. The lie that I was all alone, that no one else had ever experienced what I had, that I was *less than* – flawed, ugly, unredeemable, unusable. All lies the Father of Lies planted to keep me from becoming what God intended me to be:

He used them to keep me isolated.

He used them to keep me in the dark, hiding from 'exposure.'

He deceived me into thinking that 'exposure' equaled shame and humiliation instead of freedom.

But Romans 8:38-39 tells us the truth:

> *For I am convinced that neither death nor life, neither angels*
> *nor demons, neither the present nor the future, nor any powers,*
> *neither height nor depth, nor anything else in all creation, will be*

able to separate us from the love of God that is in Christ Jesus our Lord.

Hear this: Not one thing is beyond his reach, no situation is beyond his understanding, grace or mercy. No one thing or person holds so much power, so much influence, or has so much 'dirtiness' as to keep a person from God.

NOTHING can separate you from the love of God. Nothing you've done. Nothing that's been done to you. *Nothing* can remove His love from you, take eternity with Him away from you, or make you anything less than a precious child of the Almighty God of Creation, the God of Wonders, the great I Am. You are an heir to the throne with Jesus and always will be, and that's a fact.

These verses became my lifeline, my foundation, my security. Over and over, when I was in the deepest, darkest places I had ever known, He would speak them to my heart, reaffirming the promise that He was in control, working on my behalf. I was His child, and no matter what happened that would not change. If I trusted Him, He would make something beautiful out of the broken mess of me lying at His feet.

My Victory
Beautifully Broken

In the spring of 2006, I was touring the West Coast with some independent musician friends. All knew my story and loved me through it. At one of our stops, I was scheduled to lead worship, and my friend Kim was to speak at a women's Bible study. Kim fell ill and was not able to speak; so Pam, who we looked to as our matriarch and spiritual leader, turned to me and said, "You're on, kiddo."

Terror flooded me.

Put me on stage with a band behind me, and I'm good to go. Hand me a microphone and ask me to give a speech, and we're all sunk. Pam knew that. What was she thinking? I politely argued, "You should speak. You do it all the time. You know you'll do a better job." Really, I was thinking, *You don't understand; I've been disqualified. I'm no longer usable.* But Pam assured me she felt the Lord wanted me to speak, and she pretty much refused to step in.

What Pam didn't know was that for the past few years, I had been privately writing about brokenness. As I pulled out those notes (yes, for some reason I had packed them for the trip), I realized this was God making good on His promise – that He works all things for good.

Understanding, empathy and compassion for the broken flooded my heart – and I realized this was the beginning of God redeeming of a moment I had until then believed was not redeemable. He still had a plan for me. I could still be used for His purposes.

My journey of healing *is* my victory. Brokenness is not a destination. It is not the end of the road. It is the beginning of a beautiful journey of growth, of being shaped more and more into His image, of experiencing every day redemptive, healing God Crazy love. The victory is found in embracing the journey of being beautifully broken.

DEVOTION: DAY ONE
BE STILL AND KNOW

He says, "Be still and know that I am God..." PSALM 46:10

Sometimes it's hard enough to hear God speak through the noise of normal life. Busyness, the urgency of the immediate, the daily list of chores and errands, the demands of work – all of this is noise that can drown out the still, small voice calling us to spend time with Him. Now add in the chaos of hurt and shame; friends and family giving advice; counseling sessions; books we read because we need advice and encouragement; the internet with its infinite amount of information, both positive and negative, on the subject, which we sometimes become obsessed with; our own doubt, anger and hurt making statements and asking questions over the rest of the voices.

How can we hear anything above all this?

Perhaps we can't until we consciously make the effort. Not until we realize we are running after the wrong things, seeking out truth and promise from sources that are not capable of being a true foundation. Just for a moment stop talking, stop seeking out the advice of others, stop the busyness we unconsciously create so we don't have to think.

Just stop and be.

Be still.

This week, make time. Take a walk and notice the beauty around you. Put on worship music in the car between errands. Allow a moment in your day for your mind to be still and focus on Him. Not on your hurt, not on what happened, not on what others say you should or should not do.

Be still, and know that He is God.

Devotion: Day Two
Claim His Promises

Let us hold unswervingly to the hope we profess, for He who promised is faithful. Hebrews 10:23

I used to love roller coasters. In my younger days, I remember youth group trips to the local theme park, where my friends and I would try to ride every one as many times as possible in a twelve-hour period. Towards the end of the day, we would beg the ride operator to let us go again if there was no one else in line. Just the thought of that makes me feel nauseated now.

My journey of being beautifully broken has at times felt like that. Up and down, whipping me around corners, tremendous stomach-dropping falls and loops, making me nauseated. And sometimes, just when I thought the ride was coming to an end, it started all over again.

My faith was misplaced.

Instead of trusting in the promises of an unchanging God, I was clinging to the well-meaning words of friends and information found on the internet, and I was using my feelings as a guide. Now, I won't mislead you into thinking the roller coaster days are gone. But sisters, if you are putting your faith in anything or anyone above God and His promises, you are setting yourself up for one miserable ride instead of a beautiful God Crazy Freedom adventure.

Read through the promises in the verses below. If you keep a journal, write them down. Claim them for your own. Only the faithful promises of an unchanging God can provide the unshakable foundation, enduring hope, and lasting joy on which the God Crazy Freedom life is built!

Deuteronomy 33:37, Psalm 27:1, Isaiah 41:10, 1 Corinthians 15:57-58, 2 Corinthians 2:17

DEVOTION: DAY THREE
THE TRUTH ABOUT LIES

Be alert and of sober mind. Your enemy the devil prowls around like a roaring lion looking for someone to devour. 1 PETER 5:9

Let's just put it out there – the enemy is clever. The Father of Lies knows your weaknesses and the things that keep you stuck. He will do everything within his power to keep you in shame, fear, doubt, anger and hurt to prevent you from experiencing God Crazy Freedom. Because he knows that once you experience that freedom, you will be a shining, radiant beacon of light for the Kingdom, and his darkness cannot live in that light.

You see, he knows God Crazy love comes from a source – the God of Creation – who is omniscient, omnipresent and omnipotent. All-knowing, always present and all-powerful. He holds all the truth, He is everywhere, and He has ALL power over EVERYTHING. Satan doesn't want you to discover that.

I almost didn't go on that tour in 2006. I truly thought ministry for me was no longer an option, that my light had been extinguished. But time after time throughout those two weeks, God showed His light through me despite my feelings of being disqualified, of being damaged goods, of being less than, and the lies began to fade. My journey of victory started during those two weeks.

What lies are keeping you in darkness? That God doesn't love you, doesn't care? That you have been disqualified and He can no longer use you for His purposes? That you are less than? Write them down and get them into the His light, and ask Him to show you the truth.

DEVOTION: DAY FOUR
HIS WORK IN YOU

Now may the God of peace...work in us what is pleasing to Him... HEBREWS 13:20-21

I have a friend who is an amazing artist. During my time as worship coordinator for Journey Church in 2007, we had the opportunity to create some amazing mosaic projects for the church. For one particular project, we spent countless hours in her garage studio, meticulously preparing all the pieces for a large six-foot-by-six-foot tile mosaic. After breaking or cutting larger tiles into smaller pieces, we smoothed the edges of the pieces we would use with a grinder.

One morning, while surveying the different elements we were assembling for this project, it struck me that this was a picture of what God does in our lives. The flaws and weak spots in me – my soul issues – had been brought to the surface by a moment that left me completely broken. And over time, the Master Creator was sorting through the pieces, discarding some, and smoothing the edges on those He wanted to use.

Unless surrendered to the work of our Creator, soul issues will not only hinder our healing, but also our growth and understanding of freedom. His work cuts off the unnecessary and grinds away the rough edges, and we are prepared for something greater in His hands.

Whatever it is – pride, jealousy, insecurity, trust issues, fear or something else – surrender your soul issue to the work of the Creator. Allow Him to work on whatever piece He chooses, preparing you for the beautiful journey ahead.

DEVOTION: DAY FIVE
PEACE IN THE STORM

Rejoice in the Lord always…and the peace of God which transcends all understanding will guard your hearts and your minds in Christ Jesus… PHILIPPIANS 4:4-8

Even in the best of times we are not equipped to guard our hearts on our own. During a time of brokenness, the only thing that can begin to heal the tear in our soul and guard our heart from further bruises is God's transcendent peace. No matter what the situation, what choices lay before you, even when facing unknowns, when the peace of God washes over your soul like a healing balm you know you are safe and loved.

Having peace doesn't mean the road won't have difficulty; it doesn't mean there will be no tears; it doesn't mean you won't have questions and uncertainties. When you have the peace of God, it transcends those things. It transcends fear of the unknown, tears, and the hard decisions.

The peace of God is security. Security that even though there are challenges ahead, He is in control and you are in His hands. The peace of God is confidence that He is faithful to keep His promises. The peace of God is freedom from lies. The peace of God is a calming presence in the middle of the storm. The peace of God gives strength, courage and hope. The peace of God lets us know we are headed in the right direction.

Read through Philippians 4:4-8 again. Rejoice; be gentle, do not worry. Instead, in a spirit of prayer and thanksgiving, lay it all at the feet of Jesus. Then let go, and let His peace guide you through the storm.

GOD CRAZY FREEDOM CHALLENGE

Hopefully by now you are practicing being still, beginning to stand on the firm foundation of His promises, learning to walk in His truth instead of the enemy's lies, surrendering to His work in you, and experiencing His peace. That's a lot for one week! But there is one more area that needs attention, and I can tell you it may be the most difficult, yet most necessary step in your journey of victory over this brokenness.

Forgiveness.

To be able to truly forgive, you need to understand what it is, and what it is not.

Forgiveness is not: Forgetting, laying out a welcome mat and having no boundaries, allowing things to go back to how they were; nor is it the end of the work in a relationship. Forgiveness is not only for the other person. Consider this:

> "To forgive is to set a prisoner free and discover that prisoner was you." – UNKNOWN

Forgiveness is *for you*. Not to forgive is to allow bitterness a foothold in your heart. If it is not removed, it will eventually become the filter everything in your life runs through. Choosing to forgive is choosing to make this a defining moment *in* your journey and not to be defined *by* it.

My wish for you is to experience complete victory in your journey. Be still and know He is God. Stand on His promises. Walk in His truth. Surrender to His work in you. Let His peace guide you. *Forgive*. Make this a defining moment in your journey.

GOD CRAZY FREEDOM PRAYER

Heavenly Father,

Thank you for the cross and Your redemptive love. We are so undeserving, and yet You continually lay in front of us the opportunities to be healed from our sin and our wounds and be set free. You don't desire for anyone to be in bondage.

I lift up my sister to You now. Wrap Your loving arms around her as You did me. Envelop her with Your love. Flood her with Your peace that passes understanding. Father, You know that marriage is a soul connection, and hers has been badly damaged. Speak truth and healing to her through the power of Your Holy Spirit and Your word.

Give her the strength and wisdom not only to handle the issues that come up in the process of reconciliation, but also the soul issues that being broken reveals. Let her love as she has been loved and forgive as she has been forgiven.

Bring her into victory! I pray that everyday she becomes defined more and more by You, and nothing else. I pray that every day she experiences God Crazy Freedom! Lord, shine your light on the enemy's lies so she becomes a radiant beacon of Your glory for all the world to see and be drawn to You.

In the precious name of Your Son, Jesus, whom You so lovingly sent as a sacrifice for us, so that we would know the amazing freedom of Your love, and to whom we give all the praise and all the glory, Amen.

ADULTERY TO REPENTANCE

by Jeanne Kolenda

$\mathcal{M}$y parents said I cut my teeth on hymn books. That sounds reasonable, since my parents were traveling evangelists when I was born, and I was probably in church most nights of my life until my father settled down in the mountains of Eastern Tennessee to pastor a small church. We were part of a Pentecostal denomination that rewarded hellfire and brimstone preachers with lots of opportunity to move around, and move we did! I went to eighteen different schools in twelve years. It became a way of life, and I don't remember thinking it was odd.

Moving may not have seemed odd, but what I did find odd and intolerable were the rules and regulations of our church. "No, I'm sorry, but you can't do/go/wear/participate in (you fill in the blanks), because it's against the church's 'teachings.'" Discussing my feelings with my parents was futile, so I simply stopped trying and started living a double standard. There was the daughter they saw, and the girl I was really becoming. I lied to get to go to events like a school party or dance – things kids shouldn't have to lie about. Soon, lying and deception became a way of life, and it would be decades before God was able to bring all of me back together again, able to live in truth and authenticity.

Even with all the legalism and ridiculous rules, I knew Jesus was real and I loved who I thought He was. I just couldn't figure out a way to serve Him in the same way I saw the "Christian" life being lived out in those around me. So, I simply abandoned any effort at all to be a "Christian."

I went to a Christian university but was expelled for…you guessed it… not following the rules. In my rebellion, I became pregnant and got married. Two years after my son was born, I gave birth to a beautiful daughter. My husband wasn't a very good provider, and life was very hard. I learned to survive. I knew I didn't want my children to grow up without any chance of knowing who God really was (although I still wasn't sure myself), so we started attending church when the children were very young. They were properly dedicated, and life rocked on.

But over time, I grew bitter toward my husband, and I was still angry with the church. I didn't fit in, but I played a good game. By now, I had at least found my way out of the legalistic denomination I grew up in and enjoyed more freedom in terms of making personal decisions. Because I felt my parents were rigid and closed off in their faith, I became a parent who was determined to communicate openly about faith with my children, even when I didn't know all the answers. When they were teenagers, we continued to explore the "hard questions" of the Bible and knowing God. If I got one thing right, it was those conversations. All this honesty and openness paid off in spades, and today, my children are two of my best friends and they are following hard after God. They never rebelled, never caused me a minute's worth of grief, and I am the most grateful woman on the planet.

But I made many mistakes that would soon come to have devastating consequences on my marriage and family. As our financial pressures got worse, I got angrier. I had married so young and for all the wrong reasons. Now as an adult, I craved security, and I thought that was supposed to come from my husband. What little romance I ever experienced had long since died, and I began to crave that too. Everyone else's marriage and husband looked way more interesting and exciting than mine. I began that secret double life again – only this time the stakes were much higher.

I wasn't honest or real with anyone. I lived in my head and my emotions, all the while playing the game. A few wise and discerning people were onto me, but I ignored their warnings. I was a real "church lady," playing the keyboard and singing on the worship team, homeschooling my children, taking mission trips. You name it; I was busy with it. Of course, I was just staying busy to cover up the truth.

One day, it all changed. I met a handsome, successful, and exciting man visiting from the West coast. After a short time, we became fully involved; and I simply walked out of my marriage of twenty years. I ran away from home, literally. The irony of it all is that my children were on mission trips when I left. My son was in Mexico City, and my daughter was aboard one of the Mercy Ships in the Dominican Republic. I got on a plane and off to Seattle I went. Life as I knew it had ended.

I left wreckage in my path – a grieving husband who wasn't sure what had happened; (he didn't see the signs?) confused, hurt and angry children; church friends who were horrified; and my large extended family worried sick because I had run off with a "stranger." How was I ever going to explain this to Jesus? But He already knew more than I did.

It only took ninety days to finalize my divorce, and I married this stranger the minute it was legally possible. My father died in the middle of all this chaos. He never got to meet Leon, but they did speak on the phone before we married. I had some wonderful times with my dad before he died, although I had no idea his time was so short. Although he was grieved at all he knew I would have to walk through, Daddy surprised me and responded to my actions with compassion, love, and tender affection.

I moved three thousand miles away to Seattle, and a few months later, my daughter joined us there. She was only seventeen and missed her mom. My son left for college at the same time I moved. I buried the horror and shock I had caused other people, and I thought I was having a great time. Leon really was the romance I had been looking for. It wasn't a flash in the pan, as some had supposed. We have been married for more than twenty years now. But there is one reason, and one reason only, that we have survived all the dismal statistics for second marriages.

That reason is repentance.

It wasn't long after I moved to Seattle to be with Leon that Jesus got out of the box I had put Him in. Even in my sin, I shared Jesus with Leon and he came to faith in Jesus, albeit, a very immature faith at the time.

We had been married for about two years, and the honeymoon glow had faded just enough for us to start feeling the full weight of what we had done. We'd wake up on Saturday mornings with tears in our eyes, missing our "old lives," or at least the more pleasant parts, like having pancakes with the kids. (He had two children under the age of thirteen.) I began to earnestly cry out to God for peace. After all, I had thrown away everything familiar to me, left my family and friends, and now I wasn't feeling good about it. I panicked. I begged God for an answer. God was kind enough not to show me all my sin at one time. It was as though he lifted the curtain a little at a time, so I wouldn't be completely overwhelmed with the depravity of my soul and the consequences of my actions.

Over time, God showed me that I needed to humble myself and seek forgiveness from those I had wronged. I personally went to everyone I knew I had wounded – my extended family, my children, my friends, my ex-husband, and my former pastor (He was incredibly kind, forgiving, and even laid his hand on me, and prayed a blessing on me, my family, and my new marriage) – to apologize for all the hurt I had caused.

I thought I was finished, but God revealed one more relationship that needed repentance. It was my relationship with Leon, my new husband. We both came to realize that we had not only sinned against God and our families, but also we had sinned against each other. We knelt together before God, held hands, and asked forgiveness each one from the other. We both extended that forgiveness and asked God to keep us, to allow us to live together and be a blessing to others. That was one of the most powerful things we have ever done for each other. We released each other of the guilt and shame of adultery.

Today, we have a good marriage, and sometimes people have tended to use us as an example of how second marriages can be so *right*. We are quick to set the record straight – there was nothing right about our relationship. It was all flesh, and were it not for repentance, we wouldn't have made it this far. The only thing *right* is what the blood of Jesus offers in the way of cleansing and forgiveness. Now I am free!

My Victory

The old song "Amazing Grace" says it all, "I once was blind, but now I see."

I was guided by a self-focus that allowed me to think, feel and act based almost wholly on what I thought I needed and deserved. I put "me" on the throne in my heart, even though I was outwardly a believer, doing all the "right" things.

Mine was a secret thought-life that nearly destroyed me in the end, and caused great damage to my family, particularly my children. They had a relationship with God that sustained them and gave them grace to be His instruments in my healing and restoration from my craziness.

Through disappointment, despair, and rage, I entered into an adulterous affair that led to divorce after twenty years of marriage and remarriage to "the other man." I destroyed everything familiar in my life.

God had mercy on me and led me through a journey of repentance and eventual freedom from my bad thinking. He was also gracious enough to let my new husband get the vision. We now walk in forgiveness, unity, and God's undeserved favor. There are consequences we will always live with, but His grace allows us to live in such a way that we would never, ever consider wounding ourselves or others as we once did. We find freedom in being able to tell our story, and we are humbled by God's grace and mercy.

Devotion: Day One
Removing Self-Justification as a Barrier to Spiritual Freedom

Our natural (or flesh-controlled) mind will lead us to avoid full responsibility for our sin by concluding that we were only partially wrong, because someone else was *more* wrong. This kind of thinking will block our path to freedom quicker than almost anything. We find ourselves explaining our mistakes by pointing how another person's actions led us to do what we did. We're quick to tell our stories in that light so that our motives will appear good.

How many times have you heard someone say, "But he has a good heart." This is almost always on the heels of explaining some situation where this person was clearly behaving badly, in a way that needed this justification. I heard it just yesterday in a conversation about a man who is once again having a problem keeping a job because of his inability to work under authority.

But what does God say about our hearts?

> *The human heart is the most deceitful of all things, and*
> *desperately wicked. Who really knows how bad it is?"*
> – JEREMIAH 17:9 NEW LIVING TRANSLATION

1. Ask yourself how you have justified yourself and your sin by not taking full responsibility.
2. Are you willing to get your focus off of another person's offense to you, and deal only with your own sin? God expects it. You deserve the freedom it will bring.

Meditation Scripture: PSALM 139:23-24 NEW LIVING TRANSLATION

> *Search me, O God, and know my heart; test me and know my*
> *thoughts. Point out anything in me that offends You, and lead me*
> *along the path of everlasting life.*

DEVOTION: DAY TWO
YOUR OPINION OF SIN

As a Believer, your opinion of sin is important. It's easy to rationalize our view of sin (especially our own) when we don't fully accept what God says about it. Secretly, we believe our sin may make God unhappy, but somehow it's "worth it." We may agree intellectually with the Scripture about God's view of sin, but we don't actively live as though we believe it. We care more about how we are affected, rather than how God might be affected by our sin.

Are your feelings about sin based on its consequences to yourself? Or do you fully comprehend the insult our selfish ways are to a holy God?

Stop now and find your favorite translation of the Bible and read Romans Chapters one and two. This should give you a clear picture of how God views sin.

Now, think about these questions:

1. How do you view your own sin?

2. Does your view seem to line up with what God says about it?

3. Do you think God is just talking about others, and not you?

4. Are you willing to begin to deal ruthlessly with your own sin?

If the answer to No. 4 is YES, I have some great news for you and some great guidelines in tomorrow's devotional. But, please, don't rush through this one. It's worth the extra time you'll spend to fully comprehend the importance of your opinion of sin.

DEVOTION: DAY THREE
AN HONEST APPRAISAL

To become spiritually free, we must make an honest appraisal as to the truth about our inner life, our heart's motives, our life's purposes, our habits, our justifications and our life patterns. This must be done without looking through our old lens of self-protection or our firm determination to guard our reputation at the expense of true freedom of the heart.

Procrastination is our greatest enemy. It's just human nature to put off doing something until we "feel" like doing it. But, is obedience to God based on our emotions? In a word, No!

An honest appraisal can be frightening. After all, facing the truth about our sin is not easy, and we become blind to the lies we've told ourselves for too many years. We justify, we blame and we *procrastinate*.

Here are some simple steps to get you started:

1. Find some regular time for specific prayer. Ask God to reveal your self-life – areas of your life where you regularly go your "own way." Pray that God will illuminate blind spots in your spiritual thinking by the power of His Holy Spirit.

2. Get a notebook and pen. Use this prayer time to truly wait for God to

speak and record any thoughts or aha moments.

3. Don't allow yourself to rationalize, make excuses, or to blame.

I know it's a long chapter, but begin to read Psalm 119. In particular, pay attention to verse 59, which mentions *considering and turning* – and we'll talk about that tomorrow.

DEVOTION: DAY FOUR
MY WAY VS. GOD'S WAY

Yesterday, we talked about an honest appraisal of our heart condition. Your assignment was to begin reading Psalm 119.

Today, let's look in particular at verse 59.

> *I pondered the direction of my life and I turned to follow Your statutes.* – NEW LIVING TRANSLATION

Repentance, which leads to spiritual freedom, requires that we change our mind and our will. This will, in turn, change our feelings and our behavior. In the end, you will experience a true change in your character, which is God's plan all along.

You'll know when you've really experienced repentance which leads to a character change when you feel revulsion towards the sin you once secretly loved and justified. My secret life for years included thoughts of being with men other than my husband. This fantasy turned into reality, and I suffered severe consequences for it. I now am very discerning about this sin, and when I see it unfolding in the life of precious people who are simply deceived, I feel great sorrow. I hate adultery and what it can do to individuals and families.

1. What sin in your life do you need to repent of, and let God bring you to a place of freedom? It doesn't necessarily have to be such a dramatic and devastating sin as adultery, but sin is sin. It could be a sin of omission – simply not obeying God.

2. Have you prayerfully completed your honest appraisal?

3. If it involves others, have you made restitution and experienced reconciliation?

It's never too soon or too late to experience the freedom of repentance!

DEVOTION: DAY FIVE
RESTING, OBEYING AND WALKING IN FREEDOM

Let us do our best to enter that place of rest. For anyone who disobeys God, as the children of Israel did, will fall.
HEBREWS 4:11

When you've done the hard work of honest appraisal and have experienced repentance (with the result of fully hating the sin), it's time for your reward. That reward is rest and walking in complete freedom.

Matthew 11:28 offers this promise:

Come to me, all of you who are weary and carry heavy burdens, and I will give you rest. – NEW LIVING TRANSLATION

Hebrews 4:9:

So there is a special rest still waiting for the people of God.
– NEW LIVING TRANSLATION

When you experience this rest in your spirit, Galatians 5:13 will become your new way of living. It says,

For you, dear friends, have been called to live in freedom – not freedom to satisfy your sinful nature, but freedom to serve one another in love. – NEW LIVING TRANSLATION

John 15:4-11 gives us a clear picture of what resting in Jesus and obeying Him will do for us. It's the only way to freedom. Read John Chapter 15.

1. What does this mean to you?

2. How will your life be different after your honest appraisal, repentance, and learning to rest and obey?

3. How will you serve others? Who are we called to serve? Just those at church, or those easy to love?

I rejoice in your freedom! Reach out and take it – do the hard work, and watch God change you!

God Crazy Freedom Challenge

Now that you've had time to spend five days considering how you might gain spiritual and emotional freedom, I challenge you to spend the next week in serious prayer and contemplation as to how this kind of freedom can become yours in a real way.

You know that notebook I asked you to get on Day Three? Well, get it back out and review the notes you made. What was God saying to you?

1. Study every Scripture I have presented to you here. Read them more than once.

2. Now, turn the page and make some new notes.

   a. What does freedom look like in your life?

   b. What is holding you back from total freedom?

   c. What have you justified because of your lens of hurt and fear?

   d. How do you need to adjust your opinion of sin to line up with what God says?

   e. Are you willing to make an honest appraisal?

   f. Are you willing to "consider and turn" and have your mind, your will and your emotions cleansed and changed?

Save a few pages on that notebook to record the results. Keep that notebook handy, because this is not usually an overnight process. With a renewed commitment to go through these steps, you'll find that over time, you'll have new insights. It may take six months, a year, or even two years, but press on, sweet sisters. It's worth it!

You're welcome to email me at jeannekolenda@gmail.com and tell me your victory story.

GOD CRAZY FREEDOM PRAYER

Father God, I praise You and thank You for changing my heart, and allowing me to walk in freedom - of my past, my iniquities, and from my old ways of thinking and acting. I am most grateful You have forgiven me for all the hurt and damage I caused to other people in the name of what I thought I deserved and needed without considering how I wounded You, the One who died to set me free.

Thank you, God, for giving me the courage to tell my story and not be overcome with shame. But instead, I experience the freedom to be real, to tell the truth in order to bring others to a place of full surrender of a vicious self-life in order to gain the freedom You intended for us all.

You, O God, had plans for us even while we were in our mothers' wombs – plans to prosper us and give us a hope, as the prophet Jeremiah spoke about so long ago. This humbles me and takes away all fear of the future or fear of what others make think or say.

I'm also grateful beyond words for the forgiveness of those I wounded. I'm grateful for my dear husband who entered into this journey of repentance and freedom with me.

May all my sisters see themselves through Your eyes, knowing it's Your kindness that leads to repentance, and repentance leads to freedom.

Help us all to walk continually in the freedom for which you paid so dearly with the blood of your Son, Jesus. Amen.

CONFUSION TO PEACE
by Lisa Ostrowski

"Last-Minute Lisa." That is what my husband calls me.

But it doesn't feel like procrastination to me. It doesn't feel bad, no stress. It feels … expectant! Like I'm waiting for a present, the gift that was worth the waiting, the perfect fit, the very thing I was looking for. How liberating. No weight on my shoulders, no reliance on the brilliance of my personal skill, just waiting on supernatural, perfect Help from on High. I am following the Fire by night and the Cloud by day, so that I can travel light.

> By day the LORD went ahead of them in a pillar of cloud to guide
> them on their way and by night in a pillar of fire to give them
> light, so that they could travel by day or night. (EXODUS 13:21)

I am the oldest of five children born to a Jewish father who became Catholic to marry my mother. He had a dramatic experience as he sought the truth of the Cross, and Jesus became very real to him. My mother was raised very devout and followed the rules of her religion. When another devout family in the church ran into hardships with their children, my dad turned to a dear nun and asked for answers. Her answer came in an invitation to the Charismatic Conference in Notre Dame.

I was invited aboard the bus that would get us from Houston, Texas, to Notre Dame. As the only child on the bus, my twelve-year-old self was entertained and fell in love with a fiery red-haired woman whose name was, I am not kidding, Spark Fire. She told me stories, and we talked the entire way. When we got to Notre Dame, she went on to stay at the dorm and my parents and grandfather went off to our hotel. It never dawned on me that I would not find Sparky again in the crowd of thirty-five thousand people who were there for the conference, so when I saw a red-haired woman at the event, I ran up and gave her the huge hug she had earned on the bus trip.

The startled woman looked down at me with a puzzled expression, and I quickly recognized my mistake. The next day at the grab-your-box-lunch-and-go area, again, I met the woman I had hugged by mistake. She gave my mother a picture of her daughter who had recently been killed, the reason for her journey to Notre Dame. She had prayed, asking the Lord for confirmation that she was with Him in Heaven. The woman's daughter and I looked so much alike that we could have been sisters. God used my hug as an answer to her prayers, a confirmation that her daughter was with Him in heaven. That was the beginning of an amazing ministry with Jesus, as I knew I had fallen into the perfect will of the Lord. For me, it was all Him. How easy for me then!

I was so filled with the Holy Spirit at the conference that I practically cried the entire way home. I had tasted and seen the truth, and I would never be the same. God is with us. His Holy Spirit has been sent to comfort, guide, and be the author and finisher of our Faith. But the Lord never leaves us where He finds us, so the lesson of my youth became learning to do by choice what the little girl in me did by instinct: Go when He says go, and stay when He does not.

I definitely did not understand this in my younger years. My poor parents. I often acted first, without waiting to see what God or my parents had to say about it. I heard them say more than once, "We were just about to take you shopping," or, "We were going to let you go." Instead, I was grounded indefinitely for taking their credit card and buying what I thought I had to have or sneaking out and going where I thought I needed to go, jumping ahead of the will of my Father and never seeking the permission of my parents.

When we follow the foolish intent of our flesh and end up where we should not be, the Bible is fantastic to remind us that God steps in and turns the channel, moves the GPS address. He redirects. So true.

Later in life, God allowed me to "fall into" a great nursing program that led to a fantastic Physician Assistant program in the Dallas area. The rest of my large and very close family is in the Houston area, and we were involved in the international charismatic group called Aglow International. After moving to Dallas, I continued to go to the national and international conferences with my family; but I did not find a "home group" in Dallas.

At the international meeting in Orlando, Florida, I met a woman on our bus who asked where I attend. When I told her that I did not, she told me I should look up the president for my area. There were eight thousand women at this Orlando conference, but that night when I got on the bus, I encountered the same woman again. This time, she gave me the card of the president of the Aglow in my area. She had "run into" her at the conference and told the woman who was now handing me the card that I should call her when I returned home.

When I got home and called, the president picked me up and took me to an Aglow leadership meeting where they passed out packets for interested presidents to start an Aglow chapter in their area. What? Me, president? I just wanted to find a place to attend. Instead, the Lord was offering me a place of leadership.

I followed the Lord through this adventure like a passenger in the backseat of a convertible flying down the highway. I held on for dear life as He drove! I had a husband, two small children and a full-time job. How could I lead an Aglow chapter? It meant preparing notes, finding speakers, setting up a facility, choosing topics, and advertising. No problem for God!

I never had a moment's worry. He brought the facility, the amazing speakers and worship leaders, even the mailing list of those He wanted to come. Patients would tell me they had come for something physical and then relate the most heart-wrenching spiritual need. The door would open for me to invite them, time and time again! In ten years I never had to brainstorm for a speaker or worship leader, and each month became more amazing than the previous one. I stood in awe. My favorite scripture, John

2:9, came to brilliant life:

> *When the ruler of the wedding feast had tasted the water that*
> *had been made into wine, he did not know where it had come*
> *from; but the servants who had drawn the water, knew.*

People could come, taste and see how great the Living Lord is and marvel at the way we put the meetings together. But Last-Minute Lisa knew the inside story. I knew that the Lord had "cancelled" the speaker I had lined up in advance when she got sick and a patient of mine spoke instead. I knew that it was God's hand that made decorations just "appear" for us to put on the tables. I knew, and the amazing women who came as the Lord told them to come knew. It was all Him!

When I wait with eager expectation, the Lord moves in ways that are much more than coincidence. I learned that lesson as a child, and I continue to experience it today. When I wait on Him and follow His leading, He continues to open new doors of possibility all the time. He leads me into "divine appointments" like my bus encounter a the Aglow conference, that blossom into ministry using my passions and purpose. Today, I am filled with excited anticipation, not procrastination, as He opens new doors and shows up in "God-incidences" all over my life. God so goes before all of us who follow Him that there is no worry, no fear, only an expectant Spirit. This is because He does not call us servants; He calls us friends and tells us everything. Read John 15:15:

> *I no longer call you servants, because a servant does not know*
> *his master's business. Instead, I have called you friends, for*
> *everything that I learned from my Father I have made known to*
> *you.*

Wow! What He is doing now in my life is birthing a ministry called Connected People to use the Internet to connect Christians to new possibilities, other people, exciting events, and networks for whatever God has for us. My friend Michelle Borquez Thornton and I describe it as a "Craigslist for Christians," and I am excitedly following the leading of the Lord as He makes a way for His Bride to stay connected and supported as we see the signs of His return, the latter day Rain. He has opened the doors for God Crazy Freedom – in my own life and in ministry to other women

– so we can be healed from our habits, hurts and hang-ups.

When you are leading under His charge, His divine gift is confidence, not confusion. And with that comes – what is that feeling again? – oh yes, blessed peace!

MY VICTORY

Every "last-minute" occasion that looks like procrastination to everyone else is really just me obediently waiting for the green light, the inspiration, His direction. If I wait on Him, I have His promised peace.

> *Peace I leave with you; My peace I give to you; not as the world gives do I give to you. Do not let your heart be troubled, nor let it be fearful.* (JOHN 14:27, NEW AMERICAN STANDARD BIBLE)

It has been said that my gift is my absolute understanding that peace is not only possible, but that anything short of that incredible gift is sin. I live in it. I swim in it. And I pray that I radiate it. Peace. No money buys it, university promises it, spouse or earthly government assures it. But, Believers, we absolutely can live our lives in its contentment and comfort. The peace that passes understanding can be our experience in the midst of waking up late, a bad diagnosis, a husband leaving … anything!

Whenever I feel confusion start to rattle my cage, urgency sneak in and demand to control my day, or the clock tell me something God has not, I know it's time for a reality check. Illusions threaten the reality of the life the Spirit has for us. Can something be True when it darkens our hearts with fear, frustration, or, worse, hopelessness? No! God is only light; in Him there is no darkness at all. We just have to open our eyes and our senses and allow Him to fill them. My victory is found in 1 Corinthians 14:33 (King James Version):

> *For God is not the author of confusion, but of peace, as in all churches of the saints.*

DEVOTION: DAY ONE

I have been on an exciting educational path that the Lord put me on over a year ago. He led me to an education in nutrition, specifically eliminating toxins and adding nutrition. It seems elementary, but there is a lot to learn, and the end result is victory over fatigue and fat.

I am amazed at how parallel nutrition is to spiritual health. In our spiritual lives, we have to avoid those things that slow us down and bring the fear of death, illness, and those things in our faith diet that rob energy.

The symptoms are easy to spot, but what are the toxins? What are you taking in that opens the door for stress or fear? Whenever you are "stressed," ask yourself, "What am I in fear of?" Are you opening the door for fear by believing the lies that you won't have enough time, that the end result won't be good enough, that you will be alone forever?

God's got it! It's in the bag. He knows you much better than you know yourself. Just listen, wait and be filled with the strength to obey.

Isaiah 26:3 says, "Thou wilt keep him in perfect peace, *whose* mind is stayed on *thee*: because he trusteth in thee" (emphasis mine).

Allow the Spirit of the Lord to search your heart. What are you living in fear of today? Do you feel the word close in on you when you allow stress to cover you? Bring that thing to the Lord and allow His truth to set you free to see God in it. Then you can experience His blessed peace!

DEVOTION: DAY TWO

Eliminating toxins from our diet can seem like an obvious and easy thing, but deception in packaging, a manufacturer's wording, or public acceptance of harmful ingredients make the journey work. Once I have the knowledge of good and evil, how can I be sure that I am feeding my body or my mind the good I seek?

Isaiah 30 tells us:

Whether you turn to the right or to the left, your ears will hear a
voice behind you, saying, "This is the way; walk in it." Then you
will defile your idols overlaid with silver and your images covered
with gold; you will throw them away like a menstrual cloth and
say to them, "Away with you!"

What a promise, and always true! God not only tells us what we can and cannot eat, do or say, He actually gives us disdain for the very thing that would bring harm. He provides the way and the "want to." Many times we know the way but lack the want to. Listen to Him; He makes it easy.

Once, I was tempted through flattery to have my head turned toward another man. I presented it to God with my night prayer, and behold! I had a dream that the same man was hideous, with devil horns to boot. God is very creative, and He's always got our back.

Ask the Lord if there is deception you are feeding on. Allow the Spirit of God to move that object from desire to contempt.

DEVOTION: DAY THREE

Each day that I eliminate toxins from my diet, I free up the opportunity for nutrition to move in. As fear and illusion leave, the voice of the Lord is clear and the desire for intimacy with Him becomes like water to my soul. Intimacy with the Lord … just saying that brings a picture to my mind.

What does your picture look like? If you were brought up in a denomination that made you feel like you had to take a graduate course before intimacy was even an option, it may seem like a distant goal. If you were brought up to revere God like the Great and Mighty Oz, it may make your knees quiver like the Cowardly Lion's. If you were fortunate enough to know the God that Jesus knows, then intimacy is as close and familiar as the flesh on your own body. He is as near as that! I have longed to touch Him and have felt the closeness of my God as I brushed my own hand over my arm or felt the wind brush my cheek. Don't you know our Abba Father loves it when we ask Him to be near to us?

James 4:8 puts it simply: "Come near to God and he will come near to you."

There is nothing as nourishing to a famished Spirit. Do you feel like there is lack in your life? Feel discontent? Not satisfied with anything? it's possible your God-time is missing. Ask the Lord for time alone with Him wherever you are.

DEVOTION: DAY FOUR

With every "last minute" opportunity, the Lord often must wait for me to come to the end of myself. When I do, the Lord will get the glory that belongs only to Him.

Isaiah 42:8 reminds us:

> *"I am the LORD; that is my name! I will not give my glory to anyone else, nor share my praise with carved idols."*
> (NEW LIVING TRANSLATION)

When I have my own strength left to accomplish a task, I run the risk of requiring the glory for accomplishing the goal. So He separates me from my ability and fills the gap with His ability. Isn't it "tasty" to hear our friends tell us how amazing we are? For example, when a friend says, "How do you find the time to make such a lovely meal in the midst of all that you do?" God gets no glory for directing our steps to the sale section of the grocery store, providing just the right amount of funds, and bringing the guests over. Waiting on God allows me to know whose sous chef I am and to whom the credit goes.

When I plan a monthly meeting for our ministry, sometimes the Lord allows me to plan it a few days in advance, and sometimes it is minutes before it starts that He shows me what He wants to do. Resting in the fact that God will reveal His plan at the right time has become second nature, along with giving Him ALL of the glory for what He does.

Is there an ability you lack before you can meet with God, be His friend, or finish a task? Ask the Lord to forgive you for providing the strength to accomplish His task and rest in Him.

DEVOTION: DAY FIVE

Isn't it amazing how many cookbooks there are? Yet we still find new ways of providing nourishment. Wouldn't it be silly to reduce nutrition to one simple recipe? Yet that is what we often do to God.

We expect God to speak the way He did when we were a child, in comfort food recipes. Or to speak to us in the same way that worked so well when we first met. We may have shared an appetizer, dinner and a late night dessert with Him before we loved Him. But instead of repeating the same menu, He wants to move on and introduce something new.

Frustrated, we create the same old thing and feel disappointed when the flavor doesn't seem as exciting, the dishes as inviting. We light the candles, put on the worship tape, get out the journal and find ourselves eating the spiritual equivalent of dried toast.

God is vibrant, fresh, and alive! He is the menu brimming with tasty new delights each season. Tempting treats of wisdom and purpose that are perfect for the place we are now. We are not the same today, our walk with God should not be either.

Although Hebrews 13:8 tells us that *"Jesus Christ is the same yesterday and today and forever,"* Lamentations 3:22-23 reminds us that,

> *The Lord's lovingkindnesses indeed never cease, For His compassions never fail. They are new every morning; Great is Your faithfulness.*

God is mighty, creative and longing to go with you wherever you go. He met one at the well, one in a tree, two at the garden. He wept with his friends, ate with his disciples, and talked while He walked.

God gives us grace, the God-given ability to hear Him and do all that He calls us to do. He knows You. There will be a recipe He puts together just for you. Taste and see that the Lord is good! (Psalm 34:8)

Is there anywhere you go that God is not there? Align your senses to hear, see, and dine with Him today!

GOD CRAZY FREEDOM CHALLENGE

Do you undervalue the direction of the Lord? Is He in absolutely everything you do? Do you say things like, "The Lord gave me a brain to use," "This is not my first rodeo," or "I know what to do?"

The covering I feel when I obediently go in the direction of the Lord is like walking under an umbrella of grace and favor. There's no leaning on my own understanding, no confusion.

We laugh and feel God kisses when we discover that the cup of coffee is free, the first parking spot opens up before us, or, as I recently experienced, the world renowned cardiovascular surgeon is at the small local hospital the day before my Dad is having heart surgery. Peace!

Jesus, our example, fully God yet fully man, came so that we would know how to follow the leading of the Holy Spirit…

John 5:19:

> Jesus gave them this answer: "I tell you the truth, the Son can do nothing by himself; he can do only what he sees his Father doing, because whatever the Father does the Son also does."

I am pretty sure nothing means NOTHING! If Jesus, God's own son, leaned on the strength and ability of the Holy Spirit, what makes us think we must do anything on our own?

How can we find His peace and His leading?

LISTEN, expectantly. God speaks in many ways. He will confirm His direction.

Be empowered. Don't move until you feel peace; follow the peace of the Lord.

Then, obey. Remember, you are moving with His ability. Rest in that confidence.

Goodbye, Confusion. Hello to the wonderful words we will hear our Father say, "She listened." Then we build our treasure in Heaven and find peace on Earth.

GOD CRAZY FREEDOM PRAYER

Dear Jesus,

Thank you that your Word says you give us the victory through our Lord Jesus Christ. Help me today to align every fiber in my body with the truth that Jesus is here and He loves me. I want to surrender my all to Him. Search my heart and see if there is any part of me that says, "I've got this myself." Illuminate any place where I feel inadequate, or any place where I believe my plan is superior to your leading, Lord. Take away the, "I can do this by myself," attitude that separates me from you, God. Forgive me for all that I have done wrong; thank you for the blood of Jesus that covers me. Please help me today and everyday to listen for your leading, as thoughts of the things I have to do come to mind. Help me to listen closely and wait patiently before I move. As Mary said, "Let it be unto me as you say!" Help me today to walk confidently in the name of Jesus, with the grace of God and your total peace. I invite you into my day, sweet Holy Spirit. I want to do every minute of it together with you. Amen!

ADDICTION TO FREEDOM

by Holly Joy Renken

*W*ebster's Dictionary defines "addiction" like this: *a state of being enslaved to a habit or practice or something that is psychologically or physically habit-forming, as narcotics, to such an extent that its cessation (a temporary or complete stopping; discontinuance) causes severe trauma.*

When we hear the word addiction or hear someone speak about having an addiction, we automatically think of alcohol or drugs. But in this life I know for a fact that women have a ton of addictions that go beyond alcohol and drugs and enslave us on a daily basis.

I grew up as a pastor's kid in a non-denominational church. I loved church and Sunday school. I loved having a family that loved God. I loved knowing that our family's purpose in life was to see souls saved for Jesus.

But when I hit the teen years, something happened in our family that devastated me and made me look at God in a whole different way. I began to pull back from God because I didn't understand why he would allow something like that to happen to us, a Christian family dedicated to pastoring a church and serving Him.

At the age of sixteen, I started hanging out with friends who were not a good influence and began drinking. My grades dropped, I quit cheerleading, and I partied instead of studying. I was out of control, and my parents didn't know what to do for me. I felt out of control inside, and nothing made sense anymore. The God I thought I knew and loved all my life now felt so far away. I felt like I was living in a fog of confusion and lies.

Then, in the summer of 2000, members of the World Revival Church in Kansas City, Missouri, traveled to our church in Iowa to speak. My parents asked me if I would sing during praise and worship. This was a huge deal for me because I had never been part of praise and worship in our church. I always wanted to, but I had never done it. I didn't know if I could even get up there on that stage in our church, put a smile on my face, and make the people of our church and all the visitors believe that I still loved God.

I felt so broken and lost at that time, but I just felt God whisper to me and say, "I'm still here." So I got up there and sang with my family. As soon as I opened my mouth to sing, it was like all the hurt and pain just left. I felt God's presence and peace again. I remember looking out and seeing kids my age who were visiting from other churches crying out to God during praise and worship. All I could think was, "This is what it's all about, God. It's not about me; it's about saving lost souls."

I knew right then and there, in the very depth of my soul, that I was called into ministry for God. I didn't want that feeling ever to go away. I met some of the women from the other church that weekend and instantly clicked with them. I had never met anyone my age that I got along with like that. They had been through a lot of the same things that I had. They were the kind of people who loved God so much, it was contagious. I wanted to be like that. I wanted my fight and my passion for God back, and I felt like it was when I was around them. It says in the Bible that iron sharpens iron, and that is what happened when I was around them.

I went home that weekend and told my parents that I wanted to drop out of high school and move to Kansas City to attend the World Revival Church School of Ministry. I was just about to start my senior year, and I knew my parents would think this was a drastic decision, but it was an answer to my prayers. I finally felt God in such a real way that I knew I needed Him like I need air, and I needed a fresh start. We decided as a family that going to Kansas City would be the best thing for me.

I began the ministry school, and it was so amazing. I had great friends who loved God as much as I did and more. They became like family to me, pushed me to be all that I could be, and encouraged me to keep my walk with God strong. I stayed strong for about six months, until I discovered that my ex-boyfriend of many years lived an hour away from where I was now attending school. He and I began to talk, and before I knew it we were back in a full-on relationship. I was spending all of my free time with him, even skipping classes to be with him. I pulled away from God again and didn't even realize it.

My friends tried to talk to me, but I was so in love that I didn't want to hear what they had to say. I eventually quit school and moved away to be with him. My parents and friends from church and school were worried about me and my decision, but I didn't seem to care. I just knew that I had found the person I was supposed to be with, and he loved me. After a while, I began to get sick. I had horrible kidney pains that eventually put me in the hospital. Turns out, I was expecting.

My family was still in Iowa, and now I had to call them and deliver the news no pastor's family wants to hear from their child: "Mom and Dad, I'm pregnant." Here I was, a teenager who had dropped out of high school and a school of ministry, turned my back on all my new friends and my church, and was now living with a guy out of wedlock. Making that phone call was one of the hardest things I've done in my life. I felt like I had let everyone down, and I didn't know what to do. I felt so scared and alone.

Growing up as a pastor's kid, I knew that if I was pregnant I needed to get married. So we got married shortly after, and about seven months later Ethan Ezekiel was welcomed into this world. My marriage had its ups and downs, but my son is literally the best thing that ever happened to me. That doesn't mean life was easy. I was young, and now quickly thrust into living a very adult life. I fought with myself on a daily basis because I knew in the depth of my being that I was meant to do and be more than just a stay-at-home mom and wife. I also knew I was not equally yoked with my husband.

I didn't feel that it was his or anyone else's fault but my own. I knew it was, because I let myself slip away from God. I didn't guard my heart, and I got caught up in things outside of God's will for my life. Every day, I felt a burning, unfulfilled desire from the moment I woke up to the moment I went to bed. I knew I was called to be in ministry, but I could not see how that could even be possible now.

Soon, my marriage fell apart. Before I knew it, we were divorced. After that, I felt completely numb. I just kept thinking, *God, this is not how I saw my life playing out.* I felt like I was a body floating around earth without a spirit. I didn't know who I was anymore.

Have you ever felt loved by God but so far away from Him at the same time?

I began drinking and hanging out with friends who led me down a path even further away from God. I eventually had to move back to my parents, leaving my son in a different state with his father. Being apart from my son is by far the most painful, heart-wrenching hurt I have ever experienced.

I continued to walk away after my divorce and dated another man who was not right for me. Through the loss of that relationship, I lost all the things the world makes you think you need. Finally, I began to seek God again, and he revealed to me that I had an addiction to running from my problems and numbing my pain with the things of this world instead of running to Him in times of trouble.

It took thirteen years of feeling lost and looking for something to fill the emptiness at the end of every day before I finally realized that there was nothing in this world that could satisfy me. At the lowest point of my life, I had lost my family, ex-husband, boyfriend, house, car, career, my personal belongings, and any friends I had left.

My Victory

When you have nothing left, that's when God has you where he wants you. Not that He ever glories in your despair. In fact, the Bible says that the Holy Spirit collects your every tear. But when you have nothing left, nothing else to turn to, nothing around to numb you, that's when you can finally hear His still, small voice. There is nothing left to cover it up. I fell down on my face and cried out to Jesus. I asked him to forgive me for all the years I had run from Him. I got rid of anything that connected me to my past and the things of this world. I relinquished anything that would hold me back and cloud my vision for God. I gave him one hundred percent of my heart and life.

I am now so thankful for everything that I have been through in life. I know that sounds crazy to some people, but because of everything I have been through I have such a passion, love and appreciation for God. He has set me free, restored my life, and blessed me in ways that I could never have dreamed of before. I am now living my dream of being in ministry. I am able to use every addiction and life experience that God has freed me from to reach people and lead them to Jesus Christ. He is the only one who has the power to set the captives free and to give life, and life more abundantly!

DEVOTION: DAY ONE

I sought the Lord and he answered me; he delivered me from all my fears. Those who look to him are radiant; their faces are never covered with shame. PSALM 34:11

In life, we tend to run from our problems or fears because we think no one can understand or relate to us. We feel people will judge us if we actually told them the truth of what we have done, what has happened to us or what we are going through. We cover our problems with fake smiles and pretend that everything is okay. We suffer in silence, and our hearts become hardened and callused.

Jesus knows everything that we have been through and everything that we are going through. He knows our every thought. The scripture says that when we cry out for help, the Lord delivers us out of all our distress and troubles.

When you begin to pray and talk to Jesus, ask Him for forgiveness and guidance in your life. That allows Him to step in and be the Lord of your life. The more that you seek Him and read the Bible, the more He will begin to lead you, guide you, and direct your path in every step you take. Jesus loves every single one of us so much, and He misses no detail of our lives. Don't ever think that God is too busy for you, because you are a child of the King whom He sent His son to save – to give you life and life more abundantly.

DEVOTION: DAY TWO

So, come out from among (unbelievers), and separate (sever)
yourselves from them, says the Lord, and touch not (any) unclean
thing; then I will receive you kindly and treat you with favor...
2 CORINTHIANS 6:17

I know that as women in this world, we are pressured every day by so many influences that make us think we need to be like the world thinks we should be. We see it on TV, read it in magazines on newsstands, and hear it in school, at work or on the Internet. The world is all around us.

But God says, "Greater is he that is in you, than he that is in the world."

I know I had to let go of all of my old friends, bad habits, and anything that would influence me and pull me back into the things of this world. I knew I wanted Jesus in my life so much that letting those things go didn't even matter to me. It was easy for me to choose Jesus because I knew that He died for me, and that means that I've already been made free. I just needed to make the choice to be free in Him. Once you do, you open the door for God to pour out His blessings and favor in your life.

The scripture says we are in this world, but not of it. When we choose to live for Christ alone, we become a light to generations. People begin to see a God-change in you, and that is what changes other people's lives.

DEVOTION: DAY THREE

But those who hope in the Lord will renew their strength. They
will soar on wings like eagles; they will run and not grow weary,
they will walk and not be faint. ISAIAH 40:31

The world may battle for your heart, but the war has already been won!

Hope is defined as the following: to believe, desire or trust. We women have many things that we put our hope in. We put our hope in our jobs, men, friends, and even money. All of those things will fade, and when they do, what will your hope and trust be in then? When we lose things that we had put our hope in, we feel an emptiness.

Jesus wants us to put all of our trust and hope in him. He will renew our strength when we are weak. I know, as women, we have many things every day that are demanding of us. Job, family, church, friends … the list can be overwhelming at times. When we trust in God and read the Bible, we become strengthened. The Bible says that God is the lifter of our heads. God gives us the armor (Bible) for this battle called life. He says that we are more than conquerors. That means we have already won. It may seem like there is no way out of your circumstance, but keep trusting in the Lord, keep praying, keep standing strong. Know that the Lord your God has already won the war!

DEVOTION: DAY FOUR

Let no one despise or think less of you because of your youth, but be an example (pattern) for the believers in speech, in conduct, in love, faith, and purity. 1 TIMOTHY 4:12

In this passage Paul is speaking to Timothy about being a young, gifted minister of the gospel. Paul is essentially telling Timothy that there may be days that people don't like what he has to say about God. There may be days that Timothy won't be respected in his calling because of his age. Paul wants Timothy to know that it's okay. Jesus said that if they hate you, remember they hated me first.

Timothy stuck to what Paul told him and what his mother taught him. He stuck to the word of God. As God Crazy women, sometimes it can be hard to be in this world and believe in God. We need to keep from growing weary. We can't stop; we have to keep pressing into what God has called us to do. When we abide by God's word and live in love, faith, and purity, we set a precedence for generations of women to come who don't know Jesus yet. We can give women of all ages a standard to live by and a chance to accept Jesus as their Lord and Savior.

God Crazy women, rise up! Know in this day that God is fighting for you. God has a plan and a purpose for each and every one of you to walk in His God Crazy Freedom. It just takes one person to change a generation. Will that person be you?

Devotion: Day Five

"I'll show up and take care of you as I promised and bring you back home. I know what I'm doing. I have it all planned out— plans to take care of you, not abandon you, plans to give you the future you hope for. When you call on me, when you come and pray to me, I'll listen. When you come looking for me, you'll find me. Yes, when you get serious about finding me and want it more than anything else, I'll make sure you won't be disappointed. I'll turn things around for you." -God's Decree
JEREMIAH 29:11-14, THE MESSAGE

You may be going through things in your life right now that make no sense, and you just don't understand why bad things happen to you. Hold on to Jesus and don't give up! That is the best advice God gave us. Life can be painful at times, but I have never met anyone powerful in the kingdom of God or read about anyone in the Bible who has not been through pain. Everyone hurts, sins, and suffers loss.

On the days when you feel like giving up, know that God is right next to you. He has a plan, and you are here on purpose. He knows what He is doing. You can make it. Soon, you'll look back and think, "Wow, God! This is why I went through what I went through." Your pain becomes His purpose. Your test becomes your testimony.

GOD CRAZY FREEDOM CHALLENGE

1. When you follow God, it's hard to have worldly friends. When things get tough in life, having those kinds of friends makes it to easy to run to the things of this world instead of standing strong on God's Word. Get involved in a church. This will allow you to make new friends, Godly friends who will have your best interest at heart.

2. Find someone who can give you Godly wisdom to talk to about your problems, addictions and fears. This allows you to be able to confront all the things that hold you back in life and know that nothing is too big for God.

3. Write down all of your addictions and fears, and give them to God. Know that he can break any addiction and fear and set the captives free!

4. Ask yourself, "What does God want for me? What does He desire to do in my life?" Make goals for yourself and pray about them. You can do all things through Christ who gives you strength.

5. Every time you feel yourself giving up because things in life are too hard, and your addiction rises up inside of you and begins to tempt you to run away, start declaring the Word of God over your life! Repeat His truths, like, "God has a plan and a purpose for my life," "Greater is he that is in me than he that is in the world," and "God will never leave me or forsake me." Relax into God's hold on your life.

GOD CRAZY FREEDOM PRAYER

Heavenly Father, I thank you that I have the honor to serve such an abundant God. I ask that you break every addiction, every fear, and every chain of my past that the enemy has placed on my life. I ask that you forgive me of all of my sins, Lord. I ask that you forgive me for all of the times that I chose to run from you instead of running to you. You are the God of all flesh, and there is nothing too big for you.

I ask that you strengthen me in you and in your Word. Thank you for fighting for me and never giving up on me or leaving me. I thank you for everything that I have, and I thank you for everything that I do not have.

I ask that you would clean me up and fill me up with your love, purity, faith, and mercy. If there is anything in my life that is not of you, I don't want it. I ask that you restore my soul and teach me to forgive past hurts and pains. I ask that you use my life as a light to generations of women, so they may hear my testimony and know that only God could have changed, formed and molded my life into something so beautiful. You are the potter, Lord, and I am the clay. I give everything to you. Have your way with my life, Lord. I trust you and I love you so much, Jesus. Amen.

STRIVING TO GRACE

by Rebecca Gates

*I*ve never been the kind of girl who wears flowing dresses and twirls around. I wasn't a ballerina, and, well, the whole princess-fairy-tale thing just wasn't me. However, I had one thing that many other girls didn't: determination to survive and hope that if I could live one day at a time, I would make a better life for myself. I wanted to believe that I had value, but the world around me shouted my worthlessness. Maybe that's why I never believed in fairy tales. I knew that no one was ever going to come to my rescue. If I wanted change, I was going to have to do it myself.

I found life in my conversion to Christianity. It may have seemed drastic to those around me. Within a few months of my salvation, I was able to stop drinking, doing drugs, and sleeping around. I stopped listening to secular music and watching TV. I even stopped dating altogether … eventually. That one took awhile.

I decided I would someday get married and be a stay-at-home mom and homeschooler. I started assessing all that was wrong in the world and in my church leaders, and I freely shared my observations with others.

Then I felt empty. I asked the Lord, "What else should I give up? What else can I do to be more righteous?" I never heard an answer.

On the outside, my conversion seemed like something that I could really thank God for, but my heart still had not changed. I guess you could say I was kind of like a little Cinderella, a slave wearing my own brand of righteous filthy rags. I was doing, doing, doing for God, but missing the whole point of salvation.

When Cinderella was swept away by her Prince Charming, I wonder if she began her new life in the mansion still scrubbing the floors while wearing her "beautiful" K-mart gown. Maybe Charming tried to remind her that her place was with him, but she was unable to hear him over the sound of the vacuum.

That was my "conversion." I looked great on the outside, but it was a cheap knockoff of the newness of life God wanted to give me on the inside. He just wanted to love me, but I was too busy doing what I had always done, trying to make a way for myself.

Matthew 7:22-23 (New Living Translation) says,

> *On judgment day many will say to me, 'Lord! Lord! We*
> *prophesied in Your name and cast out demons in Your name and*
> *performed many miracles in Your name.' But I will reply, 'I never*
> *knew you. Get away from Me, you who break God's laws.'*

I never knew you, He says? Yikes! That could rock a girl's theology, since we often quote from Psalm 139 that He knows our innermost being, unless we understand what God, our Groom, is actually saying here. Just like we can be married to our husband and never be intimate with him, we can also carry the Name of Christ and not be connecting with Him intimately. We're just going through the motions of life with a little "Mrs." at the beginning of our new name.

We carry around our "bank card" that gives us access to all that belongs to God. Some of us use it and others don't, but since we have taken His name, it is ours. It is no different than when we allow cooking, cleaning and taking care of the kids to take priority over knowing our mate.

It is the marriage that is the foundation of the family. Cultivate that, and you have a healthy home. Cultivate intimacy with God, and all other relationships, success in life, and ministry will flow out of the intimacy you have developed with the Lord.

It is really easy to get caught up in doing for the Lord instead of simply being with the Lord. In this passage Jesus was talking about church people, even ministers, and He called them law breakers.

Jesus tells us in Matthew 22:37-39 what laws or commandments He is talking about:

> *You must love the Lord your God with all your heart, all your soul, and all your mind. This is the first and greatest commandment. A second is equally important: Love your neighbor as yourself.*

Just like I was doing and not doing all the right things, so it seemed, I was a law breaker because I was missing the one thing that God wanted most from me. If I had just laid aside ministry, the pursuit of perfection, and all the church functions long enough, I would have realized that I didn't even know God. Nor was I spending any of my efforts on letting Him know me. When I had something to talk about, I talked to everyone but Him: my friends, my pastor, my mentor. I wanted them to speak godly wisdom into my life without ever learning to connect with God for myself, all the while living the Christian life in my own strength.

I was like Cinderella, with access to the kingdom's best, but still living like a slave. Heir to the kingdom, having the Prince's full attention and access to the grace that covers my freedom from works, but I was still slaving away earning my keep and wondering if I would lose it all if I rested for a moment.

I'll be honest, I have three boys; and we don't watch movies like Cinderella much. What I can remember of the movie was the beautiful couple getting married and living happily ever after in the castle. I think there may have been some dancing-the-night-away kind of thing. Like I said, that stuff is so not me. But if I could relate my life to that story, I would say that when I made a commitment to the Lord, it was like the night Cinderella went to the ball. It was a magical experience that expanded my capacity to desire love and life more abundantly. But then I ran away from God's grace, afraid that He would not want me just the way I was.

MY VICTORY

It's interesting to me that in the story, everything Cinderella wore turned back into rags except for the shoe that the Prince carried in His hand. To me, that's the power of grace – my life in God's hands, changed forever. So the Lover of my soul, passionate for me, began to pursue me tirelessly. When I let myself be found, He rescued me from a passionless faith that had propelled me into legalism and exhaustive striving. He welcomed me into His loving embrace and secured me in His grace.

But the happy ending isn't here yet. I have cried more tears than I care to remember since taking His name. I am left in a world that is filled with the pains of death, groaning and destruction in the earth, and suffering of the innocent. This isn't where I am going to find my happy ending.

I'm in a long-distance romance with my King who is coming back for me. For the last twenty-plus years, He has been revealing Himself to me more and more. He has held my face in His hands while I cried. He has offered understanding when the world didn't make sense. He hasn't left me here alone, but I have had to learn to connect with Him in His Kingdom spiritually. It is there that I have found His presence and experienced His passion for me. Now is the time to know Him. I have no fear of death or the afterlife, because I am convinced that when I see my Prince face-to-face for the first time, I will finally see the One I have lived my life adoring and longing for.

This isn't our resting place. This isn't our home. And this isn't our happily ever after. This is our romance. The Bible says that all of our days are written in His book. It's our love story in the making. What will yours say? Will it read like a to-do list? Or will the readers be moved to tears as they identify with your life that was spent falling in love with your Savior? Will their heart beat hard in their chests awaiting the moment in the story when you will finally embrace all that you spent your life hoping for?

He's pursuing you, princess!

He wants to show you how your messy life, left in His hands, will be turned into something beautiful. Will you just love Him?

DEVOTION: DAY ONE
WE ARE HIS BRIDE

Read: Ephesians 5:21-32; Revelation 21:2, 21:9; Song of Songs 4:1-12

We were meant for intimacy. We are Christ's bride! A godly groom doesn't take a bride so that he can have a servant. He takes her so that he can be intimate with her. He wants to know her. He wants to share his heart, his secrets, his passions, and his future with her. He wants to be fruitful with her. (See John 15:5.)

Discovering our identity as Christ's bride sets us free from living like we are trying to earn His favor.

I know that my husband has chosen me. I know that no matter where he is or what he's doing, I can call him and he will stop everything for me if I ask. But if I didn't believe that, then I wouldn't ask. And if I don't ask, I choose to carry the burden myself.

Isn't that just what we do with God? We don't want to bother Him, or maybe we don't even think He cares enough to help. We try to do life in our own strength, but the burden quickly becomes too heavy. We end up feeling like a failure and a disappointment to God when the only thing we really failed to do was to ask Him for help in the beginning. You are His Bride. He has chosen You.

Revelation 19:11 describes Jesus riding in on a white horse. He is called Faithful and True. He is our romantic Prince, coming to save us from our distress. We can count on Him.

Who were you before you came to Christ? Have you laid down who you were so that you can become all that God has created you to be?

DEVOTION: DAY TWO
PRINCESS, PUT AWAY YOUR RAGS

Read: Galatians 2:15-21, Isaiah 64:6, Ephesians 2:8-10

I think that a lot of times people receive salvation and then want to do something to thank Jesus for His sacrifice. It's not like any of us sets out to display our filthy rags and live under the law. Maybe, like me, you aren't use to getting anything for free, including love and favor. You begin to try to do ministry and lead a perfect, pure life. These things aren't bad; they're just dead unless we are connecting intimately with our source of life.

John 15:5 says this:

> *I am the vine, you are the branches; he who abides in Me and I in him, he bears much fruit, for apart from Me you can do nothing.*

I believe that when we are intimate with Jesus, ministry and right living will naturally flow from us. It's what is conceived and birthed from our union with our Lord. Grace isn't only for our future salvation. It is meant to cover every area of our life.

I used to believe that if I was the best mom I could be, my kids would not make the same mistakes I had made. I read books, went to seminars, and developed my own formula for raising kids "God's way."

It didn't take long for me to realize that I can't be perfect enough. I need the Holy Spirit leading me as I parent my boys. His grace is sufficient for me.

In what areas of your life are you striving to be better? How can you apply God's grace to those areas to cover your imperfections?

DEVOTION: DAY THREE
YOU CARRY HIS CHECKBOOK: ACCESS IT.

My husband does the finances in our home. There have been times when I needed to go shopping, but I didn't know how much was in my account or how to access that information. This always frustrates my husband, who has shown me multiple times how to check our balance online. He wants me to be equipped so that I have all that I need for myself and for our family, but I have not wanted to learn.

God's Word is like our bank statement. He wants us to know it and be equipped in confidence that we bear His name to access it. Check your "Bank Statement," the Bible, so that you won't miss out on anything He has for you. As you read your Bible, every time you come across something it has to offer, stop. Ask God to give it to you and believe that He will. His Word does not return void but will accomplish all that He sent it to do.

Galatians 4:4-7 tells us that we are heirs to everything God has through the work of Jesus. Everything! Read Psalm 103:3-6 and consider it your benefits package as a child of God. What are your benefits? Check out 1 Corinthians 12:8-10, too. What gifts is God extending to you? Try reading 1 Corinthians 12:6-7, 12:31, and 14:1. The Bible is FULL of promises for everything we have need of. If you want to see even some of your benefits package, turn to Psalm 103:3-6. What are your benefits? Check out 1 Corinthians 12:8-10 too. What gifts is God extending to you? Try reading 1 Corinthians 12:6-7, 12:31, and 14:1. Then come back.

Now do you believe that these gifts are ALL for YOU?

Try James 1:5, Hebrews 4:16, and Jeremiah 29:11. The list goes on and on. What else does God say we can count on from Him?

Devotion: Day Four
Now Receive Your Inheritance

Keep on asking and it will be given you; keep on seeking and you
will find; keep on knocking [reverently] and [the door] will be
opened to you. For everyone who keeps on asking receives; and he
who keeps on seeking finds; and to him who keeps on knocking,
[the door] will be opened. MATTHEW 7:7-8 (AMPLIFIED)

If you held out your hand to me with a check, I am not receiving it unless I reach out my hand to take it. It doesn't matter how long you extend your arm, the check will not be in my possession until I take it. In fact, even if I hold that check in my hand, it is of no use to me until I cash it.

We do this with sincerely given compliments all the time. Someone tells us we look great when we are not feeling great, so we shrug off the compliment and think that person is wrong. Now both people are robbed of a blessing because we couldn't receive.

For whatever reason, many of us have blockages in our "receiver." It's all clogged with past disappointments, fear, unbelief, or mostly with a sense that we don't deserve God's favor or His attention.

Don't give up. Persistence is the "Drano" that unclogs our receiver pipe. Every time we ask God, we are defying the lie that has said "Access Denied." We are allowing hope to open the door to our faith.

Devotion: Day Five
Let's Get Intimate

Read: Hebrews 4:16

I usually avoid God when I feel like I have not measured up, but this passage has taught me that even when I have failed the worst, He wants me to approach His throne. I do this by imagining myself walking into His Holy place, just like this scripture implies. I envision Him rising from His throne to greet me, not with arms crossed in disappointment, but with outstretched hands ready to embrace me.

I've always wanted to be like the disciple John, resting my head on Jesus' chest. All of the disciples had their chance to sit this close to Jesus, but John was the one who abandoned all pride and fear to be called "Beloved." I imagine myself curling up with my King for a while as I listen to His heartbeat.

I don't want Him to be just a friend to me. I want to be a friend to Him too, so it's important that I take the time to ask Him what's on His heart. So often it's me He wants to encourage and love on, but other times He shows me the faces of people He wants me to agree in prayer with Him for their needs.

Prayer is a two-way conversation. I haven't communicated until I have heard God speak to me too. Through practice, I have learned to trust that I hear His voice. I expect to hear Him.

Do you believe God wants you to come boldly to Him? What assurance has He given you in scripture?

God Crazy Freedom Challenge

Day 1: If you were fully confident that you are Christ's bride and He is a good husband, how would you live differently? Write it out and begin to align yourself with this truth on a daily basis.

Day 2: Purpose to apply grace to the areas in your life where you are striving for perfection. Identify the fear that drives you and ask God to cover your shortcomings. Then keep a journal of how God comes through for you in each area. Notice how you walk in greater peace.

Day 3: What do you need? Can you find it in the Bible? Write down scriptures you have found that promise you God will provide these things for you.

Day 4: Identify lies that have kept you from receiving all that God has for you. What is the truth from God's word that speaks against each lie? Write the truth down and rehearse it as adamantly as you once rehearsed the lie.

Day 5: Come boldly into God's throne room. Imagine yourself close to Him and journal all that He says to you even if you aren't sure if you are hearing correctly. Ask yourself WHY you don't believe it's His voice. Chances are if it encourages you, makes you feel more loved by Him or expresses that you are greater than you see yourself, it is HIM. Then receive grace like you have never experienced before. Don't be afraid of making a mistake as you grow in this area. These times with Him are just between you and the Lover of your soul. Guard these intimate times together.

GOD CRAZY FREEDOM PRAYER

Thank you, my King, for loving me and rescuing me from a life of slavery. I ask that You would hold my life, every part, in Your hand and make something beautiful out of my ashes. Teach me to hear Your voice. Teach me to walk in grace for myself and towards others. Empower me with your love. I humbly ask that you would open my heart to receive every gift, every benefit and every reward that Your word promises in scripture with grateful expectation. Amen, so be it!

DEATH TO LIFE
by Christal M.N. Jenkins

In May, 2009, I got laid off from my job. I was a young corporate manager who felt as though I was on the pathway to great success. I was fortunate to be able to travel all over the world and work with top Fortune 500 companies. At the age of twenty-five, I bought my own home. I had the luxury vehicle, owned my own business and was soon to become a published author. All I could see was the mountaintop.

The sudden loss of my job was a huge blow, but I was determined to bounce back quickly. Days later, I found out that I had been accepted into graduate school. I just knew that this ultimately had to be God's plan. Little did I know, however, what I was about to encounter as I began this new journey in my life.

Faced with being unemployed and with no job opening in sight, I was forced to deplete my savings and my 401K in order to try to make ends meet. I was grateful that I had lived within my means while I worked, so that I had some funds put away. Soon, however, I felt as though I was drowning in bills – the mortgage, car payment, and everything I had worked so hard for. I held tightly to the belief that God was not going to allow me to lose my house or any of the other things I had acquired. After all, I was His child. Why would He allow me to go through the horrible pain of losing something I had worked so hard to get? My faith was strong, and I was confident that "this too shall pass." I would be back on my feet, living the high life, in no time. By spring 2010, I got word that my beloved Godmother was having complications with her cancer. I was initially heartbroken, but I knew God would sustain her. She had beaten cancer so many times before.

Over time, stress crept in and began to take a toll on my health. I ended up having to go to the hospital. For the remainder of 2010, it seemed like I received nothing but bad news. The bank foreclosed on my house, and I had to quickly move in with a friend and leave most of my belongings behind. I had to consolidate my belongings from a four-bedroom house into what would fit in just one bedroom. As difficult as that transition was, I continued to press forward. Then my Godmother passed away just a month after I lost my house. I still hadn't found a job, and I was no longer able to claim unemployment benefits. Bills began to stack up. My faith began to falter, and I slid into despair.

For a while I began to think about taking my own life to end my misery. I didn't really want to go forward because it seemed like everything I had tried to save was lost. By the end of that year, the aunt I was extremely close to started having complications with her Lupus. All I could think at the time was, *This cannot be happening right now.* But it was. In April, 2011, my aunt passed away.

I cannot even begin to tell you the amount of pain I felt. Why her? Why now? It was incredibly difficult to lose two of the closest people to me back-to-back like that. I felt like Job. God had turned His back on me. Sadly, I chose to find solace in other things besides Him. I thought we had a bargain. I loved Him, put my faith in Him, and performed well. He gave me my heart's desires and protected me from harm. Wrong! He hadn't protected me from any of this pain, and I felt duped.

I turned to relationships with men as a means to feel validation and comfort. My identity had been tied up in what I had accomplished, and now that was gone too. Unemployed, homeless, and heartbroken, I didn't know who I was anymore. I chose to use their affections as a way to mask my vulnerability, hurt and pain. At the time, I was unaware that I was even doing that, but no matter who I chose, it never seemed to work out.

A piece of me died with every man I gave my heart and body to. To top it off, people I had thought were friends began to turn their backs on me. My life felt like the game of Jenga, my structure of blocks was being pulled apart slowly by hurt, pain, distrust, guilt and shame. It would only be a matter of time before I would collapse into a heap of brokenness.

I found myself slipping into deep depression, so deep that I was operating daily on autopilot. I was unaware that I had become a zombie as a means to cope with everything I had to suddenly face. It was so bad that one day when I was driving down the highway, I contemplated killing myself by driving directly into oncoming traffic. Few people were aware of how these experiences were affecting me. I didn't want people to think I was different than the person I used to be. In public, I held it together even though I felt like I was shattered on the inside.

The reality was that I never had the chance to grieve and process any of the losses I had experienced before the next one hit. I just continued to press on, trying to lean on my crumbling faith as a means to cope. When my faith wasn't enough, I quickly abandoned it for other things that could provide me with immediate but temporary relief. I tried to pray, read, fast and worship; but it seemed like nothing was working. It got to the point where I could no longer cry about it. The pain had taken root so deeply that it had begun to plant seeds of anger. I began to isolate myself even more from others. Sure, I would hang out with classmates and continue to go to church; but even in the midst of those crowds I felt alone. I knew God was there, but it seemed so hard to access Him as I had done before.

Despite the distance I felt, I knew that God must be present because He was the only way I could have stayed moderately sane during that time. It seemed as though I was one life circumstance away from having a nervous breakdown. I knew deep inside that I had to have hope for a breakthrough, but when would it ever come?

My Victory

The light in the midst of the darkness came one day when I realized that I had gone through too much to die in the pit. I had to get out of it. David, at the end of Psalm 27, says, *"I'm sure now I'll see God's goodness in the exuberant earth. Stay with God! Take heart. Don't quit. I'll say it again:*

Stay with God."

I had to stay with God; I had to see life on the other side of the hovering, dark cloud I found myself under. The amazing part of my story is that God was always there with me every step of the way. Maybe you are thinking, *Why would God allow her – or me – to go through what we're going through?* God must be evil. In actuality, His grace and presence are demonstrations of His love for me. He kept me in times when the devil tried to take me out. He provided me refuge when I needed a place of escape. He provided me strength to carry on when I wanted to throw in the towel. Whether I've found myself soaring to great heights or trapped in the deepest depths, He has never left me nor forsaken me. God is my redeemer and my victor! He is yours, too.

The truth is that God desires all of us to be whole—mind, body, and soul. In the beginning, I was only focused on my soul—praying, reading, fasting, and worshipping. But I was neglecting the importance of taking care of my mind and body. Without taking care of those things, I was not able to receive the complete healing that Jesus ultimately died for.

I sought counseling to work through my losses and the grief that I had experienced. In addition, I began eating better foods and exercising as a means to stay healthy and reduce stress. As I began to focus on all three areas of my life, I finally began to feel the wholeness that God promised in Scripture. In 1 John 4:2, John prays that we would prosper and be in health as our soul prospers. My soul is being restored each and every day by the power of the Holy Spirit working in me. My mind is being renewed daily as I meditate on the word and allow it to take root in my life, not in isolation, but in community with others. My body is revived as I continue to take care of the precious gift of life I have been given to steward.

My life has meaning and purpose. I know that despite what I face every day my life is worth living! My identity is not in my possessions or my accomplishments but in who I am as a child of God. I refuse to allow my circumstances to cut off God's purpose and plan for my life. I will become everything that He envisioned for me to be. In Jesus, I know I have a hope and future. My future looks bright, full of purpose, love, peace, joy, victory and abundance!

DEVOTION: DAY ONE
LIVING IN PURPOSE

No one on this earth was created by mistake. Despite the circumstances many of us are born into, God predestined your life before the earth came into form. God made you with a purpose that was designed just for you to fulfill. Everyone has a distinct purpose chosen by our creator. David said in Psalm 139:14 that he praises God because he is fearfully and wonderfully made. All of us were made through God's infinite creativity, love, detail and design. You were created on purpose, with a purpose!

The devil does not want us ever to know our purpose on this earth. Once we come to understand what we were created for and begin to live it out, we become a threat to him. I know you may look at your age or your circumstances and immediately count yourself out of God's equation. Maybe you think it is too late, or that God couldn't possibly have a plan for you because of things you have done or things that were done to you in your past. Those lies cannot be further from the truth! He sent His Son to give His life so that you might have life. Your life is made new because of the life, death and resurrection of Jesus Christ. He lived the life that we could not live so that we could have the life God designed for us to live.

You are not a mistake. Your life has meaning. Live out your purpose!

DEVOTION: DAY TWO
LIVING IN WHOLENESS

God's amazing love is given to us freely, not because of what we have done, but because we are His beloved creation. In life, we struggle to find love. We look to relationships, food, substances, etc., constantly searching for a love that will fulfill us, only to come up empty-handed. The lack of true love in our lives leaves us in a place of fear, pain and isolation.

We can take refuge in knowing that God's love frees us from these dark places. John 4:18 says,

> *There is no fear in love. But perfect love drives out fear, because fear has to do with punishment. The one who fears is not made perfect in love.*

God's love is a perfect love that consumes our very being. His perfected love goes beyond the surface of our issues and pain to the depths of our core to bring healing and wholeness in our lives.

Psalm 147:3 reminds us that, *"He heals the heartbroken and bandages their wounds."* Though we may feel broken and tattered from our experiences in life, we can have hope in knowing that God will heal our broken places and our life wounds.

David goes on to say in verse five that, *"God puts the fallen on their feet again."* You may feel like you cannot get back up again; but God has the power to heal, restore and put you back on your feet. Receive His amazing love and live free of fear.

DEVOTION: DAY THREE
LIVING IN VICTORY

Every day can feel like a battle zone. Getting caught up in the whirlwind of life circumstances can make us feel like we are spiraling out of control with no hope in sight. Despite the defeat you may be feeling today, you do not have to live in defeat. We have victory in Jesus. It is not about our individual strength, but God's strength being made perfect in our weakness (2 Corinthians 2:9).

Only He has the power to overcome any of the obstacles that we may be facing in our lives. Take refuge in His strength and know that God has given you the power through Jesus Christ to be an overcomer. Romans 8:37 says this:

> *No, despite all these things, overwhelming victory is ours through*

Christ, who loved us.

The great news is that we have already been given the victory. We can face our obstacles and hardships head-on, knowing that because of Christ we will not be a defeated foe but a victorious conqueror. Stand firm in knowing that no matter what you may be facing today, you can live in victory!

DEVOTION: DAY FOUR
LIVING IN JOY

There is a huge difference between happiness and pure joy. Happiness is always circumstantial and based on our feelings, but joy is a gift from God. We can have joy in the midst of adversity, loss, grief, distress and dark times in our lives. Sometimes the trials we face bring with them seasons of tears; take refuge in knowing that it's okay. God created us with the ability to release in the most amazing way, through our tears. They can communicate what our mere words cannot.

Nevertheless, Psalm 126:5 promises us that, *"Those who plant in tears will harvest with shouts of joy."* Yes, you may find yourself crying now; but know you are sowing seeds that will produce joy. Cry if you have to, because it is not the end, but a means to the end – a harvest of joy in your life.

As you embrace the joy of the Lord in your life, you will find renewed strength. Nehemiah 8:10 triumphantly affirms, *"The Joy of the Lord is my strength."* No matter what you may be going through, keep sowing seeds and reap your harvest. You have an amazing gift from God – His joy. This joy cannot be taken away from you. Allow the joy of the Lord to be your strength today. Live your life full of joy!

DEVOTION: DAY FIVE
LIVING MORE ABUNDANTLY

It is the job of the devil to steal, kill and destroy us. We can all attest to the fact that he definitely knows how to stay employed. The good news is that despite what it looks like, there is hope. In John 10:10 the writer says that Jesus came that we might have life and have it more abundantly. Through the work of Jesus Christ, we don't have to be stuck experiencing the relentless whiplash of life. Instead, we can have an abundant life.

This does not necessarily mean a life full of material possessions, but a life that has amazing intangibles like purpose, peace, love, joy, victory, and more. All the wonderful things God desires for us to live in each and every day. Today, choose to walk in the abundance life has to offer. Don't get stuck spinning your wheels in the midst of your circumstances. Your life has purpose and meaning, and God desires to show you His amazing love. Everyday, God breathes life into you so that you can live the life that He has purposed for you to live.

Living an abundant life is not a solo experience. We were created and designed for community. Your purpose is connected to the purpose God has for all of His creation. Abundant life is a life shared in communion with others. Don't allow the devil to rob you of your place in communion with God and creation. Your life was created to live in abundance. Live your abundant life now!

GOD CRAZY FREEDOM CHALLENGE
Part 1- Choose to Speak Life

The Bible says that the power of life and death is in what we say (Proverbs 18:21). We must choose to speak life even in the midst of facing death. Challenge yourself to speak life. Get ten index cards and, on one side, write down a scripture that affirms God's truth (verses on life, purpose, love, joy, peace, etc.). On the other side, write down one thing about yourself and your life that God made wonderful and great. This can be a personal/ spiritual gift, skill, physical attribute, people, etc. Make two sets of these cards. Put one set up on your wall, mirror, or someplace where you can always see them. Take the second set of cards and carry them with you. Whenever you feel thoughts coming against you, speak God's Word over your situation and then flip over the card to remind yourself of God's goodness in your life.

Part 2- Step Out of Isolation

So much of the struggle behind suicide is the crippling effect of isolation. Challenge yourself by joining a small group or interest group, etc. Have a "Girls' night out." Do something enjoyable and fun—dinner, game night, crafting, movies, or whatever makes you relax. The goal is to surround yourself with people with whom you can build healthy relationships and who can provide you with support. Consider giving group counseling a try with a therapist you can trust. You are a child of the light and not of darkness; do not stay hidden. Come out from among the dark place you find yourself in and allow God to heal and restore you in love through community.

GOD CRAZY FREEDOM PRAYER

Dear Heavenly Father, I admit that there are times in my life when I have allowed fear, pain and my circumstances to overwhelm me. Because of this, I have even allowed thoughts of self-destruction to enter my mind. Lord, some of my thoughts have even become actions that have tried to jeopardize Your purpose and plan for my life.

Please forgive me for not putting my trust in You. Allow me to see my life through faith as You see me. I praise you that I am fearfully and wonderfully made (Psalms 139:14). Thank You that You planned and purposed my life before the earth was even formed (Ephesians 1:3-6). Thank You for Your amazing love which gives me life, forgiveness, strength, and healing through the life, death and resurrection of Your Son, Jesus Christ (John 10:10; Ephesians 1:7; 2 Corinthians 2:9; Isaiah 53:5). Thank You that there is power in the blood of Jesus. Because of the power, I can rebuke fear, self-doubt, guilt, and shame when they rise up against me. I can have peace of mind (Hebrews 10:19, 22; Philippians 4:7). Thank You that I am safe under the shadow of your wings and that no matter what I face, no weapon formed against me will prosper (Psalm 91:4; Isaiah 54:17). Thank You that because of Jesus I am more than a conqueror (Romans 8:37); and I can now live my life free, whole, and more abundantly (John 8:36; John 10:10). In Jesus' name, Amen!

ANONYMOUS TO CHOSEN
by Julia Walker Crews

$\mathcal{I}$ grew up in the Atlanta area with a Bible-believing mom and a dad who owned nightclubs. Mom took me and my siblings to the Presbyterian church every Sunday and sent us to all the Vacation Bible Schools and Sunday school classes. She delivered us to church choir practices, and we ate at the Piccadilly cafeteria nearly every Sunday after services. We were a typical, Christ-fearing Southern family. Except for Dad's nightclubs.

No matter how hard my mother tried to keep us kids on the straight and narrow, by the time we hit our late teens, the allure of Daddy's nightclubs and other clubs around town sucked us in. We wanted to be young, wild and free. In our Presbyterian church, we had learned plenty about the Bible but not about the character of Jesus. We knew a lot about God's rules, but not much about His love. We knew how to do faith; we didn't know how to believe in Him.

It was not until after I graduated from high school that I truly experienced a personal encounter with Jesus Christ. I believe it was in large part due to the effectual, fervent prayers of a righteous mother. And believe it or not, I came face-to-face with Jesus for the first time right in the middle of one of those nightclubs.

I was with a group of recently graduated seniors, dancing at one of my dad's clubs and having a wonderful time, when someone tapped me on the shoulder. I turned and looked into the eyes of a handsome young man. I smiled, hoping he was was about to ask me to dance and said, "Hi." He smiled back, leaning in so I would hear what he was about to ask over the thumping music.

"Hi," he said. "Do you happen to know a girl named Julia?"

Puzzled, I turned and looked directly into his eyes and said, "No, why?"

The young man then said with confidence, "Jesus Christ told me to come in here and tell Julia that He loves her and wants her in His Kingdom."

I looked at him like he had lost his mind. *Who on earth does that? Walks into a nightclub and looks for someone so they can tell her that Jesus Christ wants her in His Kingdom?*

I was shaken, but I wasn't going to let on. Confidently, I said, "Well, I don't know a Julia ... but if I run into her, I'll give her your message." I laughed, then looked at my friend Billy and asked, "Can you believe that guy?"

Billy said, "What guy?"

I turned and the young man was gone.

I tried to shrug off the event, but I couldn't let it go. Was he an angel? Was he real? How did he know?

You see, I always went by the name of Julie. The name Julia was too old-sounding to me. It was elegant, when I wanted to be hip and snazzy. None of my friends knew that my name was Julia. No one knew that my name was Julia.

So when the young man asked, "Do you happen to know a girl named Julia?" my heart sank to my feet. Why? Because only my mom, dad and God knew my real name.

Moments after the young man left, so did I. The next day was Sunday, and a dear friend took me to her church. It was a church in the Atlanta area that had been there for years, one of the "pillar" churches in our community. However, it was not a church you would attend if you were a Presbyterian.

Why? Because it was a Pentecostal church, and Presbyterians and Pentecostals don't mix. Those Pentecostals ran up and down the aisles and spoke in tongues, supposedly. Presbyterians sat sedately in their pews and spoke only English, albeit with a Southern drawl. Nevertheless, I was anxious to figure out who this Jesus Christ was, and I went with her. The Jesus I knew was cold, rigid, and demanded I attend church. I had found no warmth, nothing personal in Him. I had no idea that He even knew I existed, much less knew my name.

Now, He had me at "Julia," and I think He knew that I would come looking for Him after that.

As time would have it, I came to know Christ and fell in love with Him. My heart was transformed and my mind freed from any and all condemnation that the world threw upon me. God beautifully began transforming me into His image. It was such a warm, intimate time, growing in knowledge and a walk with Jesus Christ. The Word of God became my tool for living. I relied on it for every area of my life and would hold my friends accountable as well. Witnessing was so natural. As a matter of fact, I worked at the Coca-Cola Company in the public relations department; and when people would see me getting on an elevator, they would get off because inviting everyone to "my church" was just simply my way of life.

I wanted everyone to have what I had – Jesus. To me, life was not worth living unless you lived for Him.

As the journey continued and a few months went by, I met a young man who stole my heart. He truly was my knight in shining armor. He was above and beyond everything I had ever dreamed up in my young mind and heart that I hoped for in a young man. He said, "Julia, you are the greatest thing, second to Jesus, that has ever happened in my life. You are sunshine in my life."

In short, that knight in shining armor and I became husband and wife. We went into ministry, and it was blessed. Of course, there were days of challenge as we faced getting to know each other as a married couple. But Paul and I grew closer to the Lord and matured as young ministers of the gospel. Yes, our life has had its challenges; but the blessings outweigh them.

My Victory

Through all of my life's ups and downs – from my little girl choir days to my rebellious dancing in Dad's clubs – what has sustained me, I believe, are my mother's prayers. She is an amazing Christian, and she truly believed that God had a plan for my life. She trusted God to lead me and held fast to the Word of God. She prayed for me long, and she prayed hard. She prayed all hours of the day and for every area of my life.

The day I sincerely gave my life to Christ and chose to serve Him instead of the world with all of its glamour, I know my mother's heart rejoiced. She had placed her trust in a God who delivers, and He had come through, giving her her heart's desire.

What an example this has been for me as a mom of three college students. As this journey of life that God has placed me on moves forward, I realize that my faith and hope have to be placed in Him and His Word on a daily basis. Just like my mother placed hers in Him.

I know from my mother's example that prayer is powerful, and we should never give up crying out to Him on behalf of those we love. God has placed us in the positions of mom, mothers-in-law, stepmothers, aunts, nieces, grandmothers and great-grandmothers for a purpose.

One purpose is to influence for Christ the youngsters who are within our circle. The influence we have on them can impact generations to come. We can leave a legacy of faith in our family line if we persevere. God's purpose is much bigger and broader than we can imagine or think. Ephesians 3:20 says, "Now to him who is able to do immeasurably more than all we ask or imagine, according to his power that is at work within us…"

My mom prayed me through many challenges in my life, and she continues to do so to this day. My mom's prayers taught me never to give up praying and believing for my own three amazing children and their friends. Colossians 4:12b reminds us, "… He (she) is always wrestling in prayer for you, that you may stand firm in all the will of God, mature and fully assured." Pray, my friends. You are making a difference in your family's lives!

Devotion: Day One

Women are naturally caring and passionate individuals. We are thrust into the role that the world dictates to us to be glamorous, achieving, dedicated, faithful, and put together—with children who match. The reality is that we are all full of complicated issues, frailties that only we know. Some of our families are falling apart in one area or another.

So how do we deal with this as women who love the Lord God with all our heart and soul? How do we become all we can become for our family and especially for God? Ladies, here is the freedom you are looking for. Here is the key: Be all you can be for God. He will take care of the rest.

Today, go to the Lord in prayer. Seek first the Kingdom of God (His Word), and all these things shall be added unto you *and your family*. One thing I have learned over these years is that the more I try to be what others want me to be, the more I fail. However, the more I become all that God – through His Word – desires me to be, the more I achieve and overcome. He is our hope, our grace and our life.

Jesus even told His disciples in Mark 11:22, *"Have faith in God!"*

Put your faith and hope in Him. He will make all things new. Cling to His Words of promise because, as Psalm 33:4 says, *"For the word of the LORD is right and true; he is faithful in all he does."*

Devotion: Day Two
His Word is our GPS.

Yesterday we learned first and foremost to be all that God desires for us to be. This world is deceiving when it comes to women and what is expected of them. However, God's Word is more powerful than the world. He created the world in which we live, and He created us and our families.

Today, let's place our focus on who God is. He is our creator. He is our

Provider. He is our Healer. He is our Deliverer. He is our Peace.

Many days, I look to my husband to be my provider. I look to the job to be my provider. The issue with this is that when a husband loses his job or you find your life without fulfilling work, the blame game begins. When we focus on anything outside of Jesus, we lose some of our trust in Him. We rely on ourselves or those around us instead of on the One who is really in control.

Today, Ladies, redirect your focus. Right now, put your mind and heart on His words of promise. The New International Version is a beautiful translation. Read the following passages and rejoice in the promise of His Word. He is the Living Word, so how can we go wrong? Study His Word daily. Make it a priority in your life.

Psalm 119:114: You are my refuge and my shield; I have put my hope in your word.

Psalm 119:130: The unfolding of your words gives light; it gives understanding to the simple.

Psalm 119:133: Direct my footsteps according to your word; let no sin rule over me.

Psalm 130:5: I wait for the LORD, my whole being waits, and in his word I put my hope.

DEVOTION: DAY THREE
THERE IS NOW NO CONDEMNATION!

On Day One we learned to be all that God desires us to be. This world is not our home. We are just passing through. We will spend eternity with the Heavenly Father, so being all that He desires us to be on this earth is of eternal value. On Day Two we learned that His word is our GPS. He directs us to place our hope in His Word of truth. Proverbs 4:4 says, *"Then he taught me, and he said to me, 'Take hold of my words with all your heart; keep my commands, and you will live'."* His word is our path.

Today, as we take this journey, Jesus becomes our freedom from all condemnation. I am not sure about you, but there are days when I feel so guilty for things I have said and done, things I have not said and done, even the things that I cannot get done on my To-Do List. The freedom that I have experienced is found in Romans 8: 1-2, which should be familiar by now: *"Therefore, there is now no condemnation for those who are in Christ Jesus, because through Christ Jesus the law of the Spirit who gives life has set you free from the law of sin and death."*

Got that? No one, including myself, can condemn me for the past. Regardless of what we have done or not done, there is therefore now no condemnation for those of us who are in Christ Jesus. Woo-Hoo, Ladies. We are free!

How do we get this freedom? Come to Him who is able to do more than we can imagine or think. Dig into His word of promise and cling to those promises. Speak them out daily, or moment by moment, over your life and your families. He is the Living Word.

Devotion: Day Four
We are His Heirs

Day One, be all that God desires us to be. Day Two, His Word is our GPS. Day Three, we are free from all condemnation, even over the little things that entangle us and try to keep us from being all that God desires us to be.

Today, we are putting God's Word into action and moving mountains with our prayers. Romans 8:15-17 states:

The Spirit you received does not make you slaves, so that you live in fear again; rather, the Spirit you received brought about your adoption to sonship. And by him we cry, "Abba, Father." The Spirit himself testifies with our spirit that we are God's children. Now if we are children, then we are heirs—heirs of God and co-heirs with Christ, if indeed we share in his sufferings in order that we may also share in his glory.

What a powerful passage. We are heirs of the most high God, joint heirs with Jesus. If God's word is true, which it is, then this means we as women have been given the rights as heirs and the power from our elder brother, Jesus Christ, to speak to mountains and they have to move. We are His family. We are His heirs. All that God has, we have. I am jumping out of my skin just writing this.

Matthew 11:22 tells us to *"Have faith in God."* Jesus then tells us what our faith can do in Matthew 11:23-24,

> *Truly I tell you, if anyone says to this mountain, 'Go, throw*
> *yourself into the sea,' and does not doubt in their heart but*
> *believes that what they say will happen, it will be done for them.*
> *Therefore I tell you, whatever you ask for in prayer, believe that*
> *you have received it, and it will be yours.*

Today, be confident in this: you can speak to the mountains in your life and your family to move out of the way. When you do, they *have* to move.

DEVOTION: DAY FIVE
WE LACK NO GOOD THING

This is our last day of devotions. We are daily growing in the knowledge of His power and truth. Not only are we to be all that He desires us to be, but also we know that there is no condemnation for us who are in Him. His Word is our GPS – our guide and truth. We are heirs of the most high God.

Today, I would like to encourage you to trust that He is who He says He is. His word is a light unto our feet. His word is truth. The following Psalm is one of my favorites and truly has pulled me through many days:

> *I sought the LORD, and he answered me; he delivered me from*
> *all my fears. Those who look to him are radiant; their faces are*
> *never covered with shame. This poor man called, and the LORD*
> *heard him; he saved him out of all his troubles. The angel of the*
> *LORD encamps around those who fear him, and he delivers*
> *them. Taste and see that the LORD is good; blessed is the one*

who takes refuge in him. Fear the LORD, you his holy people, for those who fear him lack nothing. The lions may grow weak and hungry, but those who seek the LORD lack no good thing. (Psalm 34:4-9)

Ladies, as we move through this life praying for our families, remember always that His word will never fail you. His Word is an anchor to our souls and our families.

GOD CRAZY FREEDOM CHALLENGE

1. List the women in your family who have left a legacy of faith, Reflect on what they did to pass down their Christian heritage to the next generation. If any of them are still living, call and ask them what they did right for their families in terms of faith. Thank God for them and the "inheritance" they have given you.

2. Determine to be a praying mom. Start each day with prayers for each child. Keep a prayer journal, and ask God to illuminate the areas of prayer specific to each of your children. Ask your children how you can pray for them, and keep track as God answers your prayers.

3. Do not grow weary on the journey of doing good. Your children will not always appreciate your efforts, and you may have to wait many years before witnessing the harvest of the seeds of prayer you are planting. Don't give up! The effectual, fervent prayer of a righteous mom avails much!

GOD CRAZY FREEDOM PRAYER

Dear Lord God, we come to You with praise on our lips for this life You have given to us. Your Word is a powerful lamp unto our feet and light unto our paths. We cling to Your words of promise and trust that You will not only hear our cries, but also You will answer our prayers. Your Word says that the angel of the Lord encamps all around us and our families, and that there is no condemnation for those who are in You.

We praise Your amazing name that is above all names, and we give you the glory you deserve for answering our prayers and for empowering us to speak to the mountains in our family's lives and tell them to move out of the way. You are God. You are the Word. We are Your heirs. Wow! Praise God that we have such a Father and Elder brother. Amen

CLOSING

My dear sister –

I pray the words of this book have not only penetrated your heart, but have healed it in some way. Our desire is for you to be free, to run free, and to live free. What remains hidden and in secret is open to the adversary who goes around like a roaring lion seeking whom he may devour.

The first step to freedom is to confess with our mouth to God and to someone "safe" who can help keep us accountable through the process of walking out our freedom. The second step is to have a heart of repentance over all we have confessed. Here are a few more Freedom steps to help you walk out your journey:

1. Rid yourself of any Idols such as money, sex, power, pleasure, television, anything or anyone you are putting in a position higher than God.

2. Renounce your past participation of satanic worship, palm reading, witchcraft, astrology, spirit guides, other religions, mind control, hypnosis or sexual immorality and wrong connections with people you have been sexually or emotionally involved with.

3. Receive God's truth over everything else. Look to the Bible, your sword, as the main source of truth in your life instead of to people, books, or other sources of information. In his word it says the "Truth" shall set you free. Remember, the power is in His word. Allow it to pour over you day and night by speaking it out and listening to it on CD. Memorize as much as you can so it can begin to feed you spiritually.

4. Recognize your value in Christ. Accept Him into your heart as savior

and Lord over your life and entrust to Him the past and the future so you can begin relying on him for the renewing of your mind and heart.

5. Relinquish control into His hands. What is truly in your hands today? Give him control of the wheel and allow Him to drive your life in the direction He intends for you to go. Surrender the outcome of all things to Him and exchange old life, old thoughts, old memories, and old desires for your new life of walking in the spirit and no longer walking in the things of your flesh. You are a new creature in Christ Jesus and your old ways are no longer.

6. Remember to choose forgiveness over bitterness, and humility over pride. Forgiveness is a choice, a decision of your will. It doesn't mean you forget all that was done. Christ will heal the memories over time once you make the choice to let them go. To forgive means to set the captive free. What we don't realize is when we forgive; we are the captives we are setting free.

7. Surrender your rebellion and ask Him to help you be willing to repent. Rebellion vs repentance is choosing not to respond to God. It's saying I am going to do it my way and react the way I want. When we do this and defy the principles in God's word, we delay our restoration, our freedom. You see freedom comes in surrender. Are you ready to give up your will, your thoughts, your determination and striving, and exchange them for peace, new life, and thriving in the possibilities of all God desires for you? Are you willing to decrease so that He might increase? Where has leaning on your own understanding taken you? Are you more about making yourself famous rather allowing God to be made famous through you?

8. Respond rather than react to fear in your life. Allowing fear to control you, reacting to fear and allowing it to drive your decisions and keep you from a future, is allowing fear to enslave you. Respond to fear, irrational thoughts or lies, with the truth of Gods word. Fear is the greatest distraction and keeps us from the faith we are called to live out in order to accomplish all God has purposed us to become.

We love you, sweet sisters. We want you to have all that God desires for you, to walk out His love and His purpose in God Crazy Freedom!

Dear Heavenly Father:

I praise you and honor you today. I am ready to walk through the healing in order to find the freedom. I entrust my past, the outcome of my past, the people who have hurt me and wronged me in my past, to you, and I am asking for your strength to forgive them, and release myself from bondage. Lord, forgive me for my rebellion, for my lack of repentance. I am repenting today of all my sin, (name your sins here) and I am asking for your forgiveness.

I no longer will worship other gods; I no longer will choose addictions and idols over you in my life. I will place no other gods or people before you. You are all-powerful, all-knowing, and I ask you to fill me with your Spirit so I can begin to walk in the Spirit and not in my flesh.

I renounce the lies I have believed, lies such as: I am not worthy to know You, I am not good enough to know you, I have no value because of my past, I need to keep shame with me because I cannot be forgiven, I am abandoned, unprotected, I am guilty, I am ugly, I am not pretty enough, I am not rich enough, I am not ENOUGH. These lies will no longer have any power over me, my thoughts, my words, or my actions.

You are enough for me. I have value and I am beautifully made in your image. Today I am putting on your full armor. I submit my body as a living sacrifice, wholly devoted to you and your purpose for me. I stand against the enemy and I fight for the things that are of value to you and am offended by the things that offend you or your name. Today I begin my God Crazy Freedom journey, and I am thankful and so very grateful for your love, Lord.

> *In Jesus' name,*
> *Amen*

My Daughter,

You, my child, are a daughter of the King and all glorious within. I clothe you in clothing embroidered with gold and lead you to me in purity with gladness and rejoicing as you enter the palace of the King. (Psalm 45 13-15)

I have given you a crown of beauty instead of ashes, the oil of gladness instead of mourning, a garment of praise instead of despair, so that you will display my splendor...

I have clothed you with garments of salvation and arrayed you in a robe of righteousness as a bride adorned with jewels. (Isaiah 61:3,10)

I crown you with love and compassion and satisfy you with good things (Psalm 103:4), giving you a rich welcome into my eternal Kingdom (2 Peter 1:11) and a crown that will last forever (1 Corinthians 9:25). For you, dearest daughter, are a crown of splendor in my hand, a royal diadem in the hand of your God (Isaiah 62:3).

I have given you a new birth into a living home and into an inheritance that can never perish, spoil or fade, kept in heaven for you (1 Peter 1:3). I have made you my heir with complete access to my inheritance (Galatians 4:5-7), blessing you with every spiritual blessing in Christ (Ephesians 1:3).

I am your King and your God who declares victories for you (Psalm 44:4) - the only Ruler, King of Kings and Lord of Lords – who alone possesses immortality (1 Timothy 6:15).

I am coming soon. Hold on to what you have, so that no one will take your crown (Revelation 3:11).

See, your King comes to you…(Zechariah 9:9)

The King of Kings comes to *you*!

May the Lord bless you and keep you and shine His face upon you as you go about making him famous by sharing your story with someone, so that she too might be free.

From our heart to yours,

*Michelle Borquez Thornton
and the God Crazy Freedom Team*

OTHER BOOKS BY THE AUTHOR

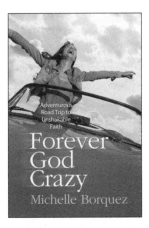

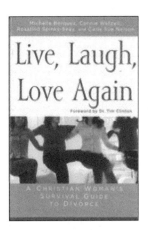

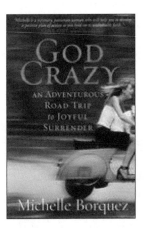

ABOUT THE CREATOR

*I*n 2005 Michelle Borquez-Thornton hosted and co-produced I-Life Television's *SHINE with Michelle Borquez* on INSP, and was the national spokesperson for Beth Moore's Loving Well Television Ministry Special. She has authored several books, including *God Crazy - An Adventurous Road Trip to Joyful Surrender* and *Overcoming the Seven Deadly Emotions*, and co-authored *Live, Laugh, Love Again, the Christian Women's Survival Guide for Divorce*. As Founder and Editor-in-Chief of SHINE Magazine for nine years, Michelle interviewed high-profile leaders such as former First Lady Laura Bush, Kurt and Brenda Warner, Chuck and Gina Norris, Anne Graham Lotz, and Gloria Gaynor, to name a few.

Currently, Michelle is the international spokesperson and co-host of the national *Divorce Care* series; host of the web TV program *Shine with Michelle Borquez*; president of Bella Women Network, a women's web TV network and on-line magazine; president of God Crazy Ministries; and co-owner and Chief Fashionista of shopbellastyle.com, a successful on-line shopping experience focused on bringing customers "adorable fashion for affordable prices."

Michelle is married to author Michael Thornton and is the mother of four almost-grown children, Joshua, Aaron, Madison and Jacob.

To find out more about the ministries and
organizations listed above, please visit:
Bellawomennetwork.com
Shopbellastyle.com
Godcrazy.org

Or visit Michelle's blog at shinewithmichelleborquez.com

To book Michelle for a speaking engagement, please go to
shinewithmichelleborquez.com

Facebook fan page: http://www.facebook.com/Keepupwithmichelle
Twitter: Godcrazy or shinemichelle